My Apprenticeship:

An Intellectual Journey

My Apprenticeship:
An Intellectual Journey

Karla Poewe

Vogelstein Press

2018 VOGELSTEIN PRESS, Calgary, Alberta, Canada
This version is an adaptation of the Cesara book (1982). It incorporates
further original research and subsequent writing.

Published by:
VOGELSTEIN PRESS
Calgary, Alberta, Canada
Book ISBN – paperback – 978-0-9949088-5-8
eBook ISBN – 978-0-9949088-4-1
Copyright © 2018 by Vogelstein Press

eBook / paperback set-up and formatting by P.L. (Trish) Kotow
cover design by K. Poewe (Author) and Trish Kotow

Cesara book first published by:
ACADEMIC PRESS, A Subsidiary of Harcourt Brace Jovanovich,
Publishers
LONDON NEW YORK PARIS SAN DIEGO SAN FRANCISCO
SAO PAULO SYDNEY TOKYO TORONTO
ACADEMIC PRESS INC. (LONDON) LTD.
24/28 Oval Road, London NW1

United States Edition published by:
ACADEMIC PRESS INC.
111 Fifth Avenue, New York, New York 10003
Copyright © 1982 by ACADEMIC PRESS INC. (LONDON) LTD.

British Library Cataloguing in Publication Data
Cesara, M.
Reflections of a woman anthropologist. — (Studies in anthropology)
1. Poewe, Karla 0.
2. Anthropologists—Canada—Biography
I. Title   II. Series
301.092'4 (expanded) GN21.P/
ISBN 0-12-164880-X

Phototypeset by Dobbie Typesetting Service, Plymouth, Devon and
printed by T.J. Press (Padstow) Limited, Padstow, Cornwall

Beneath the surface of our daily life, in the personal history of many of us, there runs a continuous controversy between an Ego that affirms and an Ego that denies ...

Now, it so happens that the internal controversy which has been perpetually recurring in my own consciousness, from girlhood to old age, led me in early life to choose a particular vocation ...

Beatrice Webb

With the exception of Zambia, its capital Lusaka, and Zambia's then President Kenneth Kaunda, all place names and personal names have been fictionalized.

PREFACE TO THE REVISED EDITION

After my first field work as a graduate student in Zambia (1973–1975), and after years of publishing and university teaching in a department of men who played a hard game of resisting my presence, I published a book in 1982 that made this research process visible. Although North America was still living an ethos "of let it all hang out," my work meant breaking a taboo. It meant paying the price and walking a long way toward a new turn. It also meant revisiting that experience, as I am doing here, to liberate it of an ideologically informed anger that distorted it. The actual research process, however, with its unforeseen events and short-comings, but also with its insights about people generally, remains available for contemplation.

The first edition of this book appeared under the pseudonym of Manda Cesara (1982). Although I had read Sartre before I went to the field, it was not until I anticipated writing the book that I took a refresher course in the philosophy of existentialism. My attraction for his thought was natural. Like myself, Sartre's existentialism is a product of WWII. His thoughts helped me hobble up and down the mountains of my mental and emotional existence in the field. What German poetry had done for me as a war-child (*Kriegskind*), Sartre's philosophy did for me as apprentice ethnographer. It gave me courage to act alone, cling to nothing, be "condemned to be free" and utterly responsible for what I could make out of what made me (Gill and Shermann, 1973, p.485–486).

War-childhood constitutes a bias. War-children were uprooted, separated periodically or permanently from parents, and handed from person to person to whoever could feed them. From an early age, I knew that I was a burden: a burden to society as a refugee and a burden to my caretakers. Although my mother was often in a different Zone of Occupied Germany, she was the one thread, especially after the separations from aunts, siblings and, most importantly, my maternal grandmother, that provided continuity.

But that "thread" was more a journey of resilience than hugs and kisses. It burned resilience into my flesh.

Since my pre-teens I grew up with one question. What in the name of heaven did adults do to make us, their children, grow up in rubble, camps, and generally a chaotic social environment? It took many decades and countries to answer that question, because first we had to overcome being refugees by becoming normal Germans, and only then become immigrants to Canada. And there—and as a graduate student in the United States with a permanent residency in Canada but with a German passport and American student visa—my uncertain and contingent past was put away—or so I thought—at least until I decided to embark on my first fieldtrip to Zambia.

How beautiful then to find a book published in 1926 that says something relevant to our time and discipline more than ninety years later. It speaks to me although, alas, Beatrice Webb (1858–1943) came from a wealthy environment and a whole country, where I came from a ruined environment and a broken country. She argued that to describe her craft, which was sociology, she found it necessary to quote from a diary that she kept over forty years earlier:

> I have neither the desire nor the intention of writing an autobiography yet the very subject-matter of my science is society; its main instrument is social intercourse; thus I can hardly leave out of the picture the experience I have gathered, not deliberately as a scientific worker, but casually as a child, unmarried woman, wife and citizen. For the sociologist, unlike the physicist, chemist and biologist, is in a quite unique manner the creature of his environment. Birth and parentage, the mental atmosphere of class and creed in which he is bred, the characteristic and attainments of men and women who have been his guides and associates, come first and

foremost of all the raw material upon which he works ...
It is his own social and economic circumstance that
determines the special opportunities, the peculiar
disabilities, the particular standpoints for observation
and reasoning—in short, the inevitable bias with which
he is started on his way to discovery, a bias which ought
to be known to the student of his work so that it may be
adequately discounted (Webb 1926:1).

The first three chapters of this revised edition show something of the
inevitable bias with which I started my journey of discovery in 1973. The
Comments at the end of various chapters were written in 1982 or now.
These comments and, importantly, the deliberate removal of strident
criticisms of the society and discipline to which I returned after the field,
make this version different. I have removed what I have judged to be an
unnecessary overlay. Kept are two things: (1) the authenticity of my
reactions to field experiences and (2) the use of Sartre's existentialism as
field work compass during the early part of the apprenticeship. This
practice changed gradually, however, as I became less blind to the general
human condition that defined people's lives in the Lenda valley of Zambia.

Today I find Sartre's existentialism that held me up then lacking. I reject
its stark individualism; and I reject the location of its final moral arbiter in
the individual's personal conscience. Any individual's conscience is
fallible: Sartre's was and so was mine. Nevertheless, if I left some of
Sartre's notions in this work, it is because existentialism was undeniably a
useful tool to keep me focused on the life *outside of* and *around* me, to
heed happenings as I *did* research, to take note of *ideological* conflicts, and
to *jump* the shadow of a past that held me captive.

In some ways, field work is liturgical (Allusion to Smith 2009:142). For
one short condensed moment of history, the researcher and those being
researched are part of one material reality in which both desire certain
ends—however they may differ. Almost inevitably, therefore, doing field

work affects the researcher and this raises questions. For example, does heeding this happening benefit the pursuit of knowledge? Is anthropological field work merely an "original mode of knowing" that plays itself out in "the person" of the anthropologist (Wengle 1983 quoting Levi-Strauss 1967:42)? Is this "mode of knowing," which is not based exclusively on cognition or reason but on the whole person, to be avoided?—One thing is certain; the anthropologist does not orbit the earth; he makes a hard landing.

The purpose of my research was to study the relationship between religion, kinship, and economic development of the Lenda peoples of Zambia. My training had emphasized quantification, British social anthropology, kinship analysis, and various methods of observing and interviewing. I did not abandon the above goal or methods as the lengthy descriptions even in my personal journal will show. But while in the field, I came to reject as dishonest the segregation of subject from object, self from other, and introspection from empiricism. I soon learned that doing field work required my whole person relating to neighbors.

This book is neither an ethnography nor an ethnology, and it should **not** be confused with them. John Wengle (1983:10) called this kind of writing "a memory of an inner confrontation that led to a birth." Indeed, had I done a suitable job of it, it might have birthed a new genre. As it is, I prefer to call it an anthropological apprenticeship because that is what a first field trip is. It is a learning journey about resilience where a student "learns something essential about himself," learns to understand "failure as a necessary condition of success," loses his way, learns "to embrace humility," but for all that remains creative, agile, and "committed to the pursuit of truth" (Riddell 2017:43).

The systematic data of the local people, which were researched by this author with her assistants, were published as two other books and several papers. By contrast, this book is the story of how a researcher bears up in a situation that she must create to reach a goal that she brought with her from another part of the world—and then become aware of what is happening to her and the people around her as she does what she does.

The book is written for ethnographic students and for those many who have transitioned or are transitioning from refugees, migrants, or immigrants to citizens of new countries. It might also speak to those United Nation Helpers that often enough jeopardize a normal family life, their personal health, and even face death, for the sake of solving stubborn political problems in violent parts of the world (Kleinschmidt 2015).

The anthropologist as source of both evidence-based research and migrating memories acts as a reminder that some social sciences consist of those disciplines that simultaneously aim to understand, explain, and discuss openly the unconventionalities of the discovery process. The event of understanding and the researcher's historicity, and here I break with Sartre, should be given a place somewhere alongside public formulation and repeatability. After all, behind the work of each researcher is a unique personal story that resonates with, occasionally hijacks, and embeds experiences in the field.

This book is dedicated to the memory of two people: David M. Schneider without whose wisdom, humanity, and unwavering support this effort would have come to nothing and Harry Basehart, my PhD supervisor who, upon having read the original manuscript, said "I understand why you had to write it." Likewise, it is a pleasure to express deep gratitude to Eugene Hammel, John Middleton, Elisabeth Colson, and Ruth Landes. They were in some form or other supportive of my general work and/or of this unusual project. I know that this book cannot be liked by every field worker. I wrote it for those who, like children, dare to affirm life, dare to make mistakes, and above all dare to pursue knowledge.

February 2018
Karla Poewe

DAVID SCHNEIDER'S COMMENDATIONS

There are really three things going in this book. First, there is a kind of self-examination and revelation of what it actually **feels like** to begin to find one's self in intensive field work in another culture. This includes, especially prominently, the problem of working out an identity of which being a woman is an important part. A part, however, which is inextricably interwoven with being a professional Anthropologist. It is not true of all anthropologists, but for a significant number of them the ability to learn about the "other," to comprehend the "other," is not only a crucial part of their intellectual trade, but it is at the same time a deeply moving personal experience. My old teacher (old! He was a young man, but older than I by a decade) Clyde Kluckhohn kept explaining that true field work, good field work, was very much like going through a successful psychoanalysis. Not that it cured you; not that it re-made you into something totally different. But that you learned a great deal about yourself as well as about the people you were spending your life with. To learn to understand takes not merely a cognitive commitment to some clearly formulated questions; it takes a deeply emotional commitment too, a cathexis. And it takes place in a deeply engaged interpersonal context. This book, I think, shows that in ways that no other book that I know of does. It is thus a very personal document, sometimes embarrassing, but never (to me) false or trivial or superficial.

A second thing that the book has going is more straightforward. It is, I believe from my own experience and from talking to others about their experiences, a perfectly normal routine "natural history" of the way in which Anthropological field work proceeds. In the beginning there are high intellectual hopes, practical foul-ups, hopeless misunderstanding. A period of utter confusion and considerable ego-disorientation takes place. Then somehow things suddenly begin to gel, and what was senseless becomes sensible. Too much so. Deceivingly so. One feels that one has suddenly "seen the light" and the whole matter is clear as a bell. This period of bliss is followed gradually by another where what was simple and clear is now clouded, more complex than one expected. By this time a sense of alienation has set in. Relations with one's own countrymen seem odd and awkward, but relations with the people one is living intimately with are not so smooth as they seemed to have been before. My own experience was one of very disturbing loneliness; Manda Cesara does not report such acute feelings, but it is there nonetheless. But the point is not to recount in detail the course of succeeding states and experiences, but rather to say that this is a document that does tell the reader what it is like to be deeply, intellectually and emotionally engaged in field work—and this is the mark of the very highest quality of field work. Many field workers go into the field with a spouse. Others are incapable of dealing with their weak egos and are threatened by the identification one makes with the natives' view and culture. Some stay in the field only for short spells, but work out of a hotel or a safe camp, safely among their own.

But my point here is that the second major point in this book is that it is a good, not atypical account of what it not only feels like, but the way in which learning another culture proceeds when it is really done well and with sensitivity. It goes without saying that one's own identity and one's own personality become deeply engaged, and so the first point and the second are in fact very closely interwoven.

The third major strength of the book is that we are given a close intimate and honest account of how inextricably interconnected the person—the self, the ego, the identity problems—and the intellectual problems are. A word about my own experience—which I have never written of and only spoken of hesitantly and cautiously—may make this clear. I had taken a course in kinship with G.P. Murdock at Yale in 1941. I hated Murdock, I hated Yale, and if I hated anything it was kinship. That this was not totally unrelated with my own problems with my family goes without saying. I quit anthropology and took a job in Washington with the federal government, fed up with the whole thing. And on Yap*, what do you suppose absorbed my attention so completely that in some ways I did not do as comprehensive a piece of field work as I should have—kinship, marriage and the family of course. This book makes that interrelationship clear, for it is not only the problems of the author's identity as a woman that was problematic, it was also the focus (despite the ostensive aim of doing a job on economic affairs) of the intellectual problem she ultimately focused most intensively on.

October 24, 1980
David Schneider
William B. Ogden Distinguished Service Professor of Anthropology

* an island of Micronesia

CONTENTS

PART I

INTRODUCTION
AND
ARRIVAL

I have met few ethnographers who were not personally affected in some profound way by their field work.

Michael H. Agar

Life yields only to the conqueror. Never accept what can be gained by giving in. You will be living off stolen goods, and your muscles will atrophy.

Dag Hammarskjold

Life only demands from you the strength you possess. Only one feat is possible—not to have run away.

Dag Hammarskjold

At Yasnaya Polyana, social injustice was camouflaged by country quaintness, the poor were scattered far apart, and sun and wind drove away the bad smells; but in Moscow poverty was walled in and concentrated, and it exploded in your face like a boil.

Henri Troyat Tolstoy

1

INTRODUCTION: CONDEMNED TO BE FREE

General Remarks

This book looks back at the description of my first field work experience in Zambia during the early nineteen seventies. That experience was first published in 1982 with the title "Reflections of a Woman Anthropologist: No Hiding Place" under the pseudonym of Manda Cesara. It was a deeply flawed book for two reasons: it used the then popular feminism as a selling point and it revealed an ethnographer falling in love. The truth is, however, the author intended neither the feminist ideology nor the matter of intimacy in the field to be priorities. Hence this revisit and revision.

The aim of the first edition was, and of this revision is, to write a narrative that everyone who is interested in knowing the world through field work can understand. And a good way to do that is to show an apprentice ethnographer gathering data for her intended doctoral dissertation. It is usually the first field trip that an ethnographer experiences most intensely and that affects him most deeply.

An anthropologist's work usually combines analysis and narrative, but not necessarily in the same work. The challenge here is to prioritize the narrative aspect of field work. And that means using ego-documents, like letters, diary entries, reflections, and notes of casual conversations, because they show most effectively the dynamic of experiencing and being affected by it. Not only do such documents reveal the ethnographer's changing reactions to fear, isolation, mistakes, disappointments, vulnerabilities, and confrontation with her specific history; they also show love merging with knowledge.

By its very nature anthropology is a risky enterprise. The profession takes "a poor primate, a beast with nerve-endings all over it, a creature with a stomach that wants to be filled, a breeding animal that wants its mate, and (says), 'Now get on with it. Become (a professional anthropologist)'" (adapted from Lewis (2001:72).

"Field work is field work," wrote the anthropologist Harry Wolcott (1929–2012). It draws on both art and science thereby making "a contribution uniquely its own" (1995:252). True, but why does anthropology, being a social science, need art?

An important part of the answer is that field work does not only raise the "how" question as in how do field workers experience their first encounter with different people in an unknown or unpredictable part of the world. It also raises the "why" question. Why do we go to the field in the first place, and why for such a long time risking alienation from our own society and, even more, the loss of friends and spouses back home? Why do we make heart-breaking decisions to leave those we love, when we know that we cannot calculate unexpected consequences down the road? Why do we expose ourselves to amalgamations of "sophisticated" with "primitive" worlds, of eating what we do not recognize as food at home, of coping with unexpected nightmares about distant pasts when we need the light of reason each morning? To recognize the turmoil suggested in these questions, and to understand the coping and overcoming it requires, field workers need resources they didn't even know they had. They need philosophy, imagination, courage, resilience, creativity, indeed, their very person.

And herein lies the biggest risk of all, for the profession or the reader may precisely not like the person. Here is the risk that the person, who is known to his mentors and examiners solely as mind or reason, is stranger than the field. Finally, here is the risk of ultimate failure, when all was done with the hope of ultimate success.

The apprentice anthropologist who goes to the field deals with three terrains: the terrain inside of himself that he did not know was even there, the terrain outside of himself that is so much there as to be invasive, and the terrain of the unspoken norm to be an atheist that expects conformity. I parked God outside of the university gates.

Sartre and I Forty Years Ago

The turmoil of leaving for the field met me again upon returning from the field. And research between those two events was so unexpectedly intertwined with my whole person and childhood memories in Germany that I knew the day would come when I would want to review that intense happening. And what better way is there than to write it down. My first obligation, however, was to finish the Ph.D. and to publish the data. Only ten years later would I review diary entries, notes, and letters of that time.

As I read through my personal journal in the nineteen-seventies, Sartre's early writings "spoke" to me as they had not done before. The reason was war. Like mine, the thoughts of Sartre are rooted in the upheaval of the Second World War. Having been part of the resistance to Hitler and dealing with the anguish of a compromised post-war France, Sartre worked out a stark choice-based individualism on the motto that "man makes himself." Instead of wallowing in guilt for the Vichy past, Sartre taught in 1945 that the future of France depended on individual choice. He meant that each citizen must choose so that resulting actions are exemplary, sit on freedom for all, and thus are responsible. To Sartre then, freedom meant choosing without reliance on outside authority because it had failed.

As the war and post-war situation was special to Sartre—so was the first field work experience special to me. It was to be enacted without regrets, excuses, and determinations.

Something of this utter self-reliance, while breaking through a dark tunnel with no guide except self-generated action and the hope that awareness will light up an indifferent world, was an element of the early part of my maiden field trip. It had something to do with the fact that my field site was at that time entirely cut off from the country's capital, its university and the research institute. The last mentioned was the newcomer's first point of contact. It also had to do with the unsettling fact that while rural Zambia was strange and vaguely threatening, it was uncannily familiar and a throwback to a post-war Germany of flight, dispersal, abandonment, and refugee camps filled primarily with women and children. My expectation to find a whole society with healthy families by comparison with what I left behind was disappointed.

It should now be clear that this account is not about field work methods. Rather, it shows the apprentice being part of, and creative in, the social world she explores. It involves reflexivity of both author and people studied, only in this story with deliberate emphasis on the author. Above all, it is decidedly not about Foucault's relationship of power and knowledge production to show how the West did in the rest. It is not an approach centered on victimization but on resilience.

For whatever reason, seeing these people as simultaneously strange and familiar unleashed many repressed memories that had the effect of driving me even harder to discover who the Lenda were, for in the discovery of them I would also discover my past and assign it new meaning (Castaneda, 1968; Jules-Rosette, 1980, p.8). For a time, the people being researched and I inhabited a common space of multiple histories not linked by common causes but by resonances of love and pain.

A Past That Would Erupt

While the intent is to show how memories of my past emerged unexpectedly during certain events of my maiden field trip, there are some things that must be told now if the rest is to be understood later.

As a child, I grew up in a devastated Germany. Our toys consisted of shrapnel and worthless money, our best food of gritty black bread and potato soup. If you had young and attractive aunts, then this monotonous diet would be enriched occasionally with sweets and salted butter from British or American soldiers. What we ate and the kind of social chaos we experienced depended on the sector of Germany in which a mother gave birth. Born into what became a Russian Zone I was haunted by all four of them, the Russian, the French, the British, and the American. But it was life in the Russian and British Zones that left deep impressions.

Our household was composed entirely of women, not because they were single, but because their spouses were at the front of World War II, taken prisoner of war, killed in action or missing. Which of these it was, remained unknown until many years later. To survive the breakdown of society, some of my aunts worked in factories, two continued as nurses, some were petty entrepreneurs trading and bartering anything in sight. My mother alternately worked in factories and bartered. Once she even bartered corsets. Don't ask me where she got them, but they were her favorite items for she traded them to buxom farmers' wives for bread and occasionally even eggs or milk.

My grandmother adored me, in part, no doubt, because I hardly ever cried or spoke. For that reason alone, she considered me to be a rare child. Most of the time I was sick. One time, when I was left alone because my grandmother was out bartering, I was tortured by the pain and potential shame of diarrhea. There were no flush toilets nor outhouses. A few pails in the basement received human waste. Filled, they would be emptied onto dunghills and the waste used as night soil. This time, all pails were full. Teary eyed and in great agony I moved from pail to pail, wherever there was a little room, in an effort not to cause my grandmother extra work or embarrassment. Since I was just six years old, my grandmother considered this a great feat. She praised my good sense and marveled at the ticking of my tiny brain. All my aunts were told and they too marveled. As reward, grandmother cooked a special potato soup with morsels of fatty meat.

Before we ate, we raised our spirits by hitting our spoons on the table to the beat of our special song:

Kartoffel Supp',	Potato Soup,
Kartoffel Supp',	Potato Soup,
jeden Tag Kartoffel Supp'.	Every day Potato Soup.

And then we ate feeling so happy that anything would have tasted good.

In my household, decisions were made by women. To the child I was then, therefore, men were occasional guests, sometimes downright strange and mysterious because they did not even speak our language. Two men stood out from the few that were left. One was our math teacher who always played the violin as he taught and who was infatuated with my mother. The other was Herr Deckwerth, the village socialist and father of a handicapped child. It is because he had a handicapped child that he took a liking to me (Poewe 1988:147–149). In his room which was painted totally pink to keep him, as he would say, awake, he taught me to speak aloud to the world through poetry. Soon I won every poetry recital contest and there were many, for Germans recited poetry at every festival, before every school play, at every inauguration, before every competition, at every demolition, before every reconstruction. My head was filled with Goethe and Schiller and Rilke and many others. Two things about these poems remained in my memory. They were mostly poems about personal freedom in the face of any kind of cultural oppression, and they were poems that lamented the alienation of the father from his child:

Wer reitet so spät durch Nacht and Wind?	Who rides so late through the stormy night?
Es ist der Vater mit Seinem Kind;	It is the father with his child;
Er hat den Knaben wohl in dem Arm,	He has the boy safe in his arm,
Er fasst ihn sicher, er hält ihn warm.	He holds him secure, he holds him warm.
Dem Vater grauset's, er reitet geschwind,	The father shudders, his ride is wild,
Er hält in Armen das ächzende Kind,	He holds in his arms the moaning child.
Erreicht den Hof mit Mühe und Not;	He reaches the farmhouse with effort and dread;
In seinen Armen das Kind war tot.	In his arms, the child was dead.
Goethe: Erlkönig	(my translation)

One day my mother packed our bags and we immigrated to Canada. It is there that I learned the cultural category "Jew" and that I should have a special affinity to it. I learned that at the sound of it I should cringe with guilt and horror and soon I did. It took a decade before I could say that Germany was not the land of poetry and strong women but that of Auschwitz.

It was in Canada too that I started the process of repressing my past. Like everyone else, I called it assimilation. I guess I began to see myself as culturally assimilated but individually peculiar. It was easy to see myself as assimilated if for no other reason than that I was white and looked much like the rest of the kids. Oh, I was reminded that I was German every so often, when I excelled in class or when I was laughed at because I recited poetry with considerable feeling. But after I performed gymnastics at cadet inspection and as the only girl in the boys' gym team, my expressiveness and the remaining accent came to be accepted.

Still there continued to be bitter reminders of a past that became defined for me as ugly and for which the only response was guilt. For example, this ugly past would re-emerge when my history teacher in high school played Nazi propaganda films which somehow fascinated him, or when I had to listen to ethnic jokes about "square heads" and people who automatically clicked their heels and raised their hands. I soon learned to laugh, not authentically perhaps, but enough to show Canadians and especially Americans, who seemed to be raised on *Hogan's Heroes* and were more adept at telling ethnic jokes, that I could take it.

But there were nagging questions. For example, how was it that Americans knew more about the people among whom I grew up than I did? Was such a thing possible? Alas, instead of answering, I filed it away—studied and stumbled forwards.

During my teens, the men who affected my existence were largely deceased authors or composers like St. Augustine, Dostoevsky, even Galsworthy and Somerset Maugham, Beethoven and Mozart. My favorite male figure, a man of extremely strong emotion and intellect, was Tolstoy. These were the men from whom I took my cues for a sound philosophy of life. Seen in this light, I was hardly a product of society. More like a butterfly, I was a young woman who borrowed her best qualities from men internationally. Later in the field, I quickly recognized men's talents, it took more effort with women.

In the late sixties, I married an American. Our courtship and marriage were part of the paradoxical practice of "falling in love in the sixties counter-culture." We became aware of one another during heated discussions about structural analysis and Levi-Strauss. And suitably, the wedding was organized by young faculty and graduate students. The man, with whom I went to buy wedding rings crafted by an "Indian" from a local reserve, was an eternal bachelor; the man who married us a Unitarian Minister; the man who gave me away our Dean. And as the Indian predicted, the stone in the ring crumbled and fell to the ground when I put it on his finger. No mothers, no fathers—it was like a marriage of refugees. But a happy farce.

My husband was at the start of his career. Our honeymoon took us to the town of his PhD supervisor, to write Bob's dissertation. I was a pre-field work graduate student, applying for papers to enable my departure. Bright and passionate, Bob fit the men I knew.

At the time of this marriage, I wanted to be American. My German past had at all cost to remain dead. Alive, it was too painful and I not strong enough, nor intelligent enough, to grasp its pain and bear the guilt. While I was in the U.S., I repressed my German childhood; later in Zambia, I repressed my Canadian adolescence and American young adulthood. It was an impossible foundation for a marriage but a surprising one for my first field trip.

Imagine, then, the shock when I entered Lenda and found myself, once again, among women in control. It was as if I were transported back into post-World War II Germany, only among Germans whose skin color was brown. The Lenda social environment had a deep, disturbing, heart-warming and, finally, liberating impact on me. While I have been accused by friends and colleagues of being a rationalist, I found myself staring at the Lenda social landscape transfixed and mystified for I was staring into my past.

The social scientist's first response to this paragraph is no doubt that the ethnographer's reaction would prejudice her research. This assumption is not without its ambiguity as those familiar with Gadamer's (1976) hermeneutics know. Gadamer argued that our prejudices do not cut us off from understanding what is strange or past, but initially open it up to us. What we tend to evaluate negatively, Gadamer saw positively. He argued, in other words, that the knower's being bound to his situation or horizons and the gulf-separating him from his object is the productive ground of all understanding. "Prejudices are biases of our openness to the world" (Gadamer, 1976, p.9). It was usually believed that only a neutral, prejudice-free consciousness guarantees objectivity of knowledge. But Gadamer points out that "the dominant ideal of knowledge and the alienated, self-sufficient consciousness it involves is itself a powerful prejudice" (p. xvi). To Gadamer, in short, understanding is not reconstruction but mediation. It is a meeting of something strange bridged by the unexpected sensation of being familiar.

Was my arrival in Lenda a grim joke perpetrated by a god of vengeance? And did this god sit there pointing a finger at me, choking with laughter as he spluttered, "You see, you see, I told you that you could not escape your past!"

So profound was the Lenda impact on me that several things followed: first, I put the relationship with my husband into abeyance. Where his tie to me in the past was real but conditional, in the field it became transformed into one that was outside of my "situation" (Sartre 1956). Second, on many occasions, but especially on those that were disquieting, I relived aspects of my past. Third, and many Lenda reciprocated, we developed an affective tie together. In terms of the human condition, and for a brief time, we were part of one another's everyday life.

One could say, at times Lenda women became like my German aunts and vice versa. And I thought my past was dead. Mercifully, all this happened slowly. The association of Lenda with my past, sort of bubbled up through my senses until it entered my dreams and finally exploded into consciousness. It was an experience much like listening to a cruel joke long in the telling because the narrator of it, watching his listeners' response, becomes aware that the cruel aspect of the joke may outweigh its humor.

Existentialism and Cultural Analysis

Having said this, the reader will now perhaps understand better my caution that this book is about the human aspects of research; that this is a study of the impact of doing research on the researcher. David M. Schneider related my experience of field work to that of past ethnography when psychoanalytical practice was a normal part of it. Under continental European influence, there was a time in American anthropological thought, when we did not shy away from the inseparable dynamic that related the person of the anthropologist to the people he studied. It was a time when we trusted that emotion, feeling and trauma enriched, rather than hindered, the anthropologist's understanding of a foreign culture. Allowing the anthropologist to be affected by those he researched as they were affected by him was part of becoming aware of the process of how we know what we know. Can we say that the person of the anthropologist, by which I mean his past, his body, his emotional repertoire, his testimony, in addition to the priorities of reason and perception, could have a place in epistemology?

Societies destroyed by war, mobile societies, and field work experiences, for example, are prerequisite conditions for existentialism because they have one thing in common: the individual's, or individual field worker's status or place is not given. Furthermore, when this condition is enhanced by the absence of metaphysics or the transcendent so that there is no sense that one is connected to a "being" greater than oneself, then the individual is left with a stark awareness that he is alone, vulnerable, and mortal. At that point, he is ready to say as existentialists are prone to do: I must create myself (as in a situation for myself) or perish. Having realized that, what does one do?

Had I remembered my roots in war torn Germany all along, I might have understood much earlier that the cultural environment could be conceived positively as one's situation. In terms of Sartre's thinking and put in plain English, depending on the individual's freely chosen project (or research goal) certain aspects of culture are re-assigned meaning and thus become his personal situation just as culture points to some worthwhile projects that may be freely chosen (1956, p.731–2). The relationship between individual consciousness and culture is not one of simple determination or constraint of the former by the latter. Rather, Sartre argues that culture can act on the subject only to the exact extent that he comprehends it, that is, transforms it into a situation (p.731). It is in this sense that the individual consciousness is the sole determinant of "being," meaning the free agent responsible for his situation.

From the perspective of field work affecting the field worker I might convert Sartre's last statements into the following: Lenda culture could only be said to have acted on me, as subject, to the extent that I comprehended it by having transformed it into my situation. Had the Lenda left me unaffected, I could not have claimed that I understood them. In other words, all researchers who have studied a foreign culture and claim that they understand it, should have been affected by it somehow. Most researchers claim such an understanding, yet virtually all of them shy away from telling how it affected them. It is like claiming that a coin has only one side.

But what about freedom? According to Sartre, freedom has structure. This is not to say that freedom has essence. It exists, that is all. Its structure is merely heuristic. In simplest terms, freedom consists of two elementary structures, a freely self-posited end or project and one's situation. The two are mediated by processes of perception and meaning. One's situation, too, consists of several elementary structures that Sartre (1956: ibid) identifies as one's place, one's body, one's past, one's position, and one's fundamental relation to others. This model structured my research. It allowed me to create a workable and dynamic situation without attaching myself to initially unrecognizable families or poorly functioning ones under stress.

One's project, which must be freely chosen, enables a person to assign meanings selectively to the elementary structures of his or her situation. When one changes one's project, an ever-present possibility, one also changes the interactions with people and assigns different meanings to various engaged aspects of one's past, place, position, relationships, and history. One may picture this account as shown below.

Most social scientists are trained in methods and techniques of data collection and observation that enable them to collect quantitative and/or qualitative data so that one anthropologist's data does not differ too enormously from that of another anthropologist who is interested in researching a similar topic. The predominant social science method is, in other words, one of analytical description. But Sartre (1956, p.726) argues that "pure, simple empirical description can only give us catalogues and put us in the presence of pseudo-irreducibles." It is not enough, he writes,

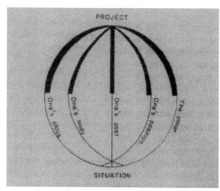

Sartre's Notion of Freedom

"to draw up a list of behaviour patterns, of drives and inclinations, it is necessary to decipher them; that is, it is necessary to know how to question them" (ibid). Such a method, which assumes that there is not a taste, a mannerism, or a human act that is not revealing, Sartre calls existential psychoanalysis. It sits on the assumption "that man is a totality not a collection. Consequently, he expresses himself as a whole in even his most insignificant and his most superficial behavior" (ibid).

In *Being and Nothingness* (1956:745), Sartre gives an example of changes in meaning by describing a "fundamental relation" of a skier (choice of being) to snow (being), a relation that consists of sliding. "The snow, which sank under my weight when I walked, which melted into water when I tried to pick it up, solidifies suddenly under the action of my speed; it supports me" (ibid). The meaning is the result of a fundamental relation in action.

A philosopher can choose any example whatsoever to make his case. It is harder for an anthropologist in a field work situation. But perhaps the following sentence might give some insight into the changes in meaning of "a fundamental relation" between an anthropologist and the other. The other who looked at me with suspicion when I arrived, who refused to help when I asked, cooperated willingly when I recognized their innate intelligence. Sartre banished the Deity to focus solely on the subtle consequences of relational action between natural man and all other phenomena of nature, and then heed what is happening.

Ethnographer and Art, not Culture and Personality

In a fascinating study, Agar (1980) states:

> Ethnographers, on the other hand, are allowed to go into a situation with no awareness of the biases they bring to it from their own cultures and personalities. This simply does not make good sense, but I am not sure how to correct it (p.42).

A quick reply would be, if ethnographers are not aware of their quirky cultural biases and personalities they soon will be. All they need to do is heed what is happening to them in their new "situation." According to Sartre, we do not need to know the whole of our culture and nervously worry about its effects on research and theories. Rather, we need to be persons who choose to act, collect data, risk being human, heed happenings, and be creative, all choices requiring both rational and affective faculties—indeed, the whole person. Three things are required of an ethnographer, namely, that he be aware that he chooses, that he choose responsibly meaning that his choices are recommendable to others and, finally, that he bring his project to fruition or be nothing.

In this sense, existentialism is an austere doctrine. For is it not inevitable that apprentice ethnographers will make mistakes in the field—but who is the judge? At best one would have to answer "freedom," because according to Sartre it is a fundamental universal value and human condition—except to judge, "freedom" would have to be personified and made transcendent, which is foreign to Sartre's thinking.

The result is anguish. Nothing legitimizes, forces, or excuses our choices. Knowing this, Sartre concludes that we are condemned to be free. But alas, today society with its institutionalized bureaucracies and bureaucratized ethics are not content with that. Rather than being condemned to be free, they understand themselves as free to condemn.

In our Western tradition, proponents of understanding, know-how or tacit knowledge, and of knowing through one's own and others' emotions and experiences, have always lived alongside those who believed in the acquisition of knowledge solely by rational means. Social science, long ago, ought to have turned the two into one unified process of acquiring knowledge. It has not. Consequently, we are often left with a superficial understanding of who we and others are. We also practice a science that tends more toward sterility than inspiration. But let us be reminded of a question asked by Thomas Mann about art, one which we should also ask about social science:

> Should we not call the one who accomplished the breakthrough from intellectual coldness into a daring world of new emotionality, should we not call him the redeemer and savior of art? (See von Gronicka, 1970, p.16; also, Mann, 1965, p.321, where emotionality is translated as feeling).

Before leaving this topic one further point must be made. To synthesize some bothersome oppositions, Agar (1980, p.13) suggests using a "'funnel' approach, with breadth and humanity at the beginning of the funnel, and then, within the context of that beginning, depth, problem-focus, and science at the narrow end." I agree with Agar when he says that "without science, we lose our credibility. Without humanity, we lose our ability to understand others" (p.13). While I was in the field, however, I found that it was much easier to do science at the beginning. Understanding came later and involved a much deeper, more concentrated, and less overtly systematic probing. But clearly, either approach works.

Summary and Prospectus

I have written a dissertation and numerous papers about Lenda behavior and social action. I have also written a book about how Lenda culture informs Lenda social action with meaning. In this, my final book about the Lenda experience, I describe how the Lenda, their culture, and their culturally-informed social environment affected the ever-changing meaning that I assigned my person, my past, and my relations with significant others. The dissonance between new feelings and old background assumptions created a small but significant revolution that would later lead to reconceptualization of the role of empathy, memory, and the affirmations of diverse genres for anthropology.

As my pre-field work project of trying to be an American and anthropologist changed in the field to understanding the Lenda in their world of religion, kinship, and economic development, so too the meaning of my relationship to my past, my husband, friends, and the people I encountered during my research changed. For the most part, however, I was merely a student of social anthropology doing "objective" research. Only gradually did the undercurrent of thought that centered on who I was as a human being and how I related to the world, change from adaptive consciousness to reflective consciousness and thus knowing something that

I did not know before. It was at times a joyful, at times a clumsy and frustrating, even angry experience.

Under the impact of my occasionally strong reactions to Lenda, I had to acknowledge that in researching "them" I was finding myself or, as Sartre would have it, making myself. But finding oneself and making oneself are not the same thing. Sartre's thinking was more on the mark toward the end of his life. During an interview, he admitted that his early writing was wrong because it addressed a limited condition, namely, that of France at war. So, he revised his famous phrase "we are what we make of ourselves" to "a man can always make something out of what is made of him" (Sartre, Audiobook). What a difference! As apprentice, however, "being what we make of ourselves" became my research model and motto of survival; "making something out of what was made of me" became the truth that emerged from my remembered experience of war and migration. Indeed, something was made of me long before I came to the field. But without Sartre's early "myth" my courage to project myself forward into the future and to make something out of what is made of me would have faltered.

The first two parts of the book look primarily at toughening mind and body not only to cope with surviving physical and emotional stress, but also with creating the conditions for solid research and comparing my efforts with those of other colleagues. It is followed by a brief description of reactions to arriving in Lusaka, the capital of Zambia. It then traces trying changes in me as I moved into the rural area, became immersed in matrilineal Lenda, and finally wound things up to return home.

2

ARRIVAL: PREPARING THE MIND, FORGETTING THE BODY

Research and Gender

When Leela Dube wrote in 1975 that anthropology was to be an integral part of the content of her marriage, I could empathize. Like her, I too was married to an anthropologist. Unlike her, I would not allow my husband to go to the field with me. That was simply not an option.

Marriage, dissertation, learning Swahili and iciBemba, paperwork and preparation, moving from state to state, and then leaving altogether was like jumping into an abyss. From January 1973 when I left for the field until July 1974, I was alone.

Before I entered the Lenda valley and during my visits to missionaries I heard a lot of dreadful stories about how travelers were beaten up in Lenda owing to the continued practice of instant vengeance. I was warned not to travel alone. One of the anthropologists who taught me the local language back in the States, described the people as being morose, unfriendly, and paranoid. The worst horror stories centered on the Zangavan pedicle which one had to cross if one took the shorter route into the valley. One was warned of bribery and theft, of the presence of aggressive guerrillas, as well as uncontrolled and unpaid Zangavan soldiers.

Naturally, I travelled alone. Indeed, at that time, I found stories like that told by Leela Dube in India, which persuaded her not to travel alone, offensive. She wrote:

> I was told about the plight of a woman sociologist who, only a few years before, had come to Chhattisgarh to collect folklore but, feeling insecure because of the behavior of petty officials and the ununderstanding and indifferent attitude of the people, had had to go back without achieving her objective. An unmarried woman travelling alone in these areas was inconceivable to the people. I therefore decided to conduct my field investigations under the protective umbrella of my father-in-law (1975, p.159).

On one hand, if it is the case that the woman sociologist was truly incapacitated, then the above quotation is a serious indictment against Indian men. They must be very different from the men in Lenda. Lenda male officials, police, and villagers were always curious and sometimes a nuisance, but none ever forced themselves on me, nor would they, once I explained what I was doing, seriously hinder my work. On the other hand, if the story is only half true, then it says something about the difference between women researchers.

First, I must admit that I tempted fate. Second, I usually worked with the assumption that no man would want to force himself on me. Third, I entrusted my life to the people and it soon became very clear that there was always someone among them who felt protective of me. Fourth, let me say it, I was naive and usually so filled with a love and zest for life that my sincerity was contagious. I really believe that this four-fold attitude, however dubious, helped me through many awkward situations. Still, one must assume that a researcher tells the truth. Which leads me to emphasize once again that Lenda men must be different from those of central India. Perhaps the fact that the Lenda are a matrilineal people had something to do with that.

There is one further point of difference between Dube's experience and my own. She consistently emphasizes her awareness of herself as a woman. "My being a woman ..." or "I must follow the norms of behavior which the people associated with my sex, age, and caste," or "I was a Brahman and a woman," or "I did not have to neutralize or minimize my femininity but presented myself as essentially a woman; even to men I was a woman interested in their women (ibid)." This constant reference to her femininity within the space of three pages must mean that she perceived herself and the people perceived her very differently from the way I perceived myself or from the way the Lenda perceived me. Only once when I thought myself to be in real danger did I use, unsuccessfully I might add, being a woman as an excuse to free myself from a tricky situation. Usually, I was oblivious to gender. That is, I was aware that I am anatomically a woman. I also observed that the Lenda were aware that I am anatomically a woman. But that fact seemed to carry no other meaning. At least, it had nothing to do with my research. It had only to do with love making. This again says something simultaneously about the Lenda and my perception of gender.

But let us pause a moment and contemplate once more Dube's story about the unsuccessful woman sociologist and Dube's persistent reference to her own gender and social status. Somewhere in that story and in those references, is the essence of human dis-ease and the failure of social science; and that dis-ease, and that essence, is determinism. Formally we no longer believe Leslie White who wrote that "Human beings are merely the instruments through which cultures express themselves ... In the man-culture system, man is the dependent, culture the independent, variable" (White, 1959, p.148–149). Informally we have long since capitulated. Had we not capitulated, we should surely have developed a theory of freedom, especially, personal freedom. Political freedom in the form of Marxism, Humanism, Liberalism, are all different forms of benevolent determinism. Sometimes the right to determine is placed into the hand of a class, or a party, or a revolutionary movement, more often it is left in the hands of churches, public opinion, parents, teachers, and so on, ad infinitum. Instead of teaching students how to explore the nature of freedom and responsibility, we encourage rebellion, wild rampages against house, furniture, and the establishment, and then we stand by as society unleashes its whips and thrashes them back into submission. Instead of re-instituting prayer, I thought, perhaps we should start each class with the following words:

> Man being condemned to be free carries the weight of the whole world on his shoulders; he is responsible for the world and for himself as a way of being … It is therefore senseless to think of *complaining* since nothing foreign has decided what we feel, what we live, or what we are (Sartre, 1956, p.707–8).

Yes, these are the harsh words of a radical individualism that I will come to reject. But open your ears, my friends, and listen. Do you not hear complaints upon complaints? The student complains about his teacher, the child about its mother, the wife about her husband, the black man about the white, and vice versa. What have we learned? Certainly, not that by choosing our project we will have chosen for the world (Sartre, 1956).

Shock, Doubt, and Help

Having clarified why I went to the field alone, how I preferred ignoring gender, and where Sartre's ideas were useful, let us now look more closely at my arrival in Lusaka. The air was moist and warm on January 2, 1973, the day of my arrival. The sky was grey as if to symbolize the mixed blessing that my field work experience would become. People of all colors speaking different languages filled the airport. An employee from the Institute for African Research met me and drove me to my place of residence. He warned that the Institute was isolated and too far from the city but did not explain how colonial its atmosphere was. Under colonialism one set of buildings and facilities were built for Europeans and quite another, little shacks without electricity or indoor plumbing for Africans. To this day, the arrangement symbolizes the presence of apartheid tendencies then, even among British intellectuals and colonial officials who employed Africans as clerks, drivers, and maintenance workers but were satisfied to keep them in inferior shelters. No doubt, my initial response to this differentiation in accommodation was like that of every liberal American. Since black researchers from Nigeria and Ghana shared the latter premises with us we soon learned to live with current realities. The goal was research.

My neighbors, the Taters from Maryland, he an economist, she a poet, showed me what to eat and where to shop. Even in city stores a lot of food looked unfamiliar or unsanitary. As one shopped one felt oneself devoured by hungry looks from hungry young boys. I was always overcome with guilt as I left the store with filled shopping bags. This guilt and the unpleasant pressure of inadequate transportation, of difficulties with money transfers from Canada to Lusaka, the inability to find a Lenda speaker so that I might continue to practice this language while in the capital; all this stress and strain, isolation and monotony, this unbearable uncertainty about the success of this venture, burst forth one day when I tried to open my door and found it stuck because under its wide bottom lay a squashed but twitching frog. I felt my endurance giving way to revulsion and yet I stared at the fluids of its body as they drew themselves out, flattened and spread across the floor, and then I screamed until the Taters came running convinced that my bungalow was on fire.

The incident of the squashed frog is a beautiful example not of neurotic projection (Jung, 1968, p.153), as of thematic unity. It was as if the fluids of the frog were charged with my feelings of anguish about Bob, poverty, humanity, life and death, as if in this viscous substance of a dying life, any kind of life, were condensed all the psychic meaning of uncertainty, horror, torment, and impermanence of life. This slimy fluid was, as Sartre (1956, p.771) noted, neither material nor psychic. Rather, it transcended the opposition of the psychic and physical and revealed itself to me "as the ontological expression of the entire world" (ibid). All this was the result of one innocent, unsuspecting motion of my arm. Here is how I recorded the effects of seeing the squashed frog in my personal journal:

   ... The image stayed with me. And for a moment I felt

recognition. A vague shadow whisked across my brain of writhing passion and defeat.

I thought of Bob. His face looked drained. I stood there stamping my feet as if crushing his will and spirit. I yanked open the door and walked through with resolve.

I thought of Zambia, of the rich and the poor. And of the boy by the entrance to the supermarket. He stood there squashed against the wall, his stomach caved in, looking furtively at bulging shopping bags of rich customers. And I turned away. In each letter, I described the twitching frog as if it were just another sensation. And I knew my friends must think me crazy to be in Zambia and focus on such trivia.

There are the rich and the poor. The poor live in picturesque but destitute shanty towns, in houses of mud walls, with pieces of tin and wood and plastic on the roofs. And everything is held in place by stones. I see lined faces and ragged clothes. And the stench of perspiration and polyester drive me away.

And then there are the houses of the rich, sprawling bungalows hidden behind lush growth, guarded by houseboys against thieves. And the faces are young and smooth, and the clothes fashionable and shapely. A chauffeur opens the door and a child slides out of the limousine and struts firmly to school. And I want to bury my nose in its black curly hair and draw in the scent …

Out came feelings of guilt about having left Bob behind and my inability to see each as self-sufficient. Out came feelings of frustration at not being able to do anything about Zambia's poverty. Out too came the admission that sweat in polyester was repulsive and that clean, polished, and deodorized bodies were pleasant. As cerebral as my goal was, the body refused to be forgotten.

These kinds of outbursts accompanied the beginning of my field work. While they may have been unpleasant they were also revealing because in them I saw the start of the process of resolving many contradictions with which my life, lived on several continents, was riddled. I bore them, as Jung seemed to when he wrote about a thirty-four-year-old American woman, a very competent analyst, who had got into a disagreeable transference situation with her patient, sought Jung's help, and experienced similar transference with him.

> I saw the climax coming and knew that one day a sudden explosion would take place. Of course, it would be a bit disagreeable and of a very emotional nature, as you have perhaps noticed in your own experience, and I foresaw a highly sentimental situation. Well, you just have to put up with it; you cannot help it. After six months of very quiet and painstaking systematic work she couldn't hold herself in any longer, and suddenly she almost shouted: 'But I love you!' and then she broke down and fell upon her knees and made an awful mess of herself.

> You just have to stand such a moment. It is really awful to be thirty-four years old and to discover suddenly that you are human (Jung, 1968, p.166–7).

My outbursts were not as severe nor of the same nature. But Jung's association of "love" with disagreeable emotions and "break down" with discovering that we are human was worrying. Disturbing too were the linkages he made within the process of moving from a lack of self-awareness to growing awareness only to "elope" with "Chinamen" or "Negroes." While it was written in the 1930's, and while we must for the moment overlook, if not excuse, Jung's own strong and embarrassing prejudices the statement is remarkable:

> We often discover with Americans that they are tremendously unconscious of themselves. Sometimes they suddenly grow aware of themselves, and then you get these interesting stories of decent

young girls eloping with Chinamen or with Negroes ... It is the same phenomenon as "going black" or "going native" in Africa (p.166).

Did I have this tendency, I wondered? Whatever, I saw it as being a politically liberal attempt to achieve absolution for bad deeds committed by previous generations that cannot, however, be absolved in this manner. To my mind, scrutinizing strong emotions helped recognize that, like it or not, body and mind both played into our research—as did the "dangerous" yearning for love. We are merely whole persons. Nevertheless, I got the point; emotional expression in matters of research was experienced as particularly disagreeable by people in the professions. In my emotional make-up, however, I identified with east Europeans like Tolstoy for whom life was art. What increasingly taxed my patience were liberal programs; to me they began to look more like rationalizations of the cerebral cortex which sat on wings and for which the whole body of human emotion and anguish was non-existent.

Changing Perceptions

Nevertheless, I became harder, became also the observer of distancing myself from intimate ties back home. Noticed it with several perceptual transformations. First, my relationship with Bob shifted from the concrete to the abstract. More importantly where I assumed that our relationship was equal in the past, I now noted its paternalism. Second, it was not Zambian culture, or later Lenda culture, that I found puzzling. What became puzzling was Zambia or Lenda nature. In the past, nature seemed dependable, now I perceived it as contingent. Finally, my distant German past and immediate American one first came to be merged in recurrent dreams and later reversed as I began more and more to relive the former and repress the latter.

I noted the change in my relationship with Bob as I reflected about his letters. At first our exchange was rather funny: I would comment about killing spiders and he would suggest letting them live because they fed on other vermin; I would describe that rice contained bugs and their eggs, and he would suggest that I float them out. More and more advice arrived with his letters: reminders to keep a daily journal, to do good archival work, to carry an identity card identifying Bob as next of kin because we used separate names, and so on. When I wrote that I had to buy a car, he wrote back advising against it, even one of Bob's colleagues included a letter advising against it. I bought a car anyways and our correspondence only meant an increase in sweat, worry and nightmares.

I wondered why Bob should have turned himself into a father figure and what I did to contribute to this change of role. I concluded that two behaviorisms were at fault. First, my letters invited his sympathy and second, he forwarded my grant money. It was easy to change the latter, in future my money would be forwarded directly from the Bank of Montreal to the Commercial Bank of Lusaka. In the event of delay or shortage I found it advisable to approach my mother for help. There were several advantages to this arrangement. My mother did not like writing letters and, given her experience in bringing me up, she had long since been convinced that I was stubborn and usually did what I thought was right and with a keen sense of survival. I was after all a refugee and a product of war. This my American husband never understood and it would be the unseen thorn in our relationship.

Nevertheless, seeking Bob's sympathy was almost unavoidable. There were real problems and advice, even when rejected, was useful. At moments of mischief, I told myself that I wrote as I did because I feared that too much positive or negative news might persuade Bob to jump into a plane and fly over. It sounds fantastic, callous, perhaps, even cruel. But something was happening, and I needed solitude. I know that if I could have wiped away our marriage with a magic wand I would have done so. I was also aware that saying this closed the possibility of being moral or making a moral decision.

But then, it was not Bob who bothered me. Rather, in the Lusaka environment, free among my equals who were all preoccupied with similar worries, the oppression of marriage hit me "like a ton of bricks." Even when "happy" couples passed through our research quarters I pitied them. I would find myself observing their every demeanor, nonverbal signs and signals used to keep the other in line. Back home I found it amusing. Here I felt repulsed. The recognition of subtle controls between man and woman merely raised this question. Can I make competent decisions alone or not? Certain is, I must risk it.

It occurred to me then that during times of mental growth and change, one must be alone. Naturally, one talks and relates to many people, including the opposite sex, but there is a quiet, respectful understanding that this time is special, that it will pass, and that much will have to be understood before it does. In such an environment, even the love-making between a man and woman is different. The strong grip of possessiveness is absent, and conversation continues into the early morning hours and is forever renewed and forever primary. For once sex appears to be quietly integrated into one's personality, and so comfortably settled is "it," that the question of its dominance simply does not arise. At least, that is how I imagined it.

What surprised me even more than my changed perception of marriage, was my changed perception of nature. North America had just emerged from the "age of the flower children" to a "new freedom." As I left the US, concerns about ecology and conservation were popular among the masses, indeed, were becoming a new religion. I fully expected to confirm the correctness of that attitude but already in Lusaka nature came to take on new meaning. Perhaps it had something to do with the deep lines on women's faces or with the presence of death in the shanty-towns near the Institute. Maybe it is just that life's contingency confronted me, as it were, in the nude.

I expressed this recognition of contingency, along with my other frustrations, to my mother. It must be understood that my mother was the only one to whom I could express such feelings openly. She and I and many others grew up surrounded by death and decay, familiar with hunger, surrounded by deformities and ruins. She knew that life sprang forth even amidst devastation. Above all, she understood that I was not seeking her sympathy but that I was trying to understand:

February 14, 1973
Darling Mama:

I feel weary. Weary, weary, and weary. I'm taking my decision-making too seriously. If I don't become more fatalistic, if I don't learn to say, "to hell with everybody, to hell with all great expectations," if I don't learn this, Mama, my brain will explode.

I bought a Datsun 1200 from Peresa. The chap is quite fatalistic. On the way to the service station we passed two accidents. "We die fast in Zambia," says he. The sun beat down on us. Sweat and blood, Mam. Sweat and blood and wailing.

And after all this bleeding flesh we go to sign all these papers. A world ordered by paper, a paper world.

I look at the shrubbery near our house. Tough, knarred branches are crawling in, cracking the stone, straining for space. And I hear the wailing from the poor section of town. Another death of course. A paper world, a temporary world and the shit comes piling in. And we're to assign it meaning.

I had forgotten that life was so temporary. How could I have forgotten, Mam?

The letter expresses the burden of being responsible and alone. Fatalism looked like a promising relief with its nonchalant assent to mortality in a world of short lives. But that attitude had to be suspended for the sake of research, personal struggle, and a more joyful and free human future.

Finally, there were my recurrent dreams. Repeatedly the U.S. was compared with Germany. Sometimes it was their wars that were compared, sometimes their people. Always, amidst fantastic colors and fantastic events I was faced with a major decision centered on freedom. I was usually offered a choice between fascism and radical freedom. What was required of me was to rupture my past. Sometimes I would be faced with several choices because each time that I thought I had grasped freedom another hurdle was put in my way. Usually I was on the brink of opting for radical freedom, once and for all, when I would wake up covered in sweat. The following is one such dream:

> In my dream, several people were comparing the U.S. and Germany after their respective wars (Vietnam, World War II). We were in a plush bar and I commented to that extent. A fellow next to me responded, "Oh, you should have seen Germany after the war, the whole capital was dressed and furnished in white to give it a look of innocence after the atrocities."

> The dream then shifted, and I found myself in a position where I and all the other people had to decide between fascism and freedom. For some reason, many people chose constraints and found themselves standing in line joining the will of the government. It was my turn to choose and I "swam" free of the crowd singing "I want freedom." When I made it through and past the crowd, an official came up to me and said, "A very important person wants to see you," and he took me to the front of a line of people into a place off to one side. There I had to wait again, and while waiting, I saw a child who had also chosen freedom and was waiting with us. The child was playing with some sort of cuddly animal which disappeared in the bushes.

> Searching for her companion, whom she didn't want to lose, the child looked around furtively, and slid through the shrubbery into freedom. While I continued to wait, an elderly woman came by, gorgeously dressed. She stood in front of a mirror and kept on

saying how absurd it was to emphasize dress like this. This expensive dress was absurd, absurd. I moved away from the crowd with the realization that freedom lay beyond the shrubs, not in this line of waiting people. Then I awoke.

Only recently have I learned that this juxtaposing of earlier with recent life events in the dreams of traveling academics is a common experience (Andersen, 1971). Agar who summarizes Andersen's research of American academics traveling in India states that she "outlines a change in dream content from an initial retreat to earlier life events, followed by the establishment of a 'secondary identity' that allows dreams with mixed, but clearly distinct American and Indian elements" (Agar, 1980, p.51). The latter type of mixture would occur in my dreams too.

A Word about Prejudice

Before I take the reader into the Lenda valley, a word about prejudice is in order. Prejudice haunts us all. Even the most just and humane are not free of being prejudicial. James Michener whose novels fall into the category of relaxed reading and, perhaps, have no place in our discussion, prides himself because he does not make "dam fool statements about other nations and other cultures" (1971, p.325). He *thinks* he does not. In fact, the very selection of his characters is a vagrant display of prejudice. For example, his Nordic characters, those that are allowed some speech in *The Drifters*, are beautiful blondes better to look at than to listen to. Germans appear only as men and then as Prussian generals with Prussian haircuts or with Prussian personalities, whatever they are. The only nation that has both sexes speaking for it is the USA, although we also hear a little from the British male. Some characters are given only physical beauty and, yes, the ability to copulate "coolly" as is becoming a cool Nordic blonde. Nature for once is "rational." Some characters only speak in commands and, yes, they drink beer, but without the usual accompaniment of colorful sentiments. Culture here is wholly "authoritarian." All this prejudice and bias comes from a man with a considerable sense of equanimity. What is he justifying and by what authority?

If prejudice in Michener is only mildly disturbing, in Sartre it is serious. Let us contemplate the following passage:

> The obscenity of the feminine sex is that of everything which "gapes open." It is an *appeal to being* as all holes are. In herself woman appeals to a strange flesh which is to transform her into a fullness of being by penetration and dissolution. Conversely woman senses her condition as an appeal precisely because she is "in the form of a hole." This is the true origin of Adler's complex. Beyond any doubt her sex is a mouth and a voracious mouth which devours the penis—a fact which can easily lead to the idea of castration (Sartre, 1956, p.782).

In *Being and Nothingness* Sartre claims that we stand revealed even in our most superficial behavior and that by our subjective choice we make known to ourselves what we are. Given that we know something of Sartre through his work and from Simone de Beauvoir, it is safe to assume that one of Sartre's major projects was the attainment of personal freedom. It is also safe to assume that he defined the feminine sex in the above terms only because he found woman alluring, indeed irresistible, and, unable to reconcile the demands of his body with those of his mind, he decided that sexual relations with woman had to be transcended. The above words and de Beauvoir's description of their relation in *The Prime of Life* would suggest that he succeeded.

We all face the conflict between mind and body and, sooner or later, most of us confront the question of how to integrate our sexuality into our personalities. None of us fear sexual activity per se, most of us fear its possible results. Most women, but especially those who see themselves as potential intellectuals, can perhaps empathize with Simone de Beauvoir when she sees in the pleasures of the flesh the "threat of being hurtled down some slippery slope to moral and intellectual ruin" (Evans, 1980, p.398). When I went to the field I was haunted by a similar fear. It is a common one to be found even in biographies of great men or women. I was familiar with it from the biographies of Mozart and Tolstoy. Like them I felt that if only I could overcome that fatal attraction to the opposite sex, if only I could overcome men, then my brain would soar freely and brilliantly across the mental landscape unencumbered by sticky emotions. The day came; and as I was bathing in the sweet victory of this overcoming, there appeared at the periphery of my consciousness, barely discernible, the icy threat of sterility and alienation. I realized then the importance of one of Sartre's distinctions. Freedom is an existence which perpetually makes itself; it has no essence. Freedom is becoming not being. It cannot be taken for granted if we want a wider sense of humanity and bring it about—but to what end?

When I first read Sartre's fantasies about how "we are haunted by the image of a consciousness which would like to launch forth into the future, toward a projection of self, and which at the very moment when it was conscious of arriving there would be slyly held back by the invisible *suction* of the past" (Sartre, 1956, p.778)—or when I read about the "moist and feminine sucking" and "the snare of the slimy" that holds and compromises man and so on ad infinitum (p.776)—I sat back and composed similar fantasies based on cerebral coitus, written from a woman's perspective who like Sartre would like to launch forth into the future without being compromised. And then I thought the whole endeavor absurd. It might look like reverse discrimination rather than what it was, namely, a surge toward freedom. Instead, I decided to tell an embarrassing story that will put our brain back into our body and all of us back on the ground.

One day I was interviewing Mr. Ngoma, headman of Kakuso village and one of the elders of Watchtower. We were discussing a sensitive political issue when I was jolted out of my preoccupations by the ferocious bleating of a sexually aroused male goat. He was in hot pursuit of a softly bleating and obviously alarmed female. I looked up from my notes, surprised and mildly horrified, just as this over-heated and over-extended male goat jumped across our wobbly table. Among those surrounding me, my response was the slowest, since the noise of this satyr was unfamiliar to my ears. Swiftly, I turned my head right and left to check the reaction of my male companions and I noted their somewhat embarrassed grins as if the male goat had exposed their very essence to the world. Two feet away stood several women bent over with laughter. And then we all laughed, men, women, and children. If nature is good to think then maleness is good to laugh. It came from the depth of our being, this laughter, and it was good because there is so little to laugh about and because nature had us again. There was not a man or woman among us who would have thought that the mortar was "voracious" without having first noted that the pestle was "greedy."

Summary

If there were a creator, he created human beings with two fatal flaws. First, he created us without letting us know who we are. The human being is, therefore, continually in search of him-and-herself. Secondly, he gave us mental tools that are inadequate to the task of sound self-definition for we define ourselves by contrast to or in terms of the other. In this search for individual or ethnic identity and in the inadequacy of our tools which allow us to see ourselves only through the other as through a lens, lies the essence of prejudice (Loubser, 1968). But if we look at it from Sartre's perspective there is no creator, and so the human being is misguided in his search for self. The self cannot be discovered; it must be made. We have made ourselves with fatal flaws, ones that lie buried in our assumptions about the nature of the human being. We cannot know who we are unless we create ourselves and we cannot expect self-knowledge unless we look inside at our plans. Only when we look at the selves of others are we involved in a process of discovery as we try to discern what their projects are and how they inform their social actions.

Liberalism, too, is burdened with a fatal flaw. It assumes, as no doubt it must, that what is good for the best, the rest should have too. Hence it requires that the poor change and assume attitudes that will transform them into members of middle or upper classes, and that women change and assume attitudes that will transform them into social men. It is not seriously required that men or the upper classes change to make mutual accommodation possible. Social change ends up being one-sided and assimilative. Yet some people seem astonished when many women run back to the kitchen (see especially Hazleton, 1977).

On one hand, we have for too long encouraged mysticism and shied away from hard thought. Too many people prefer the mystical ravings of Gabriel Marcel to the unrelenting insistence of Sartre that we must assume the burden of our freedom and with it the responsibility for what we are. On the other, we are too willing to imitate the hard sciences so that the individual finds one or the other of his qualities summarized within stated generalities. An individual becomes a collection of attributes subsumed under a fashionable concept rather than a totality that is greater than its parts. We become identities rather than human persons. I am surely not too wrong when I say that in North America the individual is the group and the group the individual. Instead of working through the painful process of trying to come to terms with disquieting aspects of our bodied human make-up, we look for a group in which a disquieting behaviorism becomes the rallying cry for more freedom. But is that freedom?

Finally, I told the last story in this section because in Lenda the claim that women are somehow more closely associated with nature and men with culture is ludicrous. It was ludicrous to Lenda women and it was ludicrous to Lenda men. It is theoretically erroneous because, of course, nature is culture and culture is nature—and that is all. But is it?

PART II

THE FIELD

There are two kinds of empiricism; one is characterized by observation, measurement, and the controlled experiment, the other is characterized by only experimenting with oneself and one's life. The anthropologist must practice both and, usually, the last of the two is more authentic.

3

LENDA NATURE

… though the human being, both male and female, was endowed with sex, and although the localization of the daemonic in the loins fitted the man better than the woman, yet the whole curse of fleshliness, of slavery to sex, was laid upon the woman (Mann, 1965, p.105).

We learned how bewilderingly the two kingdoms [animate and inanimate nature] mimic each other. When Father Leverkuhn showed us the "devouring drop" … What he did was as follows: he took a tiny glass stick, just a glass thread, which he had coated with shellac, between the prongs of a little pair of pincers and brought it close to the drop. That was all he did: the rest the drop did itself. It drew up on its surface a little protuberance, something like a moment of conception, through which it took the stick into itself, lengthwise. At the same time it got longer, became pear-shaped in order to get its prey all in, so that it should not stick out, beyond, and began, I give you my word for it, gradually growing round again, first by taking on an egg-shape, to eat off the shellac and distribute it in its body. This done, and returned to its round shape, it moved the stick, licked clean, crosswise to its own surface and ejected it into the water (Mann, 1965, p.18–9).

I ended the last section with the bold statement that nature is culture and culture is nature. In this chapter we must look more closely at its meaning, and try to decipher it.

According to Sartre (1956), being is the ever-present foundation of the existent. Being is everywhere in it and nowhere. Being is. Consciousness can pass beyond the existent toward the meaning of this being. And this "meaning of the being of the existent in so far as it reveals itself to consciousness is the phenomenon of being" (Mann, 1965, p.25). By saying that nature is culture I am talking about this "phenomenon of being" which is immediately disclosed to consciousness.

Since the phenomenon of being can be disclosed to my consciousness, I should stand before it in an attitude of interrogation. Unfortunately, most researchers do not take such an attitude with them to the field. Rather, we take with us an attitude of knowing. We do not question so much as measure nature.

There is a difference between approaching nature from the perspective of objective as against existentialist thought. Thinking of nature as a "thing," we make assumptions about its functions. On one hand, we may assume that nature is passive so that we can force upon it modifications of which it is neither the source nor the creator. On the other, we may assume that it is active so that it can force upon our behavior modifications of which we are neither the source nor the creator. Usually, the interaction between nature and culture falls somewhere between the two extremes and cultural ecology has given this dialectic expression.

The distinction between an objective and existentialist perspective may be seen in the different perception the Lenda, the government, and I had of the main north-south road and the many winding paths to women's fields in Lenda. The road is passive. It is nature conquered by the bulldozer and subdued by the grader. By contrast, paths are there almost by default. A field is made and its shape adjusted to avoid particularly immovable obstacles, like big tree roots. Cassava is planted right to the edge of the field thus leaving a footpath. The path adjusts its growths according to the constant traipsing of many feet and one's feet adjust their hold on the ground in line with the recurring growths.

If you ask a boy to take you to his mother's field, you do so at considerable peril to your life and well-being. He has no sense of this space. It is not part of his tacit knowledge nor consciousness. Instead, he relies utterly on verbal skills to find his way around. With him by your side you will continually find yourself standing on knolls, listening to his calls for help. I shiver at the memory of it. By contrast, little girls have a strong spatial sense that is utterly nonverbal. Her know-how is embedded and implicit as if she were absorbed by her surroundings. Her confidence is inspiring. Sure-footed, never veering from the course, and in tasteful silence, she will lead you to your destination.

I went to Lenda with a scientific disposition. It remained a priority. But doing field work made me aware that reflection, discernment, and acquiring know-how were also important. A subject's observation of objects is different from consciousness deciphering the meaning of what is out there. It is thus that nature became puzzling. My perception of it jarred with my functionalist assumptions. I first became aware of the role of my consciousness in the perception of nature when it presented itself to me in the form of eidetic reductions consisting of unusually vivid mental images that sprang loose from their archaeological sedimentation at the sight of lacerated dogs, crippled men, and emaciated women.

I became aware, in other words, that nature looked differently (a) when I assumed a scientific stance and looked at nature through the eyes of my western education and its interest in results, or (b) when I adopted an existentialist approach and perceived nature in terms of my consciousness colored by my past and present projects, or (c) when I adopted a phenomenological or cultural approach and perceived reality from the perspective of the ethnographic other (Stoller, 1980, p.427). Before I describe my preoccupation with nature in the sequence in which these encounters took place, I shall relate some examples that make clear the distinction between the above points.

The Lenda and national government perception of space is not only contradictory; it is also part of their respective political philosophies and models of society. For the government, north-south constitutes the dynamic relation between Lenda and the national capital. It has been government policy since the 1950s to break the dynamic relations between east and west in Lenda. For the Lenda, the river by that name is even now their primary mode of communication among themselves. By contrast, for the government it is a national boundary separating Zambia from Zangava. For the government, land has become capital which can be owned privately or publicly, and which is measured in terms of square miles, soil fertility and quality to assess its monetary value. From their perspective, land is limited in quantity and high in value. By contrast, for the Lenda, land is kin ties, it is a network of human relationships that span across unlimited time and distance. Time and space are unified in a chain of births that starts and ends in infinity. The conception of limited amount of land or of land shortage is absent among many Lenda. Land is abundant, without boundary, just as there can be no boundary to womb. It is, therefore, not land that is wealth but children who are wealth (*ifyumu*) (Goody, 1976). To the government, land is the reification of capitalism and socialism. To the villager, it is the reification of matrilineal ideology. Space is constituted space. What space is, its being, discloses itself differently to its different interrogators.

The identification of land with kin is particularly clear in the story of the missionary-witch. This missionary, a woman in her sixties, tough in spirit and sinewy in flesh, lived in a two-story mission house. It was one of those magnificent sun-dried brick structures that had the ingeniousness of the human brain imprinted in every nook and cranny. She lived alone in this house on a hundred acres of land that separated two villages. When she first settled here villagers visited regularly, brought their prestations, and expected some in return. And in those early days she gave not only food, but also precious religious booklets written in Lenda or booklets which she translated into Braille. At times, she gave clothing or other goodies that were sent from donors abroad and, then, she gave generously of herself and her time as she drove the sick to distant clinics and hospitals and cared for them at home.

Age caught up with her and, like many missionaries, she began to suffer from severe calcium deficiency so that her spinal cord became brittle and driving on corrugated roads unbearably painful. Gradually she withdrew from the people. Where she felt one with them in the past, she now felt their visits burdensome. Nor could she let them know of her pain. Instead, she assumed more of her British identity and less of the Lenda one. Perhaps she knew only how to interact with the Lenda from the vantage point of strength, and with that strength gone, she gave up her footing in a society that she knew intimately but to which she had not been totally assimilated. Visitors were sent away or kept waiting in the yard or servants' entrance and slowly their view of her changed. As she broke her ties with them they regarded her ties with the land broken too. It began to annoy them that this "stranger" should sit on their land and many soon clamored to have her removed. As I walked through villages I often heard talk of the missionary-witch, until one day she was gone.

4

THE FIELD

… Western glorification of man's reason at the expense of his non-rational energies and needs has made a profound fissure in his total being. Normatively divided into a 'higher' and 'lower' self, he must live with a schism in his soul … (Gill and Sherman, 1973, p.17).

The Scope Between The Familiar and The Strange

From Lusaka, I drove north to Nhunda along a tarmac road. Gradually urban cement turned into mud-and-thatch or wattle-and-daub huts. In Niassa Province, people practiced shifting cultivation, a form of agriculture that entailed movement and makeshift structures.

A couple hitched a ride and I used the opportunity to practice the local language, *ChiBemba*. In Nhunda I stayed with the Patricks, the last known people by name on this trip. Apparently, my arrival called for refreshments for I was steered to Nhunda's social club, a cement hut offering beer and chairs. The history teacher Patrick, the District Governor, the Chief of the Nhunda area, as well as extension and agricultural officers drank Zambian Castle beer. A lively discussion about corruption ensued.

During the evening meal in the Patrick home, our conversation dwelled on difficulties of teaching rural Zambian boys. Sarah, a clearly disillusioned woman, mentioned that she gave up teaching because the behavior of local boys toward her, a woman, was too raucous. Hearing that upset me. A disgrace, I thought.

But of course, my judgment was too harsh, which prompted me to look at Sarah's young, pale face again. Since I saw no drive, since the boys were young men rough, earthy, and defensive about their lack of book-learning skills, I could understand how Sarah, unable to discover receptivity for her "creative" teaching methods, began to hate some students and stopped teaching. In this decision, she was honest and had my sympathy.

The morning of March 3, after first testing muddy roads, I left for Cassamba. From Nhunda I drove on dirt roads that were terribly difficult to traverse. Surviving potholes required full attention. Cassamba's government rest house was a welcome sight. I made myself known to the police, or they to me, and quickly retired. The following morning, I introduced myself to the District Governor, District Secretary, and local chief. My aim was to explain my research interests and start the search for an appropriate village.

Satisfied with my initial introductions, I drove south from Cassamba to the provincial capital, Mboua. The intention was to make my presence known at the Cabinet Office. On the way, I had my first flat tire. At the sight of my competent maneuverings, for I practiced changing tires in Lusaka, a crowd gathered quickly. Women were "aahing" and "oohing" about my efforts. They were also intently examining my goods.

When the exercise was almost over, two men stopped. Women nudged them to help. Remembering how, on leaving the repair shop in Lusaka, the newly replaced wheel came off, I declined. Unfortunately, that increased their time and excuse to study my wares. It made me nervous to have people peek at the gear, but I decided that their interest in my activity prevented theft. They even helped return to the trunk my pots, pans, mosquito nets, cot, air filters, tubes, brake and transmission fluids, fan belts, oil, cans with petrol, and the rest of my mobile garage.

The tire replaced, I continued to drive south. Feeling hungry, I stopped to buy some bananas. Two little boys had waved them at me. No sooner had I stopped but an old, ratty looking man pushed his head through the open car window and demanded 10 Zambian Kwacha. I told him that I didn't have 10 Zambian Kwacha, least of all would I hand one out on demand. I looked him straight in the eye, unfortunately, with failing courage. His increased proportionately, and a menacing hand grabbed a blanket covering suitcases in the backseat. I slapped his hand, yelled no, and tore off.

The experience left me shaken. I came to at the sound of violent thuds. I had momentarily lost consciousness. Disoriented and disbelieving I stared at tree stumps rapidly approaching the car. It took a moment, then I yanked the car off the embankment back to the road. My heart pounded violently in my throat. I stopped the car, no one was around. All I need is a broken gas tank, I thought, crawled under the car, and slowly inspected the metal. There were a few dents, but no ruptures. I opened the trunk, released built-up vapors from the petrol which was stored in plastic cans and covered the cans with a damp blanket to reduce the heat. "Dumb," I breathed, "I wouldn't have known what blacking out means."

An Oasis of the Neglected School

In Mboua, I stayed at the Mboua Inn. It was expensive but clean and it offered good facilities. The Minister of State and Cabinet Minister were on tour, so I left them a note informing them of my presence in the Province. That duty done, I walked to the White Fathers' mission in search of conversation and a Lenda dictionary. No one was home, but as I left I met a Catholic nun who introduced herself as Sister Teresa. Initially, she regarded me with some suspicion. I explained who I was and what I wanted at the mission. She explained that there were no Lenda dictionaries anymore. She told me about herself and finally mentioned that she was looking for a ride to Katumba. I was overjoyed to offer her one. We planned to drive north a day after tomorrow. Back at the Inn, I studied Lenda from my notes and quickly fell asleep.

March 5th, I checked with the Bank in Mboua to see if they had received a letter of introduction from the Commercial Bank of Zambia. They had not and I was unable to cash my check. Where I felt frustrated in Lusaka, I now merely waited.

A day later, Sister Teresa and I drove to Katumba. It is the name of a district and its capital. Sister Teresa taught the blind at a mission school just outside of Katumba town. The convent and school were run by nine sisters, all but one was Dutch.

Lenda is known as the valley of the blind. I guessed that one in ten people had eye problems and many of them gradually became blind. Government reports read in Lusaka suggested that blindness was suffered by 2% of the population. No one seemed to be certain of the cause. Some physicians and nurses blamed the blindness on measles, poor diet, or African *muti* (medicine). It looked like infection or inflammation, somehow. Sister Teresa thought the eye problems worsened considerably during the dry season when dust lingered incessantly in the air.

Before we arrived in Katumba, we stopped at a blind settlement, a little lush and shady spot off a few miles from the dusty road. The settlement was organized into two compounds. Blind inhabitants gardened communally. Cultivation exceeded local consumption, and the government supposedly bought surplus products through NAMB (National Agricultural Marketing Board).

Despite their handicap, the people were rather lively as they moved between garden and home. Some used sticks, others were guided by children, most were so familiar with their surroundings they needed no help. A man who was bitten by a snake lay on dire bedding beside his grass hut. Snake bites were not infrequent. Huts contained no furniture, nothing but a few old cooking pots. Some had grass-filled mats for bedding. A minimal existence.

Children born to these people could see and ran to welcome Sister Teresa who glowed with joy at her reception. As usual, women carried their babies in a sling. Though women were raggedly dressed, one breast was usually exposed ready to feed the baby. Older children, energetic and dressed in tatters, helped with cultivation. They received no schooling. People were growing tomatoes, maize, pineapples, and groundnuts. They managed, but life was harsh and accidents and disease but a step away.

At the mission, Sister Teresa, now relaxed and joyful, invited me to share their lunch. I was relieved to hear sincerity in her voice and see kindness on her face. She told me that traveling whites abused mission hospitality and I feared being one of them. In comparison with tinned food, this was a splendid meal, including beef, potatoes, vegetables, pudding, guavas, and passion fruit. If an admission is necessary, then I confess that I remembered the meal more clearly than Sister Teresa's personality. Nevertheless, missions, I was learning, were like an oasis in the desert, an oasis of "the neglected school" (allusion to Lewis 1940:49–51). It refers to the long Christian tradition that many scholars resent but locals welcome for its health services, education, words of hope and guidance. For me, at this moment, it offered calmness and an escape from poverty and hunger, dust and thirst. Finding food, I knew already, would be a major problem.

Reconnoitering, Bad Food, Shabby Nature

I left this oasis reluctantly to inform the District Governor, Mr. Feta, of my research intentions. He was young, friendly and intelligent. He pointed out, what I didn't know before, that the old Katumba District had been divided into three administrative areas, Nzubuka, Zongwe, and Katumba itself. It was therefore suggested that I travel further along the valley, not only to decide upon a village, but also to determine its District. A District Governor would then write to the Chief and inquire about a village house and assistant.

Mentally preparing myself for extensive reconnoitering, I returned to the convent and asked to store my equipment. I was tired of worrying about it being stolen. The constant looking and checking by locals strained my nerves. The work to be done in this country! How to rid it of this poverty, how to produce more, direct the products to markets, generate jobs—it all was overwhelming.

That evening, back at the Katumba rest house, I ate the usual—tinned tuna, tinned apple sauce, tinned peaches—supplies from Lusaka. Local stores were out of tinned tuna, and tinned Chinese meats, jams, or vegetables made starving a gift from heaven. I was desperate enough to taste them once.

Local dirt roads were not only corrugated, they were also full of holes. And then there was the dust, an unbelievable amount of it, red and threatening. It was everywhere, in the car oil, in my books, and in my mouth. My mouth had become dry, stiff, and difficult to move. My jaw felt locked. The whole body was covered with dust, everything but everything was covered with dust. My nose bled from it and dust clogged my ears.

Katumba rest house looked poor, its facilities run-down. There was more crud on the toilet seat than in the bowl. The bath had a tub but no plug, a layer of filth decorated its interior. And tomorrow was another long, dusty, and who knew what sort of day. I tuned up my psychological gear. My eyes were closed to nature, it no longer had the power to renew me. I saw only dry, red dust, worn faces, and deformed people wobbling along the road. Even women's breasts looked worn and arid. Nature deformed people, sapped them of their energy, and desiccated the land.

Several diseases plagued Lendans and explained, perhaps, the population's preoccupation with reproduction. Topping the list was malaria. The presence of malignant malaria and sickle cell anemia reduced fertility and may have resulted in a high frequency of unviable fetuses. Endemic diseases like malaria, bilharzia, and hookworm appeared to contribute to the presence of serious anemia and anemia-related deaths from blood loss as well as nutritional inadequacies. The hospital records, which I was later able to study, indicated predominant human wastage from these causes. Falciparum malaria was hyperendemic in the valley.

March 7th, I prepared to return to Mboua for money. At the gas station in Katumba a young man, holding a baby in one arm, asked for a ride south. I liked him and his two pretty "cousins" with their closely cropped hair. One of them was the mother of the baby which he cradled in his arms. They had a lot of luggage; the car was cramped. Not far from Katumba it had rained, and the dirt road was a sea of mud. We simply skidded along—at times it took our breath away.

Nevertheless, I had a good conversation with the English-speaking passenger from Niassa Province. "Why," I continued, "did Zambian men not take their wives or female companions, to social functions?" A typically stupid Western question but fit his description of local life. At the time, I still accepted that all humanity rotated around men-women couples in love with and attached to one another. He was polite. "The reason is simple," he hazarded, "if a man takes his wife, or potential wife, he does not feel free to go and talk to other women. If he did, his escort would be jealous and walk off. Women do the same. Why create problems?"

The conversation turned to the unemployed youths of Lenda province. He felt people of this province were stubborn, not very co-operative, and tribalistic. He suggested that many of the youths were not working because they didn't want to marry, implying, I guess, that they had no incentive. Marriage was a joke in Lenda, he claimed. Women handled the household. Then, many men were lame; they didn't want to leave the area. They only wanted to fish. "Are the two provinces friends or rivals of one another?" I asked in jest.

In Mboua, I stayed at the Mission school where I felt safe. My bath, although it took place in an austere setting, was a luxury, as was the light dinner. Two sisters and I sat by candlelight and watched young Zambian students as they sang their funeral songs. The mood was eerie but peaceful.

I feasted my eyes and spirit on the beauty and joyfulness of these young girls. Their dark skin blazed as if freshly polished with Vaseline. I knew enough of the starkness of the valley to recognize that they were privileged.

Saturday morning, I went to the bank. The letter had arrived and I was able to cash a check. This done, I thanked the Sisters, paid them 2 Zambian Kwacha for the night, and drove back to Katumba. The roads were better; most of the mud had dried, leaving but unpleasant holes.

It was noon when I checked in at the Katumba rest house. A policeman came to see me and asked for my I.D. I showed it to him. He asked endless questions all of which I answered. He suggested that women were dangerous spies. It sounded absurd to me, but I didn't say so. He told me that a soccer game was being played at the Government Secondary School and suggested that I see it. But the roads had no names and his directions were unclear. I headed for St. Mary's Mission.

I was grateful to be offered coffee and given a chance to relax in a familiar setting. Several nuns had left for Wafema, a lake and swamp area to the southeast where the completion of a new church was being celebrated. I stayed at the mission until about 5 p.m. It was hard to leave. I particularly enjoyed the conversation with Dr Van Gella, a handsome Dutch physician stationed at Kakuso. We discussed Lenda illnesses. He, his lively French wife and exquisite children were visiting this mission. I began to learn that whites formed a network up and down the valley. One could survive in an almost totally white environment if one knew the spots.

On my return to the rest house, two policemen stopped me again wanting to see my I.D. By now I found police suspicion of strangers amusing. Sometimes I wondered whether they were interested in the woman rather than their duty. I decided it was safer to behave in accordance with the assumption that they were doing their duty, that way my distance would remain intact. So far, the police had been very humane, so I had no cause to complain. Being white, alone, and a woman, I was rather incongruent in this setting. Most white women traveled in pairs and were recognized as sisters of several religious orders.

It was Saturday evening, and I was at the rest house. My dinner consisted of tinned sardines and an orange. I was glad Saturday was almost over. Not being settled yet, weekends looked desolate. There were, of course, young men around but I surmised their motives and kept them at a distance. First, I must know the community. Not unlike Sarah, I too judged these young men to be dull of mind and incapable of perceiving the impersonality of friendliness. The heat worked against the need to look cold. Even here nature seemed to determine psychology. I couldn't tolerate men who attempted to violate my autonomy.

Nzubuka District: First Impressions

I arrived in Nzubuka by Lake Tana Monday, March 9th, and saw the District Secretary both regarding housing and an assistant. It was suggested that I move into a small house which, during colonial days, accommodated servants. They were trying to move someone out and prepare the house for me. I explained that I didn't want to live in the *boma* or administrative center that I was looking for a house in one of the villages.

While I waited to meet my assistant, I looked in at the Fisheries Department. The staff was at a meeting, so I watched fish being sold. Mr Pili showed me the different species. He asked questions. It was difficult to explain to people what I was trying to do. They were not used to having a researcher around.

Being a stranger and out of place, I made enquiry into housing my major motive for looking around. Nzubuka *boma* had quite a few bars; bare structures, but functional. Its two general stores, Muteta's and Chisaka's were well stocked with everything but food. Only tinned food was sold, and not much of that.

District capitals and hospitals had electricity, though it frequently malfunctioned. Villages did not. This created a storage problem. I went to NAMBoard in search of potatoes or any sort of vegetable. They had none. Finding food, I realized, would be a serious problem.

I was eager to move about, familiarize myself with people and their routine. As I did so, I wore a long skirt. I sewed it by hand the day before. It created quite a sensation. For one thing, villagers and local politicians didn't see Europeans wearing long skirts (minis were the fashion). At first, I thought the women were laughing at me. They expressed themselves rather noisily, clapping their hands and throwing their heads back with thick guttural laughter. But several women and men commented that they liked the skirt and asked for a pattern. I promised to show them how to make one. The District Governor was visibly impressed. "So you are not like the other Europeans. We don't like miniskirts here. But expatriates don't listen, and our young girls copy them." His words relieved me. My first clumsy attempt at gaining rapport was seemingly a success. I had surmised that modesty centered on thighs not on breasts. The latter were frequently bare, while women, even when they wore a short dress, wrapped around their waists colored cloth which emphasized their full hips but hid their thighs and legs.

I wanted more contact with people, but felt that an assistant would help explain better what I aimed to do. My local language was still clumsy. Not wanting to say the wrong thing, I admonished myself to exercise patience.

In Nzubuka, most fishermen fished for the government and lived on a government compound. They followed a work-week routine, fishing from Monday through Friday. Their houses, refugee-like structures, were oval huts made of tin. Although temporary, these huts have been there since 1968. One saw no gardens. Furniture in these tin huts usually consisted of several easy chairs, a bookshelf, and a table. Sleeping quarters were separate huts, as were kitchens. Most of the women were away visiting their kin.

I finally met Banachile who was to be my first assistant. Banachile walked in from Booke's village 15 km to the north. Despite my concern that she was selected to assist me by the District Governor, I took an immediate liking to her. A woman still in her early twenties, she already had three children. I was struck by her linear beauty and quiet vulnerability. I did not see here the bucolic, rustic manner or stoutness of body of other women. Her face looked almost angelic with its wide brown eyes and slight flush of her light brown skin. I feared that this harsh environment would do her harm, knock her seraphic manner out of her. A tragic figure she seemed to be.

Her name meant mother (owner) of Chile, her first-born daughter. Banachile's English name was Grace. Grace's husband was presently staying at the Industrial Belt while she lived in Booke village with several "mothers." Mother referred to several kinds of women: what we consider biological mother, mother's sisters, grandmothers' daughters, and so on. It took me some time to learn that what we meant by biological relatedness and what the Lenda meant by it were not quite the same. But this discovery of a difference between "our" and "their" biology did not occur until much later. Also living with Grace were several brothers and sisters, individuals we would usually call cousins. I quickly learned that "marriage" was loose and that both men and women had, in fact, several partners—at least, when they were not Christians.

The slopes of Lake Tana hugged Booke's village. Its mud-brick and grass huts extended westward to the beach where women washed and soaked cassava, and men washed and repaired nets. The better houses, usually built of mud bricks and covered with grass roofs, stood every which way between guava and olive trees. Paths were never straight as they turned and twisted around trees and huts. Each house was surrounded by a small garden in which green beans, pumpkins, soya beans, potatoes and groundnuts were grown. It was hard to distinguish a garden from the rest of the landscape, as if the latter were changed as little as possible.

Woman in Cassava Field

Cassava fields, and cassava a starchy root crop was the staple food, were located to the east of the village. Beyond the fields was bush. There were several small stores in the village and four or five churches. All were rectangular mud-brick structures barely distinguishable from the usual homes. Churches included Seventh-day Adventists, Christian Missions of Many Lands, United Church of Zambia, a Catholic Church, and Jehovah's Witnesses, all these for about 500 people.

Some men were in the village repairing or making nets. A tailor with his manual sewing machine sat in front of the store sewing clothes for his customers. One man ran a clothes repair business in his hut.

Stores were frequently owned and run by women. As I learned later, many women, even when they had husbands, did not pool their resources with them. An economic parallelism, not to be confused with segregation, prevailed between men and women. Storeowners were referred to as *bakankala*, rich people.

Several women were busy preparing cassava. The pungent odor of wet, almost fermenting, cassava lingered in the air. Once the root was dug out of the ground, it was peeled, soaked in water for several days until soft, then broken into small pieces and left to dry in the sun. The process was said to eliminate hydrocyanic acid found in the roots. Once dry, women pounded the chipped cassava into flour. Most women prepared enough to last about three days. I was fascinated by the sight of two women leaning over a mortar, alternately forcing their pestles down to crush or grind cassava into flour.

I counted 32 houses in Booke, some of them looked abandoned, apparently because their families had gone to the Industrial Belt either to work or sell sun-dried fish.

Returning from Booke, I went to see the Assistant District Secretary (A.D.S.) to ask for a letter of introduction to Chief Kikombo. I wanted the option of doing research in Kikombo's village at the mouth of the Lenda River. Kikombo was the lush "capital" of his sub-chiefdom which, in turn, was part of the paramount chiefdom of Catote. Mwata Catote was the paramount chief in Lenda. His village, the chiefly capital, also named after him, was located some 80 km to the south.

With the letter, Banachile and I went to meet chief Kikombo. A *kapaso* (servant) let us through the gate of the fenced palace grounds. He disappeared to inform the chief of our presence. We greeted the latter's wife, and both kapaso and wife invited us in. The house consisted of several rooms and contained a few odd chairs, bags, and clothes hanging from a wooden pole suspended between two mud-brick walls. The chief himself, a large man with a large, pale brown head and face, was ill in bed. He was covered with blue cloth, the same cloth used to make schoolgirls' uniforms. His feet and one hand were in bandages. He asked us questions about my research. Our answers apparently satisfied him, for he gave his blessings. On our exit Grace knelt and clapped three times. I bowed, having been ignorant of the ritual and gestures involved in greetings. Grace would later teach me how to greet a chief properly. Mind you, other Europeans failed to follow such indigenous customs.

Kikombo village was large, studded with olive and guava trees, and divided into several sections. Its total population exceeded two thousand. We walked through one of the northern sections and observed several women preoccupied with their tasks. Two were busy whitewashing the floor of their house with a mixture consisting of water, cassava, and cement. Some were preparing cassava flour. Others still were processing oil from the fruits of local olive trees. The fruit was boiled twice. A first boiling turned it into an impure orange substance. A second boiling cleared it. It tasted, as one would expect, like olive oil.

At times, I felt like a Pied Piper as a horde of thirty or more children followed me around. Some screamed at the sight of my white skin. I was absolutely horrified at this expression of emotion. Somehow, it hadn't occurred to me that anyone might find white skin and blonde hair frightening. A few touched my exposed flesh, or felt the texture of my hair. All took interest in my writing. Some children who could read and were accustomed to white skin, checked my spelling of Lenda words.

The houses were as the anthropologist, Ian Cunnison (1923–2013), had photographed them during his fieldtrip in 1949. Most were made, here as elsewhere, of sun-dried bricks, plastered with mud and covered with grass roofs. Some had glass windows of which usually several were broken. Front verandas, sometimes covered with vines, or flanked by shapeless gardens, created an earthy atmosphere.

Colorful bachelor huts added gaiety to the scene. Some were decorated with messages which read "welcome kitts." The latter word was meant to read "kids," and really referred to those very raucous youths that terrorized Sarah and now leered at us like so many whimsical satyrs. When we entered the hut of two such youths they clapped their hands and threw back their heads with uninhibited joy. "You can live here," they suggested to me. We left them and their youthful nonsense and walked on. Stores and tailors lined each side of a main, copper-red path. Everything added to the sensuality of local life.

Most men were away, either fishing or selling their produce at the Industrial Belt. Here and there a young man repaired his nets. Most women too were off cultivating their fields. Only of youths and children was there an abundance.

On our return in the afternoon, following a lunch break in Nzubuka, Grace and I walked along the south section of Kikombo. Women asked us to sit down. It was their time to rest. Most thought I had come to help them organize clubs as prescribed by UNIP's policy of cooperation. It was difficult to awaken them to the idea that I came to learn not to teach. I was told that cooperatives or clubs didn't work anyway. The local population was too individualistic in the production of wealth. As I would learn later, the communal aspect entered the picture only when products were shared among matrikin.

A social worker for Community Development explained that UNIP (United National Independence Party) supplied these women with cement and other materials to build a community hall. Once a hall was built, however, it was up to the women to maintain it by earning money. Lack of money was exactly what women complained about. They had to earn it weeding gardens of local *bakankala* (the rich). They considered the work too hard and its remuneration too little. In fact, weeding was strenuous work and required the use of clumsy, heavy *ulukasu* or hoes. I tried weeding and tired quickly.

Ask a social worker what women needed to learn most urgently and she would answer nutrition and childcare. I pointed out that while women were being taught how to sew, cloth was outrageously expensive. I was told that some women bought directly from factories, but factories were stationed in urban centers and difficult to visit. Nothing made sense around here. To understand what was desirable or problematic for the local population I needed a different perspective. First, I felt, I must understand Zambia's existing differences in wealth. With UNIP making itself felt in the rural areas, I had to sort out what the goals of the government and its sole political party were. What is good for the nation, may not necessarily be good for its rural dwellers. To discover whether such a discrepancy existed, I needed also to understand the goals of villagers themselves.

Nature Kills

Lake Tana was attractive. A welcome exception. Its beaches were flat to the southeast where Nzubuka *boma* and Kakuso were located. Going north, sandy beach gave way to gentle slopes. Booke village sat on one of them. If my description of nature has been dearth it was because I found it for the most part overwhelmingly ugly, insistent, and relentlessly present. At this point the idyllic sensuality of Kikombo village manifested itself but rarely and then only for a moment in the shade cast by the gentler morning sun. By noon, the heat was brutal; disease, crippled limbs, dried breasts and listless animals revealed themselves. I was afloat amidst a sea of sickness, blindness, decay and insanity, and expressed my feelings to my mother.

March 10, 1973
Darling Mother,

How could I ever have idealized nature? How did its danger, its ugliness escape me? It maims, mother, and it kills.

Quite a few people are crippled, possibly from polio. Men's legs generally look spindly, possibly from sitting in canoes where they use primarily arms. Women's breasts look dry; there they hang exposed, their purpose stripped of all illusion.

When it's wet, mud bricks melt away, the village loses its familiar appearance. When it's dry, red dust hides the world from view, refracted light beats down on us. The blind, irritable or defeated, sit endlessly by straw huts. Lepers walk about as do the insane. Infants suffer from diarrhea and when they deposit their crap, flies feast, and mothers clean it all away.

Wailing sends shivers down my spine. And through the dust I glance a crowd carrying a corpse away. Nature kills, Mam. How could we allow its reign without control? I'll never idealize nature again.

I wrote that letter following one of my many trips to Booke's village. I alternately visited Kikombo on the river and Booke on the lake. Since people began to know me in Grace's village, I began my first efforts at systematic enquiry there. It took weeks before I lost my fright of those hordes of children and the one or two insane adults who inevitably followed me. I couldn't think of a single rule or gesture of etiquette that might relieve my fear or clumsiness. I simply had to wait until they lost interest in me, registered our shared humanity, or recognized my development of immunity to their mental suffering. The insane truly reminded me of those biblical figures, possessed by demons, in need of being exorcized.

It was not merely the human condition which sent my mind and emotions reeling. The physical rawness and lacerations of domesticated animals unavoidably jolted me out of the present and rocketed my memory into the past. It burst the seams of my rationality. The rawness of Lenda nature brought me to the very boundary of my existence – as if that's how it should be. Only I kept creating a new routine, anything empirical, in fact, to prevent breakage. And so it was this Sunday morning as I drove to Banachile. We planned to attend church in Booke's village. Not only was my visibility important, but I was also interested in villagers' religious activities, especially those in churches led by Zambians themselves. As I drove along I noticed a dog standing in the middle of the dusty road maintaining a peculiarly immobile posture. Dogs were very emaciated, largely fended for themselves, and lethargically moved about. As I checked his behavior, for one had always to watch for animals and, even more so, people on the road, I noticed that the front part of his snout was gone. He was dripping blood. My stomach contracted into one heavy, threatening knot. I lost all sense of where I was.

It seemed to glance at me from the corner of its eyes. I slowed down and stared it fully in the face and its eyelids drooped and it looked at me with an expression of unfathomable suffering. For a moment, I felt recognition as if the face of this dog had turned into that of a human being. The memory stayed with me for a long time and haunted me even after my return.

We sat in the bar. She came over, glanced at me, and took possession of him as if he were married to her and not to me. She didn't know I was his wife. To her I was but another woman threatening to steal her mate and I saw her fumble for his hand and it remained immobile. My eyes screamed at him for an explanation, and I saw his body grow catatonic and his eyelids drooped and he looked at me with unfathomable sadness. What was done was done, they seemed to say.

I drove on and murmured to myself a rhythmic incantation, "oh my god, oh my god, oh my god." And the pain spread across the landscape and the heat waves carried it along. The land looked desolate and I heard their wailing.

It was a relief to arrive in Booke and see Banachile, her three children, her numerous brothers, her sisters and her mothers. Her baby huddled contentedly in a cloth on its mother's back. I looked at it and it smiled and broke my heart. I felt inundated with pathos for the babe and its unknown destiny, its inescapable fate. Can he make himself—of course, he must?! But my sense of certainty was broken.

Grace took the baby from her back and handed it to her grandfather. I kept my eyes glued to the pair until his cooing soothed me and erased the screaming from my ears. I closed my eyes and felt the flood of emotions recede, allowing my brain to spew out mundane things. It occurred to me, life being relatively monotonous, babies were one of the real joys in this valley. I remembered Van Gella jest that procreation was the sole creative Lenda act. I laughed at that, laughed the pain away.

CMML's church was a very simple structure, its floor, pews, and altar made of cement. CMML stood for Christian Missions in Many Lands. Drumming informed people to prepare for services. Church leaders included a local preacher, a choir of six people (two men, four women), a prayer leader, and deacons who took attendance and such. The congregation included about 16 men and 15 women. Children moved freely about the church. People sang and prayed and listened and sang some more. Later, I would record services and discussions, then transcribe and translate them. So time-consuming was this task that I did it whenever I felt weak or ill. I needed the rest of my time to be among the people.

Today, I was only looking and persuading people to get used to me. A little boy urinated during the service, and the urine spread unhindered along the floor. Children brought bread, a piece dropped into the urine. They picked it up and ate it anyway. Women and men sat through a service lasting three hours. Babies were breast-fed intermittently. When they became restless, children were sent outside to play. One slept on the cement floor.

People loved cleanliness like a precious god. I observed children and young people wash their heads and faces, arms and legs at the well, using much soap. For a bigger wash, they bathed in lagoons. The better off used buckets. One man built an indoor bathtub from cement. People loved clothes, men especially preened themselves. When they could afford it, they wore the latest in fashion. The clothes of most villagers, however, were badly worn and torn; many rips and holes, some mended, most not— then, mending would be so much wasted work.

I missed green vegetables. They were hard to find, even in season, and mostly non-existent or grown by villagers for their own consumption. Villagers ate the leaves of cassava plants, pumpkins, and potatoes. Later on, I would drive 130 km just to find a cabbage. Anything to help maintain my health.

There were the blind and the lame, lepers and the insane. Every deformity nature had wrought upon its people paraded before my eyes. As rapidly as it generated birth, it killed. And when nature was finally generous and turned the soil fertile, it increased the parasites that devoured its growth. No one could tell me that nature, untouched by humankind, was beautiful, at best it was indifferent and usually it killed. Lenda was not only the valley of the blind, more appropriately, it was also the valley of death. "We die fast in the valley," was a common refrain.

According to existentialists ... much of the life of any person
remains (unexamined). Comfortably insulated by habit and
routine he dwells in a state of philosophic oblivion, blindly
unaware of the real conditions of human existence. Suddenly,
however, there comes a moment when a direct encounter with life
is inescapable (Gill and Sherman, 1973, p.22, word in bracket
added by author).

For me, there would be many such moments in this valley when a hint of
life expiring would increase my dread and focus attention on myself and
the human condition. At such times, I would find myself tossed into the
past, overcome either by feelings of guilt or bursts of anger. There was the
unfathomable pain of mere existence. My nicely ordered world would
dissolve into a slimy morass of nothing, oppressing me with its
senselessness. At those moments, I experienced not only the meaning of
being abandoned but also that of being finite. It's this realization of the
possibility of my not being that persuaded me, again and again, to learn
who I was and what it meant to exist. And to do that, I stuck with Sartre's
"map" and its implied admonition to follow my goal.

I think about the valley all the time,
but of course it is my mind and
momentarily, no doubt, the instinct to
survive that selects what I describe. I
remind myself that being here is like
the gift that I always wanted, and yet,
it is strange, prickly, resistant—above
all, living its own life, indifferent to
me. Something is missing.

**Missionary, Anthropologist,
and Local Chief**

5

A LETTER ABOUT LOVE FROM THE FIELD

I was born inside the rain on a day of wonder
Deep inside my brain memories of thunder
I grew up a refugee, my life not fixed or free
I know the world's not to blame
Cos' everybody carries my name

Johnny Clegg

The need to find accommodation kept me moving among people and villages. That was important. It's too easy to withdraw. I now lived part of the time with Banachile and her children in her hut, the rest of it in the government rest house. A multiple residential pattern was maintained throughout field work. As I became interested in housebuilding, I organized a team to build me a third hut. What I learned in the process was invaluable.

Mingling with people was important. Too many researchers escaped by reading novels, hitting the bars, or quarreling with their spouses. My friend Peter, whom I met at the Institute back in Lusaka, would later start his research in Lenda. He remained one week, became ill, and never returned.

Sometimes for weeks at an end, I'd forget my own existence so absorbed was I in the puzzles with which Lenda presented me. The need to understand drove me. Then I'd grow restless, pack my bags, and drive off.

There were moments when it seemed that everything I was doing was right, but with those precious moments gone I had grave doubts.

Upon arrival in Zambia, and for a considerable while, most of my associations were with expatriates. Their stories about malnutrition, family problems, conflicts and crimes among locals made me feel uneasy. I was always suspicious of people's illusions, including my own. All along, therefore, I knew that only more contact with Zambians themselves would alleviate suspicions and fears. After all, research based on fear results in a different sort of understanding and knowledge than that based on direct contact.

On Tuesday, March 17th, I decided to check with the local magistrate to enquire about the possibility of studying local court cases. Having collected archived cases, recent conflicts would allow important comparisons. Cases point to areas of life where conflicts are inevitable. And contradictions in the social fabric, to which conflicts point, are the essence of social dynamics.

The court clerk gave his permission to look at notes of recent cases. As I sat down and opened the first page, the magistrate entered. He queried my curiosity, checked my letter of introduction then suggested that I watch court proceedings to give me a better idea of what to expect from written records. I did.

I was quite taken by the formalities and amazed at the continuation of procedures from colonial times. It was a connection to a familiar part of civilization.

During recess, the magistrate asked me into his office for a chat. I looked at him for a long time. His gestures fascinated me. He smoked a pipe and my eyes followed his fingers pack the tobacco. He stood there leaning against a desk; his shoulders sagged a little and his belly was softly rounded. A big forehead graced his face and encased a lucid brain. I watched his eyelids lift and felt his eyes sink into mine. And they stayed there. A soft breeze embraced my body. He crossed one leg over the other and slowly extracted his glance.

As from a distance, I heard the clerk of court blaming the assault on the woman. "She took his beer and that gesture promised him company," he was saying. "But she swaggered over to another man and nuzzled up to him. So, he followed her home and beat her up."

"But she wanted a divorce," I said, "and you didn't give it to her."

"She only wanted a dress," he replied, "You don't know our women."

"You see then that I must live in a village," I said.

"Try chief Catote's village," the magistrate suggested. "I'll introduce you. Catote is my friend." I watched the sparkle from his large dark eyes blend with a ray of sunlight that had just slipped past a moving curtain. "Tomorrow I hold court in Zongwe," he continued, "drive down with me, we'll pass and stop in Catote's village."

I spent the evening with CUSO friends, Tom and Judy, when the magistrate came by to say that he couldn't go because there was no transportation. Government Lorries were always in short supply. I suggested we use my car. He agreed.

Tom and I were outside sucking sugarcane when Paul Kupeta, for that was his name, arrived. The sun set quickly across the lake. Judy came home from the hospital just then, and Tom invited Kupeta in. We had cokes, chatted and agreed to leave after lunch tomorrow.

Wednesday April 18th, I filled the car with petrol and took along tinned food. At three the magistrate arrived. His houseboy carried his luggage. I put it into the trunk. We said good-bye to Tom and Judy and took off. I felt nervous somehow as if something glorious were to happen.

It was the 21st, two days following our return. I sat by candlelight, sipped

Zangavan beer, and dreamt the hours away. I glanced impatiently at Catote's unruly chicken in the kitchen and turned to stare at a ghostly sort of grasshopper sitting on melted candle wax. Reluctantly I hammered on my typewriter. The letter grew pages in length, the longest letter I'd ever write. My mother, as always, would understand.

March 21, 1973
Darling Mother:

I've spent nine years among academics, as student or wife. Nine years. I'll spend many more among them as their colleague. But now, I have an overwhelming desire to live, just to live ...

I reflected for a long, long moment. Have I gone crazy, I thought? Then I continued to write.

... The man's name is Paul Kupeta. I know you are smiling, Mam. I know, that you know, when I'm screaming for life, I'm announcing an outrageous act. Outrageous to the general mind, not yours, Mam. To live, to love, to express emotions, it's all the same to you, am I right?

But let me tell it. The telling will clear my brain. We took off for Zongwe by way of Catote. I drove first, that is important. I honked the horn to caution a cyclist of our presence, but he kept on cycling erratically and I had to slam on the brakes and steer the car into a sandbank, missing the cyclist and the lagoon by a few inches. The car stalled, wheels buried in sand. Kupeta got out and ran toward the boy, grabbed him by the collar and slapped him across the face, from relief more than anger.

The boy cried, of course, and a mob gathered and Paul gestured and explained. He had them all organized in minutes and they pushed the car out of the sand. I turned and leaned against the car, my knees were shaking. My God, Mam, had something happened there would have been instant vengeance! The D.S. was recently violently beaten when his driver hit a villager. I held out the keys to Paul and he took the wheel. Nestled in the corner of my seat, I watched him as he drove. You understand the role reversal.

Catote's palace was built of fired brick. A dense palisade blocked it from view. We sat silently under a shelter until the kapaso *invited us in. Three chairs stood ready in the shade. I watched Catote's jerky movements and reflected that it lent him grandeur. Everything about him spoke of distance and grace. His cheeks were flushed and the tip of his nose held tiny pearls of perspiration. His hands and arms trembled from abuse of alcohol, but you know Mam, it enhanced his charisma. Kupeta kneeled and slowly clapped three times, and so did I.*

Catote didn't like the letter from the A.D.S. in Katumba. It should have come, he argued, from the Minister of State in Mboua or from the Permanent Secretary. But these, I felt, were minor irritations. What really bothered him was research being done in his area. Worse still, the A.D. S. wrote that I would do historical research, which, of course, was not the case. I should have checked. I didn't know then the meaning historical research and history itself had for the Lunda. History and ethnopolitics are one and the same. The past is the present and in the same way is subject to manipulation. You don't want it on paper, permanent and static. Then, Mam, Catote claimed that Cunnison got people drunk to extract information. I knew that to be slander. Nevertheless, he insisted that Cunnison's book is banned in his kingdom. He still referred to the valley as his kingdom, and has not accepted, at least not willingly, the new hegemony. I explained that my primary interest was in the economic activities of the people.

The conversation ended. He would make enquiries about me, he said, and left abruptly. I thought the meeting was over and prepared to leave. Paul held me down. Wait, he said. We waited a long time, Mam, until Mwata Catote returned as abruptly as he had disappeared. His kapaso *followed him with a live chicken which he, following a gesture from Mwata Catote, handed to me. Not that I knew what to do with it, or how to hold the damn thing. But to be given a chicken was to be honored. Kneeling and clapping, somehow, we left.*

Paul assured me that everything was alright, that Catote likes me. At the car, he covered the trunk with paper. The chicken would relieve itself, Paul pointed out. Catote's pearls of perspiration, his tremors, the kapaso's *sinewy legs; their communion through gesture as much as words. It's this contact with nature, Mam. Everything cerebral becomes flesh and blood. It's intoxicating.*

Walking through Catote village, visiting its bars, I got the impression that this area had reached the height of its civilization and was now experiencing its decline. Everything looked proud and everything was decaying. And you know, even the decay held me enthralled. We are surely wrong to assume that "civilizations" of this part of Africa did not also rise and decline. I am reminded of Muggeridge who loves to flagellate himself and the West which he argues has become a society no better than a pigsty. He thrashes the West for its disintegration into a morally appalling and spiritually impoverished affluent society "with its accent everlastingly on consumption and sensual indulgence of every kind" (1969, p.145). But what is sensual indulgence? It's hardly what we have in the West, we who preach "die in the flesh in order to be reborn?" Why are we such despisers of the body? Have we forgotten that our virtues grow out of our passions? Finally, the West is hardly sensual in comparison to this.

Well, we arrived in Zongwe's rural development rest house and were shown around by an animated manager. The rest house was attractive, almost plush. One brings one's own food, and cooks prepare and serve it. The lounge and dining room were spacious and breezy. There was an uneasy moment when Paul and the manager teased me about rooms. Signed in, we took food to the cook and Kupeta made arrangements for dinner. You know, Mam, he thought I would have brought more and better food. The expectations this man has. But I forgot, decent food signifies respect and acknowledges high status. While he took a bath, I rested. Dinner was pleasant, though the food came from tins.

After dinner, Paul suggested that we seek out a bar. We drove along the dirt road under a full moon. Before today, I couldn't have told you whether a moon shone over Zambia, but it shone tonight. I had to shake myself to confirm that I was indeed in Zambia and not at some marvelous resort. The bar was magical with its lit candles, dark customers, and long shadows. We had Simba and were absorbed in one another. We talked, though I couldn't tell you about what, and the bar closed and we moved to a side room and continued. And then we noticed that people were listening to our conversation and we finished the beer and left.

I opened the door to my room and entered. He leaned against the frame. I looked at us, looking at one another, and I experienced a deep sense of peace. It enveloped us like a soft blanket. In Lenda nothing is ever purely cerebral, it is always mingled with flesh.

He told of his childhood. How his father would take him to the Industrial Belt and how he would roam the streets and rummage through refuse cans of Europeans. And I watched the skin around his large, mellow eyes crinkle with laughter. I could see him bent over a garbage can and look up surprised upon being reprimanded by a stern European. He would stand and look steadfastly into the pale man's eyes. "Your garbage are our riches," he would say.

He told me about his peculiar European friend who always took his cocktail to the verandah where he sat for the longest time watching the sunset. How peculiar, he said, to watch the sun for hours when I want to see smoke stacks. And in the process of talking to me, he made me watch our own culture. We despoil the earth and then prize the bit that is left to view. But earth and sky, life and death that is the essence of Lenda.

"Why should anyone sit and watch the sunset?" he said. I became the observer of our attitude toward nature. We worship it. The Lenda know its danger.

I was up first and had the cook prepare tea. Paul got up around eight. Seeing him made me feel warm all over. The same and continuing ease on his part caused me to marvel. He discussed food with the cook and while he gave his instructions he leaned sideways against the counter and slowly turned the end of a match in his ear. We soon ate beans, porridge, and drank tea.

He went to the court but returned quickly, for the prosecutor had not arrived. We collected our things and drove around Zongwe. I was unbelievably aware of his presence, so I put on my rational voice and told him that I enjoyed our stay in Zongwe. He put his hand between my breasts and asked me whether what I said came from there or from my mouth only. And I shoved rationality aside and answered from there and burst into laughter, laughter of sheer joy. And I stood there and my arms enveloped the earth. My cocoon has burst for good. I've been rattling at my cage, Mam. But I'm in Zambia now and something is breaking out.

He had to inspect the prison and took me along. I watched him as he talked to the officer in charge, with that relaxed sense of authority, all along slowly cleaning his ear with the back end of a match. We entered the prison. Guards did not wear guns, and Kupeta shook hands with the prisoners. He asked them if they had any complaints; they said no. The prison was simple but very clean. No furniture, just a set of blankets on a cement floor. Women's cells were empty.

We walked toward the garden, which was well looked after though in need of fertilizer. Back in the officer's building Paul recorded his observations in a book. In the meantime, two prisoners, upon instruction from the officer in charge, washed the car. When all was ready, we left, and I looked at him as he drove.

Authority makes Paul generous. In Zambia, Mam, I can read a person's status in his face. Facial lines are different, and eyes hold a different message. The poor wear hostile, defiant, tired, and dull expressions. Their bodies move without pride.

I mentioned already my first meeting with Catote, and how he kept repeating that he didn't want historical research done in his area. History was sacred and part of official philosophy and not public knowledge. You remember, we had left with the hen.

Thursday the 19th of March, we made our way back to Nzubuka, again stopping at Catote's. He had intended to radio the D.C. and/or D.S. in Katumba to enquire about me. I wanted to know the result.

Around noon, we collected the hen from the cook of the rural development rest house where we had left it, and once again put it into the trunk. We drove further around Zongwe meeting some of P.K.'s friends. Several were sitting on low benches or turned over buckets, drinking Simba. We sat down with them and were offered beer which we gratefully accepted. Bopas, a friend of Paul, was a prominent businessman. The business, he told us, was started by his sister who sold fish and with this capital started a store. Two brothers then joined in and expanded it—perhaps too much. The family, a group of siblings, now ran several different businesses; bars, hotels, bus services, and stores, in Nanyuki, Lusaka, and Zongwe. They owned stores in other towns which have, however, gone out of business. Bopas, who looked as if he had never left the valley had traveled across Europe—England, Scotland, Germany, and France. He didn't like England—too impersonal he said. He liked Scotland, people invited him for beer there; and he liked Germany where people told their children to call him "Onkel." France, he didn't care for at all. He went to these countries on some sort of business-training program.

We moved to the bar and had another beer. Bopas complained of "eyes." He and his family were suffering from eye inflammations, which occur, as I said, frequently. A person who has eye, leg, or stomach pains, for example, simply says he has "eyes," "legs," or "stomach," as if the pain made one aware of only that part of the body.

Before leaving Zongwe, we met one of Paul's many female friends. She was a middle-aged woman of mixed Greek-Lenda parentage. Her house was the usual mud-brick structure, with her mother's house next to hers. Her father was dead. She was a striking woman, divorced from her husband who resided in Zangava. My Lenda allowed me to follow only part of the conversation, so I looked around. Looking, as you know, gives me the greatest pleasure. Why do we need to talk at all? The living room contained three simple well-used chairs, one table, and a homemade cabinet with a cloth. And that was it but for colorful curtains that danced in the wind. The bedroom was separated by a wall and the entrance was open. I saw a bed. The latrine was outside, a hole in the ground, surrounded by wattle-and-daub walls with roof and an open entrance. And then we talked about mixed marriages and white men who impregnate black women and run.

Paul insisted that I meet several other women on the way to Catote, some were young, some were older, and they were all women whom he openly admired. Which Western man, mother, would drive through a town and show his female guest its prominent women? To begin with, he wouldn't even know such existed. And if they did, they would be a different kind, young and fit to be revealed only to a male friend suffering from sexual deprivation. These women were admired for their capability and personal strength. They are admired for their power and their independence. Lenda call it "amaka."

As we drove on, I smelled the air and the charcoal fires and felt the dust and the heat. He held my hand. The magic of it. The only thing I dreaded was seeing Catote again. We arrived at his palace and the kapaso left to announce us and to ready the chairs. And we waited and then were escorted in. We knelt, and slowly clapped three times and Catote saw my eyes flicker with mischief. He cocked his head sideways and his hand jerked and he sat there staring at me. The silence of it.

Generous shadow cooled us. And it felt as if Catote's tremors set waves in the air and it enhanced his grandeur. Ten feet away his kapaso *remained standing throughout the meeting. Our conversation stayed light and did not touch upon my request to conduct research here. For the most part no one talked at all, as if words were unnecessary. I saw that his attitude had mellowed, and he was satisfied.*

He got up suddenly, as he did yesterday, without saying a word and walked off. We sat. Feeling very tired I asked P.K. whether we needed to wait for the chief to touch on my research. He didn't answer. We sat and the chief returned. He had changed into a pale brown suit and donned a colorful headdress, which enhanced his grandeur. He wanted a short ride with us, and I directed him to the front seat. I saw Paul glance at me but it was too late. Prominent persons sit in the back.

But we drove him to the bar and he steered us into a room which contained worn-out easy chairs with a fantastic assortment of cushions. They all had different shapes, sizes, and color and I was reminded of a bordello in ancient Rome. The atmosphere was unspeakably romantic. We sat down, and the chief disappeared. The waiter brought two beers and we paid, and I thought that one beer was meant for P.K. and the other for Mwata Catote, and none for me. I asked for a coke. Paul looked surprised and pointed out that one bottle was mine. Then he remembered that I was unfamiliar with customs here and explained that Mwata Catote drank in his private room. There was dignity in that and all understood it but me.

Nevertheless, I gave my beer to a primary school headmaster, whose face carried the expression of a poor man. We sat, both very tired. The chief came in, and his hand jerked, and his head was cocked, and his cheeks were aglow. He checked that we were alright.

But I was very tired, and told Paul that we must leave and he told the chief. So, we said good-bye, and I heard the chief tell Paul to take good care of me. I saw him raise his arm and silence the chatter and he told the guests my name and said that I would do research here. I was confused and asked

P.K. whether he understood this man. He said if I get the letter from the Cabinet Minister or Permanent Secretary in Lusaka and bring it to Catote things will be OK.

We drove off. The heat was unbearable, and I was tired. On arrival in Nzubuka, Ephraim sat on my doorstep. All felt somewhat uneasy, so I suggested to P.K. that he not feel constrained and go about his routine. He stayed, trying half-heartedly to fix my Tilley lamps. I grew irritable, as I always do when behavior becomes irrelevant. Paul noticed and left. Ephraim, a biologist here, who also helped with the lamps, followed Paul's example and left too. I took a bath and went to bed.

And so it was, Mam. As if everything took place in slow motion. I sat and sensed it all. Sensed it, because body and brain were one. Remind me of this description when I'm home.

Comment 1982

Even now I can still hear the Lenda as they "touch" rather than discuss a topic, or "move" rather than walk with someone, and so on. The Lenda lifestyle reminded me of Gauguin's style of painting—colorful, sensuous, simple, and yet filled with mystery. Too much of my time was spent surveying villages and fields. I looked, measured, and counted everything that was somehow related to the problem I had come to study. Sometimes I wondered how I was trained to be so arduous an empiricist. And then I would sit back and ask myself what of Lenda life I understood. To my surprise, the word "understand" brought out a totally different attitude and mood. Why, for example, did I think that I understood the Lenda better when I took in their gestures—even the mere gesture of greeting the chief—than when I calculated their earnings and counted their divorces?

And then there is the intimacy. Usually, for anthropologists, it is bar talk. Men tell *risqué* stories; women do not. I mention it because it is inevitable that some ethnographers in certain settings should experience such an encounter. Even more important, I would argue that the love for a particular individual of a people among whom one conducts research aims at laying hold of the culture in its entirety through that particular individual (Sartre, 1956, p.719). To lay hold of a culture through one's love of one individual may be an illusion, but there can be no doubt that love became a fundamental relation of my thoughts about, and perceptions of, the Lenda world and myself. It engendered an attitude that allowed me to move freely in this society. Fear turned into compassion. "The German thing" that I had become in North America broke, and the attitude of love for these people helped this research forward to its conclusion.

Comment 2018

It is more than forty years since I left the field, and I still wonder about this letter? Should it be there at all? Has not maturity disqualified its presence. I think not. For only now do I understand how easy it is to confuse the love of friendship, or of charity with one another and worse, with the instrumentalization of sexuality. It is stories about such instrumentalization that we hear daily in the news. What did happen was a surprise meeting of kindred souls. What we shared was a common vision of a flourishing valley in a just world. Our origin from different societies played no role at all. Need played no role either; meeting of the mind did. And though the voice is solely mine, we both valued the unexpected consequence of an opening of the door from lab to life and from valley to world. This was its fruit.

Although we were man and woman, and the love of friendship merged with that of Eros, we experienced what Lewis calls "the kingliness of Friendship" where friends "meet like sovereign princes of independent states, abroad, on neutral ground, freed from all contexts" (2012:70 [originally published 1960]). Here I must also quote Susan Neiman and not because I seek an excuse. It is good to remember that "We are finite and fallible and struggling, and we are nonetheless the source of moral reasoning" (2008: 424). To the onerous task of finding food was added that of contingency, choice, and moral struggle.

The people I here call Lenda have a long history. Once a dynamic center of a dynasty with a history of battles and intrigues, they later traded with Greeks in Zangava and have now become a backwater of capitalism. What reminded me of post-war Germany on first arrival is simply seeing human beings struggling to make a fresh start in a world of which they are a part but which has nothing in place to provide solid and sustained economic growth.

6

EMOTIONAL TURMOIL

Father in Heaven! Hold not our sins up against us
but hold us up against our sins ...

Kierkegaard's Prayer

The next two evenings P.K. came by, first alone and then with several friends and cousins. I didn't feel as relaxed as in Zongwe. On the other hand, when I didn't see him at all, I grew restless. Being emotionally tied-up was exactly what I wanted to avoid during research. Except, damn it, it has let me see Zambia through different eyes: warmer, gentler, less fear-ridden eyes, in short, from the changed perspective of love and wonder.

My mind had been so free to play with research strategies and dwell on anthropological puzzles. There were times when I was totally absorbed by them. Now I found myself dwelling on a relationship. I was furious with myself. My rationality castigated my feelings. It was the old split—one so obvious in Malinowski's *Diary*, one so typically normative of my origins in European culture, the obsession with one person, the inability to relate to this desire gracefully, to explore the world and its people freely as if we really did what we all do, die of old age, if not before. I've rebelled against it. I haven't resolved it, and so my preoccupation now. I was back to the dying of the flesh to set my spirit soaring. In short, I was in conflict within myself, with the tradition that shaped me, and with the profession that regarded that very tradition with disdain.

So, I sat and stared into space. I had to admit that P.K. opened for me the gate to Lenda. I don't mean that he introduced me to his friends. I mean that he opened my heart and mind. I now moved among its people free of suspicion and fear. I felt a sense of equanimity. I knew some people would threaten me, but I also knew they would threaten others. He gave me that kind of freedom for my current unease, as if he exchanged one kind of liberation for another, one sort of bondage for another.

It was Sunday. I resolved to write. Instead, I remained sitting as if paralyzed. I disliked week-ends. They held no meaning here. A feeling of utter desolation swept over me, as if the parched land had dried my soul. Let it dry. Loneliness was intimate too, no use to run away. It held out a stark beauty which I soon learned to appreciate too. I let its beauty sink in.

Monday I felt restored. It was a holiday. I decided to spend it among Europeans. Caro and Jacque Christeau were part of the French rice growing scheme. They had invited me to spend the week-end with them and I was curious to learn whether the project was successful. When I arrived, there were other guests. We drove for a picnic to Cuito Falls, about 60 km southeast of Kikombo. McFaran, the bank manager of Barclay's in Mboua, promised to arrange my use of the traveling bank. It would eliminate driving to Mboua.

Among the guests was father Twela, a gentle Anglican priest from Chipili mission. He's been in Lenda three years. I appreciated his candor when he said that things were going backward for the mission. Church-held marriages no longer occurred, the bloom had worn off. Marriages never were important in this society and monogamy is only attempted by a few Christians, and usually Jehovah's Witnesses. It seemed that people did not buy Christianity wholesale.

He felt heartened, he continued, by the fact that local preachers taught the Bible pretty much as they were taught it by Anglicans. "Something must have sunk in," he said.

"Do sermons address the circumstances of rural people?" I asked ever the functionalist.

"They do," he said, "but the white community is not really close to the people and being here, they are rural too."

Ah yes, I thought, a useless question and a subtle critique. We looked at one another. I studied the other guests and recognized in the Provincial Medical Officer an uninteresting and seemingly flippant man. I turned to listen to his wife tell of the high murder rate in Catote.

That night, March 23, I slept in Booke village. Early next morning Banachile and I went to cultivate. We left at 6 a.m. and returned by about 11 a.m. Harvesting cassava was hard labor, not only was the *ulukasu* heavy, but the soil was unyielding and the sun hot. Before leaving the field, we peeled cassava and stacked it into a basket. So heavy was the basket that two women had to lift it onto the head of the one who carried it home.

At noon, we drove to the rest house to eat and freshen up. The afternoon we spent looking for a house in Kikombo's village. We were directed to a section headman. The latter, however, was away visiting another wife 10 km south of here. When we found him, he told us that there was a big two-story house which we could rent. His maternal nephew took us to it.

One look at the house and Banachile whispered that she would have nothing to do with it. This, even though it was imaginatively built. Grace behaved as though she was afraid. The house was owned and built by Pela, a Jehovah's Witness. When I prodded her to say why she wouldn't live in it, she just repeated that it was not good to live in. After all, one didn't know why Pela had left.

"You believe in evil spirits then," I teased, "and I thought you were a Christian."

"What has belief in evil spirits to do with not being a Christian? There is the story when Christ ordered the evil spirits out of a man and they entered a herd of swine who then ran violently down a steep hill and were choked. The bible is full of stories like this which confirm our beliefs." She looked at me calmly with her big brown eyes. If nothing else her flushed cheeks persuaded me. Besides, she was right and I was tired. "Alright, you win. I'll reconsider your house," I said. "Let's go. Let's look it over again." It occurred to me that Christianity probably dovetailed quite easily with certain local beliefs, especially those centered on witchcraft, spirits, and theories of disease. All those aspects of the bible that were themselves tribal. Then I wondered, just for a split second, whether her father's sister, the *mayosenge*, wouldn't be trying to pressure Grace into persuading me to live with them. There would be rent and the *mayosenge* was shrewd. We drove to Booke village.

It amused me to find that every time I looked at an unfamiliar structure it looked dirty, dark and run-down. Then it was explained to me and the structure changed its appearance, as if words could change the sense of sight. That is how it was with Banachile's home. The house belonged to Banachile's father's sister or *mayosenge* whom Grace, nevertheless, called mayo or mother.

"I call her mother," Grace whispered, "lest she be insulted." Kinsmen from her father's side are not her biological kin since they are not of the same blood as Grace. They do, however, prefer to be treated as if they were. Nor should it be thought that Banachile's father was the head of the household. He was not, as I learned the hard way. His sister was. She "owned" these houses and the fields. Her brother merely brought his wife, Grace's mother, to share in his sister's wealth.

Several windows of the house were broken, the kitchen was smoky. Usually kitchens are separate huts. In this case it was part of the main house. A whole house is often no larger than a good-sized Western living room. Its separate rooms were empty except for two beds, one for Banachile and one for her father's sister. The kitchen contained a charcoal burner and a few pots and pans. There were no tables nor chairs. Its dark interior depressed me.

Banachile noticed my sour mood. "The house is good, you'll see. It just needs cleaning," she said.

"But the walls are cracked and filled with spiders and other deadly insects." I sat down, perspiration was trickling down my face as much from depression as from heat.

"You don't understand what I mean by cleaning. We plaster all the walls and floors with fresh mud. There won't be any insects. You'll see," she said.

I set up my cot and mosquito net and stayed the night. The next day we plastered the walls and floor. Banachile was right; the house looked in order. It also felt cool and fresh. How beautiful these women are, their hands express such care.

Toward evening, worn down from heat and work, I drove to the rest house. Exhausted, I sat and stared. Hours ticked away. Then I pulled myself together and took a bath. Dogs had chased Catote's hen again. I found it and put it back into the pen. It was soaked in dog saliva, ugly beasts those untrained scavenging dogs, obnoxious.

Everything took much time and patience and constant mental adjustment and re-adjustment. At times, it felt as if I had to prop up my spirits every half hour or so. I had constantly to convert the unknown and ugly into the known and attractive, without really knowing it. "You should eat," I told myself. Instead, I continued to sit and stare, wrapped in silence.

Finally, I pulled myself together and prepared a dreadful meal. Scrambled eggs with canned Tanzanian corned beef and peas. The food wouldn't go down. I sat and stared some more.

It was dark. I lit a candle and looked over my field notes. It is probably easiest to learn the structure of the valley economy first, I reminded myself. My mind began to drift but I harnessed it and reviewed my accommodations. I decided that dual residence might be useful. I'd be in touch with politicians and government employees as well as with villagers. I also realized that I would need periodic escapes into the privacy of my own room where I could monitor and adjust my mood without causing misunderstanding. The rest house was often empty but for me. Once or twice I noticed male villagers hiding to observe me. Sometimes I was afraid of the many empty rooms, the impenetrable darkness, and the distant toilet, which required that I cross the courtyard and confront bats. But I welcomed its silence. Having reached a decision about housing, my brain returned to work.

I reminded myself to make a special effort to meet more of Nzubuka's people and noted down:

1. Must join Club

2. Must meet Sinyongwe (rice scheme officer)

3. Must meet Chisaka, one of the big local businessmen

Regarding conditions people live in, I jotted down:

1. Unless housing changes there is no use to emphasize mending, cleanliness, neatness. Note: no cupboards, electricity, irons. (Later, I'd learn just how carefully groomed people could emerge from these dwellings. There is no end to human imagination.)

2. Fishing and especially cultivation means one is dirtied in no time. The soil is hard to wash off. Even sitting and peeling cassava is dirty work.

3. By the way, today for the first time I had a mad desire to get into good clothes. I think this is significant. Donning good clothes symbolizes a kind of freedom from incessant poverty. I seem to

be feeling their poverty. Clean clothes are a relief, a freeing of oneself from a hard, tiring, and monotonous existence. A return from their existence to my own.

4.   Review economic situation. Men primarily fish, women cultivate. Both men and women own stores, bars, but independently of one another. Trade generally is important. Rice scheme requires checking into.

I fell into an uneasy sleep and vaguely worried about having the courage to face the next day. I knew that I needed whatever psychological strength I could muster. At 6 a.m. I awoke to the tune of two dogs chasing my chicken. I cursed out loud, "Damn it, it'll have to be eaten."

After breakfast, I sat and thought. I could stare and think an hour away without even being aware of it. Last night I had yet planned strategies for today and that planning, made me feel more at ease. It also became a habit.

The sight of the D.S. (District Secretary) cheered me. I informed him about my housing decision and next research focus. There is something very capable about him. His demeanor is very European making it easy to relate to him. We sat and puzzled a bit about how much money villagers might have and how they spent it. He was pleased to have me stay at the rest house at least part of the time. I understood, as did he, that in this rural setting each human being with brain and imagination sparkled like a star. Departure of just one such individual generated a sense of deep loss. Here, at least, human being, not machine, not raw nature, was everything.

I had not seen Paul these last few days. I wrestled with my feelings and started to exorcize his ghost. It didn't leave willingly. He'd reached more deeply than I wanted to believe.

During lunchtime, the court clerk brought a letter from Paul written in quaint Lenda-English. I sat back and read.

27th March 1973
Dearest Karla,

I right away feel good at the thought of writing you. I pray that you are OK and at ease with everything.

I am very sorry that I was unable to come last evening. Someone gave me a lift to Kakuso and promised to come and collect me back before 8 p.m. The punk never turned up till 10 p.m. I had by now given up and I was already in the booze business. I was annoyed and now I have to get my car.

As I mentioned to you earlier I am on my way to the I. Belt and then to Lusaka. I felt I should drop you a note in case I have not the chance to say goodbye in person and so not touch your lips. You are a lot on my mind my dear. Anyway I will be back either 1st or 2nd April. If I don't you can check with my clerk of court.

For now best of luck to you special one. Please think of me once a day if you can be so kind, for me it's going to be more than six times a day.

Yours, Paul

The rat, I wrote in my diary, he seems to savor his feeling and, why can't I? I left the thought unanswered, I didn't want to know.

Comment 1982

When we are caught in the uncanniness of what existentialists call dread, we often try to break the empty silence by words spoken at random. Non-conversations take place as was shown by my silly comments to Grace about the house or the bible.

In dread, there is retreat from something, although it is not so much a flight as a spellbound peace. Frequently I simply sat in silence while something was being resolved. Usually, a practical course of action appeared to my mind's eye and the dread would recede. I took such a moment or insight as a tacit way of coming to terms with, and accepting, life's inevitabilities followed by a sense of release and a return to a clear focus on research.

Comment 2018

Anthropology is all about meeting the world around us and then it is social science. It is all about the art of field work and then it is empirical. Finally, it is all about the meeting of bodies, and then it is about analytical distance. Are we more comfortable with the oppositions or their fusion—with exclusivity or inclusivity—or why take note of it at all?

I am reminded of the importance of the body as a bridging symbol. For example, the anti-apartheid South African singer Johnny Clegg (b. 1953) did not only fuse African and Western music; he successfully mimed the gestures of Zulu dancers. The impact on the audience was magnetic—at least as I observed it while attending his performances. The love between the magistrate and the apprentice was such a bridge. The feminist movement missed this bridging between man and woman, black and white, Africa and Europe, kinship and mission, art and science, emotion and mind, among others. The love described here was framed by field work. It was as genuine as it was innocent and as innocent as it is questionable.

But it is a picture that stays in the mind. And not only in my mind. I am reminded of the lino-cuts by the graphic artist John Muafangejo (1943–1987). I met him during my later research between 1981 and 1983 in Namibia. It is from him that I bought several lino-cuts including the one relevant here. What fascinates me is that his lino-cuts work with seemingly obvious binary oppositions, like black/white, traditional/modern, male/female, religious/secular, love/war, Afrocentric/Eurocentric, and visual text/literary text. One of his lino-cuts shows a white woman and a black man holding hands with Muafangejo's words: "They are shaking their hands because they are longing each other." His art seems driven by a force that makes conscious the inner confrontations of his own life, and his lino-cuts seem to bridge these two levels of experience, as does field work itself. Is corporality the essence of this longing, or is corporality an expression of a longing that far exceeds materiality?

I am inclined to see something lyrical in the longings of some Zambian men. A reminder of something like this: "I could not long for you so much did I not long for greatness more" (an adaptation from Lewis, 1960, p.124). Independent Zambia has, perhaps, created a new ambition. Or maybe, it was always there but missed by previous researchers.

7

PROJECT RESEARCH

The next three nights I spent in the Booke home. I followed two rhythms, that of a rational "robot," which I insisted I was, and that of the Lenda. My organization was impeccable. The Sartre model helped. Following lax periods, I became willful, tenacious, and organized. Grace looked at me once and knew. We worked. The first morning we observed male fishers, the second female cultivators, the third male fishers again and finally female cultivators. To observe transactions of fishermen we headed west to the lake; to observe agriculture we headed east to the bush. To observe traders, we headed up and down the valley, in the middle. We talked, helped, and met new people. We needed their rapport for the time was nearing when we would have to ask systematic questions, try out questionnaires, and do life history interviews.

Afternoons we spent taking census and attending churches. I drew a map of Booke and its adjacent fishing camp, Dukana, and noted each path and house. I quickly learned who lived where, how many in each house, and how they were related to one another. I marked down stores and churches and, for the first time, discovered village bars, which served brew prepared and sold by women. All this was yet very preliminary, but people became aware of my presence, and our mutual ease increased.

It is Monday morning, March 30. I finally surveyed the rice fields. Sinyongwe was with me. With his help, I could measure the fields. We met with rice growers and reconstructed their labor and marketing routine.

Labor appeared to be a major problem because it was organized on the principle of non-existent nuclear families.

In need of some silent staring, I decided to lunch at the rest house. Cooks now prepared lunch for me. After lunch, I returned to Booke's village eager to translate letters that people read in the church last Sunday. Grace explained that when people from another village visited Booke, their home church would write a letter of introduction. The visitor attended church, read the letter to the congregation, and was welcomed. In case of an emergency, pastors and congregants knew who the individual was, and where to find them. The church did more than that. It also helped people defray funeral expenses.

We had a simple dinner of tinned hot-dogs and beans. Then we prepared to see a movie, which the government intended to show at the *boma* that evening. By "we," I meant of course Grace, her two older children, her stern *mayosenge* and a sister. More would have come had there been room in the car. When we reached Nzubuka, however, officials told us that the film did not arrive from Mboua. This lack of co-ordination in the valley was only too common.

I fetched a few things from the rest house and on return found the D.G. talking to Banachile, no doubt about my activities. Government, party, and intelligence officials kept close tap on my activities. So far, they were supportive. Back in Booke, we relaxed with Grace's mother. The children loved teaching me Lenda from their schoolbooks and I enjoyed encouraging their reading. We used a hurricane lamp to light the room, and the atmosphere, though dark, was warm and pleasant. I grew to love these people.

We retired to the house owned by the sister of Grace's father. Banachile bedded her two older children and her sister on the floor and took the baby to sleep with her on her bed. I huddled in my cot under a mosquito net. When the *mayosenge* arrived, she locked the doors, prayed out loud, and bedded down. I rested, thinking in the dark. It was a pleasant day, and these people were earthy and sincere. I lay sleepless for many hours, thinking, listening to noises, feeling safe enveloped in my mosquito net. Chibwe cried and his mother breast-fed him.

At 4 a.m. I was already awake waiting for the sun to rise and cocks to crow. Light spread slowly within the hour. Banachile got up, swept the yard, and started the fire. She was very busy at this time in the morning. I came out to relieve myself, having needed to do so for at least the last, endless 90 minutes. I feared the dark.

Mornings were chilly. Children hovered around the fire, which began to burn brightly. Grace cut wood first, placed it among three stones, and lit it with paraffin and matches. She put water on for our baths. As I washed, everybody left the house granting me privacy.

Banachile washed next and then bathed her children. She sent one child to buy four big buns baked by Grace's sister-in-law. We ate these with peanut butter and jam, drank coffee, and added an orange. As is custom, the children took food to Banachile's mothers and sisters. Finished we again collected the *mayosenge* and three of Grace's sisters and drove to Nzubuka to observe the Labor Day ceremony. Life was peaceful, almost idyllic, like the calm before a storm.

We arrived at the ceremonies early. I collected my camera and tape recorder. After much organizing and waiting for people to arrive in Lories from the more distant villages, festivities began. Attendants invited Grace and me to sit on the platform among the officials. The D.G. was the last to arrive in his white Ford. The D.S. and A.D.S. arrived just before and other government personnel earlier still. Members of the Youth Brigade performed "native" dances. A blind man performed acrobatics on a 30-foot pole. I took pictures. Chibwe, as usual, cried and even the breast did not help; and I so much wanted his mother to take notes.

The D.G. spoke of work, holidays, and help to those in need. Like all political speeches, this one had no meat. It was national policy that politicians may not make promises, a response, no doubt, to the rising expectations theory.

He ended his speech with the refrain: "One Zambia," to which the audience replied, "one nation," whereupon the D.G. continued with "One nation," and was answered with "one leader," he ended with "that leader," and the people replied "Kaunda." Ceremonies were soon over and reached few hearts. We returned to the rest house to translate and transcribe the speeches.

While we worked on the translation of the main speech, a staff member announced that the D.G. wanted to see me and would come by. I felt rather nervous because I assumed that he wanted to enquire about photos when I had just ruined one film. He came and I started to explain how I had ruined the film. Halfway through my babble, however, I perceived that he must have come for another reason. I stopped talking, expecting him to explain his visit. He did not. Instead, he left saying we would meet when I was not busy with Banachile. Neither Banachile nor I could make sense of it, so we resumed our work.

Fisherman and Chief Elder of the CMML

We had another monotonous dinner and drove to Booke to see Mr. Mumba, a preacher and chief elder of the CMML church. More importantly, he was a successful fisherman who employed three men. I wanted to persuade him to let his men take me out on the lake so that I could experience fishing activities first hand. His wife invited us into the house to look at their newly born baby. However, babies did not interest me, so I assumed my observer role and counted, and appraised household contents.

The interior was comfortable, even attractive with its small couch, three easy chairs, four straight chairs, and dining table; a small round table with tablecloth, shelves, framed photos and a charcoal drawing of Mr. Mumba. A person with money tended to overwhelm his living quarters with furniture. About six other women visited, all but one with babies. We looked around the garden where I counted three orange trees full of fruit, each fruit sold at one penny. Then there were two pawpaw trees, three mango trees, and a small banana grove. He owned several chickens and geese the latter fenced in. The house was quite big, which means that it was, perhaps, the size of one and a half of our living rooms. It sat on a slope overlooking the lake.

Mr. Mumba, a handsome, elderly and somewhat worldly man, although humble in demeanor as became a leader, returned from a prayer meeting. We sat outside, away from the chatter of other people. He agreed to my going fishing with his men. He himself had fished for twelve years, though he did not do it anymore.

He summoned his fishermen to meet me. They were rather amused at my wanting to go out on the lake. They told me they leave around 4 a.m., stay out on the lake until 10 or 11 a.m., then cruise to INDECO in Kakuso to sell the fish, and return to Booke around 2 p.m. They emphasized that they sit in the boat for 6 to 8 hours. I finally understood what worried them. They were worried about having to urinate. I promised not to look when they did. They told me that they did not eat on the trip and were concerned that I, being a European, bring some food. When they were satisfied as to what and who I was, we returned to Booke's village, where word spread quickly that I was going on the lake.

My attempt to retire early that evening failed. In fact, I slept not at all and heard time tick away slowly, too slowly. Banachile's daughter, Chola, was breathing with great difficulty. Chola was suffering from some sort of deep chest cold. Banachile told me however that she would not take Chola to the hospital. A villager gave the child an injection of, apparently, liquid chloroquine or penicillin.

Villagers believed in injections. Since the hospital did not always administer them, locals regularly sneaked hypodermic needles and medicine from hospital premises and administered them in secret. Before I fell asleep, Banachile's *mayosenge* brought a village "dentist" to discuss the *mayosenge's* toothache and the expense of native medicine. The *mayosenge* decided that he should try his medicine first, if it worked he would be paid later.

It was useless to fall asleep. The village, I discovered, woke up in the evening. People visited back and forth to gossip or to sell something. Two women dropped by with the express purpose of looking at me lying in my cot. Banachile's father sent a message that he would like to sell me some duiker meat for one Zambian pound. He was a hunter. I dressed and went to his house and looked at the meat. It was dark and cozy in the hut. The meat sold, Banachile's father told his favorite stories about the hyena and rabbit.

We got up at 4:30 a.m. to meet the fishermen at 5:00. Grace was terrified to pass the graveyard in the dark and I promised to keep the car windows rolled up. When we arrived in Liwan, the village immediately adjacent to both Booke and Dukana, Mumba's workers were ready and waiting. Grace stayed in one of the fisherman's houses until daylight. She did not want to press her luck twice the same morning by passing the graves again.

Nets had been set the night before. This morning, therefore, fishermen would only haul in the catch. One of the fishers explained that if it was dark they followed a chosen star. He pointed to it. Once it was light, he continued, land formations guided them. For example, where the mouth of the Logirim River looked "wide open" they knew they were somewhere in the center of the lake. There they aligned net markers with some such formation. In fact, the fishers found their destination very easily and directly. It took 1 hour and 45 minutes by boat to the nets. Once there, it took another 1 hour and 30 minutes to take in the fish, 15 minutes to start the motor and about another 1 hour and 45 minutes to return to Dukana fishing camp. In Dukana, fish guards weighed the fish and recorded the weight and species. This is part of the government scheme to rationalize fish production. They brought in one basket weighing 29 kg, and another weighing 48 kg. Of the types of fish, bream predominated, although there were also catfish and several other species.

Gentle clouds covered the sky early that morning and the air was unbelievably mellow. Before we reached the boat, Mumba's brother, Kosa by name, repeated that I would have to excuse the men should they have to urinate. He said they troubled about that problem a bit. I promised that I would close my eyes in such an event, and hold in where I was concerned. They pushed the banana boat into the water and gave me a seat. Kosa, a young man whose face was alive with energy and humor, suggested I sit on his coat for the seat was wet. Feeling quite at ease, he sat beside me.

The water gave the illusion of being a soft carpet gently undulating over a wide space. I felt quite secure in that mellow atmosphere even though it took some time and trouble to start the motor of their boat. On the way out, Kosa explained different fishing methods, involving nets, traps, and beating; government authorities forbid the last. He was very eager to learn how men fished in Canada. Unfortunately, I knew little about it. He explained the boundary with Zangava, and the government's justification to include Sese Island in Zambia.

We discussed divorce, a favorite topic in Lenda. Apparently, there was a recent divorce case involving a woman whose husband lived in the Industrial Belt and no longer sent her money. She had already married someone else. The magistrate had no choice but to grant the divorce.

"Are your women like that?" he asked.

"Do you mean do European women marry a second husband while still married to the first?" I said. "No, they can't; unfortunately, it's illegal," I teased. He enjoyed our exchange of banter.

"Ah, our women, they can't be trusted. Today they love you and tomorrow they throw you out," he said.

This is great, I thought, and decided to agitate him with questions that pictured the constraints on the behavior of Western couples. "Would you like to be married to one and the same woman all your life and not sleep with others?" I asked.

"By my mother, no! That would be absurd," he said looking simultaneously surprised and alarmed.

"Would you like to take your wife to friends, beer drinks, dances, and hold her hand and show the world you love her?"

"That's what you do, really?" he asked. I nodded affirmatively. "No," he said. "If I took my wife, I could not talk with other women. I could not explore what others are like."

I looked at him with as much gravity as I could muster. "Would you like to be ostracized from couples when you are single? Upon meeting a nice married woman, would you accept that you cannot marry her? Would you like to feel alone? Would you like to feel that there are few women, or that you may never find one because most are married?"

He looked at me with great fright. "No," he said.

I took a deep breath and laughed. "Then don't complain about your women," I said. All were silent so that I could not resist adding, with a combination of humor and piety, "be grateful that you can always and at any time meet a woman, and she a man. You see, in our society many are lonely, sexually frustrated because one man and one woman are each other's exclusive and private property." I looked deep into Kosa's eyes. "Ah" is what they seemed to say. I hoped that some of their mystification of Western culture had melted away. It was not my task, perhaps, to remind them of the restraining side of our life. However, I disliked mystification and I knew that other whites presented the West in a flawless, even idyllic light.

We listened to the droning motor and the splash of tiny waves against the boat. But for these sounds, it was noiseless for a long time, until Kosa's face lit up again. He heard, he told me, this man in rags that some Europeans, scientists and the like, did not believe that God created the earth and life on it, what was this thing people believed in instead.

"You are referring to evolution?"

"Yes, that's it," he said. "You Europeans are funny. You come here and teach us Christianity and just when we've learned, other Europeans come and say the first ones were wrong. Tell me; what is this evolution, then?"

I tried to explain the theory of Evolution. However, to explain the history and logic of evolution to people who had no background in biology, chemistry, archaeology, or genetics, is an almost impossible task. The theory began to look more enigmatical than anything written in the Bible did. In fact, my explanation sounded absurd in the context. I tried repeatedly to refine it, but it was hopeless.

"How many years did it take you to learn Christian teachings?" I asked, exasperated.

"Many."

"Well, it would take even longer for you to learn all aspects of evolution." This is taxing, I thought, and marveled at Kosa's unending curiosity about our way of life. But then, I thought, so much of our life is already part of theirs—just poorer and with a curious mix.

Last night, they told me that they did not eat or drink while fishing. I took it to mean that they did not want to encourage a bowel movement or such. However, when they discovered that I had brought a bun and something to drink they asked whether I meant it to be for me only or whether they could share it. I told them the whole thing was for them, and after some disappointment at discovering that I brought orange juice instead of Fanta, they nevertheless devoured everything, sharing it equally.

During the hauling process, two men stood in the boat, the other two paddled the boat along a 1000-yard net, all this with considerable gaiety. They simply lifted the net out of the water, freed the gills and fins from the net, and threw the fish into baskets. These nets belonged to two different owners. Respecting that fact, the men threw the fish into separate baskets. If a big fish struggled, he clubbed it over the head. Upon completion of the task, the men added another net, left them in the water, and returned.

On the way back to INDECO, the fishers continued the discussion of the Bible, evolution, poverty, and ended with their concern that I did not have children. We solved the last problem more easily than the previous ones.

"Your children belong first to their mother and then also to her brother, is that right?" I said.

"Yes. They belong to the mother. But a woman and her brother are one person, so he has some interest in her children as well," Kosa said.

"Each child is legitimate, no matter who the father, is that right?" I said. "Yes. The father makes no difference," he answered.

"When we have such a system, I'll have children," I said. They appreciated my mischief and laughed.

Upon return, the fishers stayed in Dukana. They weighed the fish and distributed some for immediate consumption. Kosa insisted that I take a share. I accepted, knowing that Banachile would be delighted.

In my notebook which I carried with me always I wrote that I must buy them socks, for one of the fishermen discovered that I was wearing men's socks and asked whether I had more than one pair. I had only the one pair.

The conversation ended. I was becoming used to the oblique way in which people asked for gifts.

In Booke's village, Banachile cleaned three fish for me to take to Nzubuka. The rest remained. Not having slept the night, I was tired and craved the solitude of the rest house. It was not to be and I had lunch in a busy atmosphere. Several men painted the dining room and lounge in anticipation of the arrival of Mr. Jomo Mutanga, then, Minister of Rural Development.

In the afternoon, I went to the court to look at cases for the year 1971. I had already recorded cases for two years prior to this date when the court was established. Of the 28 cases heard during 1971, almost half involved assault. The rest included stealing, driving offences, and bribery.

My cheeks flushed at the sight of Paul. I could not deny that I went to the court to both record cases and, perhaps, see him. He stood there leaning against the desk, his arms held out to welcome me. Work was much easier after that.

Toward evening, the D.S. came by with mail from CAIU and Bob. I settled back to read.

CENTER FOR THE ADVANCEMENT OF INTERNATIONAL UNDERSTANDING OTTAWA, CANADA

April 3, 1973
Dear Miss Poewe:

Thank you for your letters of February 21 and February 30, 1973. You will be notified shortly of the deposit of $91.47 for the receipts you have submitted for publications and tape recorder accessories.

The Centre cannot reimburse you directly for the cost of your car, insurance, car repairs, etc. Instead, when a grantee decides that his field travel must be undertaken by car, he is reimbursed a fixed amount per mile. I therefore suggest that you keep a record of your mileage, which you can submit periodically to us. The exact amount per mile, which the Centre will pay, is still under discussion; however, it will certainly cover costs of gas, repairs, and depreciation.

I am pleased that you have been able to sort out the various problems you encountered on your arrival and shall look forward to your first progress report at the end of May.

Sincerely yours,
Peter Paladin
Associate Director

Need I say that I found this letter frustrating? Since money was important, however, I did not dwell on the frustration. I simply reviewed all my travel and calculated the number of miles covered to date. Feeling confident that I could adjust without loss to this new demand, I read Bob's letter. He wrote that he had accepted a position at another university, that he loved and missed me, and that there might be a possibility of a position for me too.

I felt simultaneously glad and worried about Bob's decision to move to Morissa. I was happy because he had made the decision alone. I was worried because the letter contained too much optimism and emotion. He was obviously surfacing from his own dejection. I was suspicious of optimism unless it was grounded either in the probability that an event might occur, or in an overall plan, project, or philosophy of life. His optimism, that there may be a position for me at Morissa or in the vicinity, I dismissed as self-deception. Instinctively, I felt that there is too much built-in cruelty in our social arrangements to allow so smooth a solution. As for the rest, I had to admit that I did not know just what Bob's philosophy of life was. All I knew was that he tried to act in accordance with a set of battered Christian-based principles that, seen from my current uncertain situation, seemed too optimistic. Having been a refugee, nothing in my life was ever easy, nor could I ever take anything for granted. My first remembered childhood experience was sudden loss. War tore the ground from under me and denatured trust. The nineteen-sixties counter-culture continued the trend.

Comment 1982

Slowly I began to learn three things:

1. From the magistrate I learned that most cases are related to material want and are played out in quarrels between men and women and between kin of the parental generation and their offspring.

2. From politicians I learned that most conflicts are over concentration and movement of resources with government officials pushing national democracy and traditional leaders favoring regional chiefdoms.

3. From people generally, I learned that the source of strength to survive and shape their lives comes from different religious and ideological sources: It comes from Christianity that attracts both men and women but is becoming seen by women to favor men; and it comes from their Kin-based history that leans toward favoring male descendants among Lenda's "aristocrats," but is matrifocal for the general valley population. The valley population has its uncertainties and conflicts and I had mine, but theirs were and remain far more serious and long term.

8

GRIEF AND RECALL OF CHILDHOOD MEMORIES

I slept in the rest house to talk with Roberts at the Fisheries Research Centre the following morning. The Minister of State Mr. Muela arrived, an important event because one could take a hot bath. The rest house only functioned adequately on arrival of VIPs.

Early Saturday morning I drove to Booke's village where Banachile and other club members were already at work in the rice field. The aim was to earn one Zambian pound per woman for the club from the female owner of the field. Rice was harvested local style and not with a sickle as taught by extension officers. Eight women with pocketknives cut plants just below the rice kernels. Women were anxious to earn funds for the following week's visit by the Minister of Rural Development, Mr. Jomo Mutanga. He telegrammed that he would visit Chade's and Booke's women's clubs and villages. Community Development people were out in full force organizing for Mutanga's visit.

We left the field about 10 a.m. long before the others ceased their work to attend Seventh-day Adventist services. SdA organized their services differently from those of CMML. For one thing, SdA was more dynamic. Because CMML did not require the payment of tithe, it appealed largely to the poor. Like Catholicism it did not seriously change, or aim to change the life of rural dwellers. Jehovah's Witnesses and Seventh-day Adventists were more effective in matters of change, although differentially so.

During SdA service, people formed several groups with their own leaders who taught them intensively from the Bible. The congregation was encouraged to ask and answer questions. In contrast with CMML, SdA members preferred talk to singing.

The SdA building was similar in structure to that of CMML. Its benches consisted of wooden planks placed across blocks of cement. A wooden table decorated with cloth and paper flowers constituted the altar. Four people sat on a bench behind the altar facing the audience. Ushers told me that they were the visiting preacher, local preacher, deacon, and a deaconess. Services lasted three hours and gave me a sore back.

Banachile joined me for lunch at the Nzubuka rest house. As constituency secretary of UNIP, she had to attend a political meeting here. UNIP officials were planning to check the ownership of party cards. Those without, were to be disallowed to buy fish at the market.

During lunch, I met both the Minister of State for Lenda Province and the Minister for Community Development. We discussed family planning that both discouraged. I could sympathize with their view. The infant mortality rate was too high. That topic exhausted, I asked the former for a letter of introduction following Catote's request. He agreed to have one prepared.

Judy dropped by. I was tired and somewhat depressed. Nevertheless, I welcomed Judy's suggestion to go to the boat and relax the rest of the afternoon. Once on the water, however, I found, to my own astonishment, that I had nothing to talk about with my white friends. Still, placid waters soothed my spirit. I topped this excursion with a visit to Van Gella. There too, I found myself restless and without anything to say. Hans sympathized and left me wrapped in silence.

Upon return, I found Banachile at the rest house and was relieved to see her. We had supper and drove to Booke's village. Her father told folktales while Chibwe crawled along the floor. I watched his shadow grasp the

Chibwe

door. Chola looked ill and worn. She had slept all afternoon as if life had bid her farewell.

For the next five days, my routine varied little. I stayed in Booke's village and rose about 5 a.m., following the demands of my bladder. Each morning, I watched Banachile start the fire. Children came to huddle over it until the heat spread to melt the morning chill. Then Banachile prepared water for us. Each morning, we waited for freshly baked bread and ate it with peanut butter and jam. In addition, we had coffee, which B. drank only for its sugar. Her children ate and drank with us, but their coffee contained mostly sugar and instant milk. Each morning, Banachile sent a child to take bread and coffee to her mothers.

My contacts increased. Banachile's brother-in-law, a preacher and carpenter, built us furniture and wrote the history of the local church. Women who could write recorded their purchases, barter, and gifts. Such records increased in number, and I checked them each day and they became valuable data.

Then I felt drained and drove to Nzubuka to sit and stare. I repaired the D.G.'s tape recorder, which was the reason for his past visit. The D.S. explained the structure of the local government, or that aspect of it, which he was free to reveal. Then I wrote to Lusaka, for the time was nearing to return and write my first report.

A longing stirred within me and, in my mind's eye, I watched his finger pack the tobacco. Then I remembered that I had court cases to review. I saw him standing in his office welcoming me and I ran to him.

He told me of his plans. They were right and good, but deep down, I choked with sorrow; less than a month and he would be gone. Paul explained the adult education program, which the government had introduced for those who missed their chance of an education during colonial times. He would attend the University of Zambia within a short time.

I stood there, paralyzed and overwhelmed with a sense of loss. There is no progress in love. I saw Paul rarely, but knowing that he was in the valley lent a certain eloquence to this stark environment. He spoke for it. His grace and quiet authority, his sensuality and deep sense of responsibility, his fierce sense of autonomy, his dignified manliness, his appreciation of the dignity of woman, all these qualities had their roots in this hot, unruly valley. He was a son of its earth.

"You write your report in Lusaka," he said interrupting my thoughts. "Can't you drive down with me?" My hopes rose. Then I was angry with myself. He had given me everything I could have wanted, why should I want more. Above all, why prolong the end? Yet, I was unbearably sad at the loss of this man from this valley.

I forced myself, dragged myself to Booke. With each mile, I felt as if my gut, hooked to Nzubuka, was being pulled out of my body. I hurt, that was all. I hurt and felt desolate. Inside me, someone moaned through the night. Therefore, I sent myself through a rigorous routine next day. I did research with a vengeance to quell pain with pain, but my spirit rebelled, and my straining exhausted me. For a moment, I wondered whether I would be mad enough to follow this man and slow down or ruin my research. Despairing, I wrote to my mother.

April 10, 1973
Darling Mother:

I am torn between intense feeling and cold reason. The tension is awful. At times, I feel like one of Thomas Mann's characters who, in his quest for truth and understanding, is questionably guided by his senses and Eros. You remember Aschenbach (in Death in Venice) who says:

> *For you must know that we poets cannot walk the way of beauty*
> *without Eros as our companion and peremptory guide. We may*
> *be heroic after our fashion, disciplined warriors of our craft, yet*
> *we are all like women, for we exult in passion ... (and so on).*

I know that I am not a poet, and yet I am straining for a breakthrough, an
escape into freedom. Describing artists who face similar dilemmas,
Thomas Mann describes the solution as the miracle of a dialectical process
by means of which the strictest formalism is changed into the free language
of emotion. It is a miracle of the birth of freedom from total conformity and
order (Doctor Faustus).

My parting with P.K.—for I have determined there must be an end—is but
the parting, in human form, with anthropological literature, childhood
memories, the white community here, Bob and friends back home. An ever-
growing gulf is beginning to separate me from my immediate past, even
from my discipline. I have become very impatient with anthropological
literature. Instead of the thrill of discovering new ideas, reading
anthropological papers fills me with a deep sense of nausea. The formalism
upon which anthropologists insist is remote from life and irrelevant to
anything I am currently experiencing. How very tiring conformity is.

Having written that letter, I felt better. From the dizziness of my brain rose
a decision. Once surfaced, it calmly rode the waves of quiet pain never to
be drowned again.

The night was pitch black much like a tomb when I entered the club. Paul
was there. Charles came and left, and Ephraim did too. Then we were alone
with nothing to say.

He accompanied me to the rest house. There too, I found nothing to say.
He had malaria and felt weak and sick. Beads of perspiration trickled down
his face, and as I looked at him, I felt some recognition. It stirred my
memory and took me into my past for I saw in him the image of my father.

He returned from the war when I was little over six years old. He was simply there one day. The hair of his head was shaved, his face looked wan, and he was weak and ailing. As he greeted my mother, cold sweat ran down his face, and my mother burdened him with me. I too was sick and he took me to my grandmother to recover. We crossed the Russian sector. The train stopped. He carried me to the platform and went back to fetch our bags.

I saw the train pull off with my father still on it, and I felt as if someone was strangling me and my stomach was torn asunder. I stood there screaming for help and stamping my feet. Terror spread through me, my screams radiated through the air, and the echo of them came back to me. Reddened eyes followed the train.

Paul left. We had nothing to say. I mourned for the loss of him and tomorrow I would mourn again.

He came in the evening. He sat on my bed. Beads of perspiration played on his face and pain shot through his head, and he held my hand. "I have a dream for us," he said. I looked at him surprised, and my glance sank into him. "There can't be a dream," I replied. The sound of those words was familiar, and as I looked at this proud son of the earth, I recalled an image of my father and mother.

Mother sent my sister and me to play outside, but we peeked through the low window of the hospital and saw our mother with that man. My father sat in bed. He was dressed in white. Cold sweat ran down his face. He looked to his neighbor who moaned and groaned and said he was sick and would die. My father held him by the arm and stared. "You must want to live," he cried out. Then he leaned back and his head turned to my mother. "I have a dream for us," he said to her. They looked at each other and then he turned to look at me. A ray of light shot from his eyes and it was so strong that it touched me. I held my breath and reached for his hand, but he lay back and died. I remembered my mother shiver and moan through the nights. Five years she had waited for his return and he came back to meet not her but his death.

Comment 2018

This was a period of deep turmoil. I began to feel alienated from the white community at a time when I could not yet be a full part of the black community either. Just when I resolved that my involvement with P.K. had reached its end, he dreamt of a new beginning thereby also acknowledging an end. Our reaction to the inevitability of parting was so like that of my parents that I relived, as in a dream, the traumatic death of my father.

My father was a businessman born into a family of people in diverse professions from pharmacy to horse raising. His father and father's father raised Trakehner horses near Gumbinnen, East Prussia. Apparently, the family had migrated to Prussia from Alsace-Lorraine during the 1800s. French by birth, they became German. Although my father was twenty years older than my mother, he "joined" the army or Volkssturm—or so it seemed. My search for records, provided no answer as to which it was. Only in 2001, a year before my mother died, did she show me some of his letters.

Commenting on the refugee crisis in December 1944 he wrote to my mother, "And now a thought about the evil (*bösen*) times. Thousands are worse off than we." He saw the treks of refugees from Memel and other East Prussian border areas, but could not describe details owing to military censorship. Instead, he wrote abstractly "One must try and help oneself as best one can. There is no alternative but to think clearly and to concentrate one's thoughts on the problem of survival. Too much worry weakens." Then he was gone until four and a half years later when he returned to die. He had gangrenous lungs.

To capture what I felt then, I left this chapter filled with emotion. It evokes not only the rhythmic wailing of Lenda women that I heard so often during sleepless nights, it also evokes haunting scenes as I learned to face, ever so slowly, the debilitating memories that have haunted my assimilated existence. The exchange of a willed for an unwilled sacrifice itself was curative. Life was never about permanence.

9

ALIENATION, SEEING, AND FEELING

It was mid-April. I drove to Booke's village to attend the three-hour CMML services. Many more hours were spent recording and transcribing them. I am particularly curious to discover whether the Lenda are learning a different ideology to that of their matrilineal one or whether during church services they merely express old values in new ways. It is already becoming clear that services among Jehovah's Witnesses, Seventh-day Adventists and CMML are very different. Jehovah's Witnesses tend to teach the bible as if it were a record of historical fact, an ongoing stream of human corruption leading inevitably to a new social order, Gods kingdom on earth (*ubuteko Wawanesa*). Seventh-day Adventists, by contrast, tend to sermonize, relying on analogy and metaphor to make their points. They portray the human condition by means of narratives about local circumstances, but within a universal context devoid of time, specificities, or numbers. It would appear, therefore, that Jehovah's Witnesses are learning a whole new way of seeing and organizing their life, while SdA and CMML tend to be somewhat more syncretistic; new values are added but old ones are not necessarily discarded.

In the afternoon, Banachile and I conducted preliminary interviews with two female storeowners. I was under the impression that these women started, controlled, and ran their own small businesses. I was particularly curious to discover whether husbands had anything to do with the business.

Women rather smiled at me when I discussed husbands. They behaved as if to let me know that I was assigning importance to a relationship that it might not have. Indeed, I began to feel that my assumptions about family, in the sense of husband, wife and children were wrong. Certainly, families are not neat little economic units based on committed complementary relationships as I knew them back home. For the moment, I put the problem aside.

Toward evening, I decided to visit the Van Gella home. I needed to get away, to clear my brain. As I drove through Kakuso, I saw Paul dressed in his Sunday best driving his car. He was taking Muteta and Muteta's daughter to Katumba. He looked well, I said so, and he agreed. A truck passed. I drove off and in the mirror, I saw him drive off too.

I was relieved to find Van Gella at home. I expressed my need to escape. Hans understood; he always did. We puzzled why we were here and expressed our dissatisfactions with things back home. Hans observed that we were like characters in Simone de Beauvoir's book *The Mandarins*. That sort of realism, which Hans termed sad, was the only kind of philosophy with which I could presently empathize.

"But at least," I said shifting attention from Beauvoir to Camus' book *The Plague*, "you are the great figure of humanitarian work because as physician you reduce real pain and suffering. You are not an ineffectual intellectual." He looked at me with his usual kindness. "In that sense, you too are a humanitarian worker."

"At best, a dubious one," I said, "for like a journalist, I will leave when my assignment is done. Then comes a long slog," I sighed. "You will stay and heal and train nurses to carry on."

Nicolas, their two-year-old son, wanted to play with me, so we ran about in the banana grove and then stood there staring across the water. From the distance, we heard wailing and knew it was another death.

Van Gella asked me to stay for a barbecue and I gladly accepted. I did not want to return to the rest house and dwell on Paul. Following a meal of delicious tender loin, Father Leo brought three short French films. He borrowed them from the French Ambassador, and the white community gathered to watch. Several secondary school teachers came, two Dutch sisters, two Dutch volunteers, three Catholic priests and so on. All I remembered of the films was their incongruity. Suddenly I felt the company stifling and got up to leave. Hans turned and held my arm. "Are you alright, Karla?" he said. "It's crazy, Hans. I can't stand the white community for long and I had to escape from the Zambian one as well." I kissed his cheek and left. Restlessness took over. Everything was unsettled inside.

Monday morning, I still had a mad desire to escape a sense of dread. Instead, I got up very deliberately. It was 6 a.m. The Minister for Rural Development, Mr. Mutanga, who had arrived last night, also rose at this hour. We ran into one another on the way to the bathroom. He greeted me and asked several questions. Realizing that the rest house would be crowded with people, I drove to Booke's village where the Minister would look at the women's club.

Local women had decorated the club and even whitewashed it. The women were rather excited. I had a quick piece of bread with peanut butter and jam when I heard that UNIP people were arriving. Banachile ran off. She was to read a little speech. I fetched my camera and followed her to the club. Women were dancing and ululating. Even Booke's oldest woman danced though with the support of a stick. We waited. The women continued to sing and dance. Men stood off to the side.

Around 9 a.m., the Minister arrived. I photographed women decorating him with flowers, and with my camera, I followed him as he entered the club where he would read his speech. Conversations became informal and the Minister prodded the women to grow vegetables. They were not shy to reply that they needed a well for that. Some had to walk a mile or more to fetch water. Coming that distance, it was too precious to pour on the ground.

Outside, and for the benefit of the press, women displayed various articles that they had made; a little dress, for example, a tablecloth, a small rug made from remnants. Someone gave the Minister a chicken, a stalk of bananas and groundnuts. Officials returned to their Mercedes, which raised dust as they left.

The club stood empty but for some women and two village men. A woman called for silence and announced that one of the men wanted to speak to them. He reminded them of the time when the club was first built, when men and women worked together. Apparently, they did not do so now. However, the club needed latrines, and the men promised to work with the women to build them. "We shall even fetch water and help make bricks," he promised. The promise sounded sweet to the women's ears.

The atmosphere was relaxed. People broke into hearty laughter when told that the headman's mother had run to hide. She was very old, but had nonetheless joined the women in their dance. When she saw the entourage of cars and police, however, she ran away. I see her still, the old woman with her eccentricities, walking, bent with age, checking that no evil spirit followed her.

Banachile and I returned to the house and finished our breakfast. Seated on bamboo mats in the shade we reviewed notes from last Sunday's sermon. They were stories about Jesus' deeds and man's misdeeds and the forces of nature, and most of it was about life and death.

We rested. The shade of the mango tree was generous. Its coolness cleared my brain. I asked Banachile to read the sermon again and suddenly it all made sense. I saw how the story would appeal to fishermen. Banachile even used appropriate examples.

Chibwe crawled about naked and defecated on the mat. Banachile ran for a cloth, wiped it off, and placed her baby son in the sand, which cleaned his bum. His big eyes shone mischief as he came crawling back. I loved the silly little fellow with his tiny penis, hands, and feet. His popping belly struck my flesh. Chola cried. I took her in my arms and put her on my lap. She cuddled quietly. People touched more freely here. Everything was closer to nature. Contact was easy and warm. I wondered why these people listened to a chilling biblical morality only to follow that thought with the question why I saw biblical morality negatively? And why did I suddenly romanticize nature when its starkness was overwhelming?

My thoughts fled to Paul. I saw us, but could not remember a single word we said and yet we talked endlessly. I realized that my field work so far was primarily seeing and feeling, especially seeing. Even what I saw, was bereft somehow of structure. It took a long time to distinguish visually local poverty from wealth, a field from the bush, a path from landscape, a village bar from a dwelling. I saw no couples, no families, no parents, no husbands, and no wives.

They did not walk together in pairs as we do back home, and except for Jehovah's Witnesses, many did not live together permanently in single dwellings. I learned to see all over again, and what I felt was somehow wrong too, that much at least I knew.

In the afternoon, I gathered census material at Liwan village. I counted fishermen and bakers and observed the sole mechanic. I studied their boats, motors, and nets, and recorded the cost of it all. I even counted the kinds and numbers of fruit-bearing trees. Finally, I summarized everything and wrote to Professor Justin.

C/o P.O. Box 1
Nzubuka, Zambia
April 16, 1973
Dear Professor Justin

I know that my infrequent writing to date will not please you. I have been preoccupied. As well, I have very little privacy, not because I cannot have more, but because at this point privacy can too easily turn into isolation.

The Institute for African Research was completely uninformed about this area, and with frequent changes of personnel in government departments, volunteer organizations, and hospitals they lost contact with people in the valley. In short, I came into the area alone and have had to meet everyone from scratch.

What was formerly Katumba is now divided into three districts: Katumba itself, Nzubuka to the north and Zongwe to the south. This has meant that I have had to drive some distance to the respective bomas, *administrative centers, to meet government officials and inform them of my presence.*

My central location, therefore, has been Nzubuka itself—it is the boma *for the district and houses mainly government personnel, secondary and primary schoolteachers, and fisheries personnel. Fishermen themselves live in various villages. Many fishermen seem to be moving north where there are said to be more fish, especially bream, which is more expensive and better tasting.*

If a study is to give even a fair picture of life here, the researcher must maintain contact not only with the villages, but also with the boma *and with central "commercial" locations as, for example, Kakuso where Lakes Fisheries (INDECO) is located and where fishermen sell their fish. To begin to know the region has been my first concern.*

During the last few weeks, then, I have been living part of the time in Booke's village, which is the home of the young woman assisting me, and part of the time in the rest house at Nzubuka. In addition, I have visited several other villages including chiefly capitals.

Booke's village consists of 32 houses along the main road. Most of its people are not fishers, rather they are carpenters, mat makers, rice farmers, small storeowners, and so on (report will give details). Continuous with Booke village to the west and down the slope to the lakeshore is Dukana fishing camp where most of the fishermen live. At Booke's small fish market, fish guards weigh and record distinct species of fish for government records. This procedure starts upon fishermen's return from the lake and before any fish can be sold to villagers, to Lakes Fisheries, or to fish traders. Villagers who do not fish buy their fish in this market. Mind you, only some fishermen sell their fish here. To the north and continuous with Booke, along the main road, and on the slope to the lakeshore, is Liwan, a village with about 70 houses. Here again one gets the usual composition of fishermen, small storeowners, a tailor and so on.

Villagers are selling, or perhaps the word is hawking, everything in sight. For example, about 30 feet away the treasurer of the CMML church owns several banana trees (among others). A Booke villager might go there, buy two green bananas for 1 penny, take them home to Booke and let them ripen and then sell them to villagers or people sitting along the road waiting for the bus. Now the price has doubled.

The government has supplied women in the villages with materials to build a clubhouse—a small square structure of mud bricks, but whitewashed, and with a tin roof. Working for wealthier villagers, women are then supposed to earn additional money to buy materials and learn to sew and cook. Infant nutritional needs are taught. Usually, women stitch decorative doilies, or such, which are placed just about everywhere in the house. Why they are taught such useless things only the British can tell us. It has no doubt to do with their conception of women as housekeepers, not with the Lenda conception of women as providers. Women are always trying to sell things they make to other villagers and passing strangers. Men or women walk, hitch rides, or cycle great distances to buy something at one price and then sell it at a slightly higher price elsewhere. I suspect, but do not know yet, that I am talking about the poorer women here.

Economic activities of the sexes revolve around different resources and space. Women are the cultivators; their work takes them east each morning. Men are the fishers and their work takes them west. Both sexes seem to own businesses and both trade. What women own, appears to be quite separate from what men own, although Jehovah's Witnesses appear to function more like small Western-type families. I seem to be misreading women somehow. Anyway, it is a darned lot easier and more pleasant to work with Lenda men than with Lenda women. The men are the talkers here. Women are taciturn, proud, and, I would say, managerial. Sometimes I have the impression that women see me as foolish for talking to men.

I have not looked at kinship yet and the answer to my puzzlement about the sexes may lie there, but I am determined to discover kinship first through their behavior. I want to know whether it is a living reality. To ask questions about it now and from one informant creates the danger of treating what may be mere memory as if it were ongoing reality. Now my attitude is, if it is alive it will reveal itself, and then I will pursue it through intensive enquiry.

I am under the impression that young men are free of any responsibility until late in life. They wander aimlessly about while young girls are busy helping their mothers. Many older men too sit about doing nothing. Where exactly they live is also hard to determine. Some of them remind me of bees fluttering from flower to flower. In the afternoon people look more rested although, some women prepare food, which takes unbelievably long.

I must say that I had to waste much time because the Institute is uninformed about basic procedures—especially those that concern contacting government hierarchies to gain their consent to do research in areas under their jurisdiction. This carelessness on the part of the Institute is especially out of place since this country is status conscious and status seeking. I have found that as I move into an area people already expect me to know them and I have run into one problem, which I must go and correct in Lusaka. It involved a slight mistake in the title on my letter of introduction—I knew better, but did not want to squabble with the Institute's Director Vandenberg who is too damn irascible.

In short, then, this coming Monday I am on my way back to Lusaka straightening out various details, including servicing my car. The car is vital to my research.

I might mention, by the way, that I feel a constant tension between learning Lenda and getting data. At this stage, at least, the two do not coincide all that much and I say this even though I learned Lenda before I came to Zambia. There also seems to be a tension, at least at this point of my research, between exploring the "minds" of Lendans and observing their behavior. It seems to me, I have been primarily observer to date. Yet, I know, as I glimpse more of their cognition that it makes me see differently. I am still blind, however, to much of "their reality."

P.S. Measurement of gardens, food, etc. will constitute a bit of a problem— Len will no doubt have some suggestions.

Upon the completion of this letter, I prepared to leave for Lusaka. The first report was due. The Institute in Lusaka is a better environment in which to write it. If I'm lucky there might be some feedback from other researchers. As well, my body could stand decent food. If that sounds as if I am treating my body like a tool in need of maintenance, then I expressed myself clearly. Nutrition is a general as well as a personal problem in Lenda.

10

LUSAKA, LETTERS, CONVERSATIONS, AND BARS

April 19, 1973
Hello Bob:

I am back in Lusaka for a few days. I must get a new letter of introduction, write the report, and service the car.

Writing the report irritates me. It is difficult enough to keep my emotional balance, and to cut myself off to write the report is disquieting. I find that the only way I can keep my spirits up is to move constantly among people. I get out there and stay out there all the time—except for the odd moments of absolute silence, which I need even here.

I feel that I am still only scratching the surface. In addition, I will have to decide when to move to another area and village. The river valley is more conservative than the lake area where I am now.

By the way, could you send a copy of Rappaport's Pigs for the Ancestors*? Please, send Chayanov's book too. Maybe they contain something useful. No rush, though.*

Now, here is something that needs to be sent AIRMAIL to Nzubuka. The RUBBER ENGINE MOUNT of my car is broken—split halfway across. I cannot find one in all of Lusaka never mind anywhere else. It is just a small part, you know, it supports the engine to absorb vibrations. Remember, it is for a 1972 Datsun 1200.

This is, by the way, the most status conscious and status seeking country I have experienced, although I suspect that "status," "position" may mean something quite different here. The struggle for position makes sense; opportunities to succeed are still there. Should you ever decide to visit, give me ample notice, I should like you to bring presents. For example, cassette tapes of the most recent American music are a precious good. Fishermen would appreciate a few nice pairs of socks, although I have already bought some for them here.

Having finished the letter, I sought out Vandenberg, the Director of the Institute. Much to my surprise, we managed to have a very fruitful and stimulating discussion.

"It seems to me," I told him, "that two sorts of populations highlight Zambia's problems: the poor and women. In Lenda, when men are fishermen they receive loans and recent technology. Women who cultivate do not seem to receive loans or technology. When cultivators are given loans, they are given to male heads of households, but, I'm not sure such male heads exist." We dwelled on this and decided that I should continue to study the economic and social structure of two kinds of communities, fishing and farming ones.

"If you're right about loans and Jehovah's Witnesses, check whether farming villages form a different sort of population. Could they be primarily Jehovah's Witnesses?" he said.

"Jehovah's Witnesses are more likely to be fishers," I suggested.

"By the way," he continued after a pause, "do you feel that the men are improving their economic well-being largely through the economic efforts and acumen of women?"

I thought about that. Was there a sort of economic parallelism in Lenda or were the women supporting the men?

"Aren't men piranhas," he said.

"And here I thought you would stick up for men," I teased. "But yes, it seems that many business ventures are started by women, not to mention cultivation and all that. It is not clear to me yet which men are primarily benefitting. Probably brothers more than husbands, if the matrilineal business means anything." I also wondered what happened to the interaction between men and women in situations where men are wealthier or become politicians. Is everything calculated, I wondered? What about the longing? I said nothing.

He suggested that I focus my attention on women's activities to elucidate the strife and struggle for wealth and positions among men. An interesting twist; are women being used or are they in control?

In rural areas, women provide cheap labor, reliable labor, and continuous labor. As already mentioned, much of the strife for positions among men, in a status seeking setting, is possible because women provide basic securities. Not just that, but women start business and fishing ventures which may be handed to brothers to manage, not to husbands. But is this a uniform pattern? In towns and urban settings, the men–women interdependencies change again. Only one thing is certain. Women must provide for their children. And here the phrase "we suffer" (Cliggett 2005; Evans 2016) comes in. What does that tell us about the economy of responsibilities?

The economic activities of men and women and the conflicts that arise when both find themselves in similar situations are one of the more fascinating aspects of Zambian life. For example, in Lusaka the battle of the sexes was raging over the issue of marketing which women saw as their domain but which men began to invade. In urban areas, trade and barter was one activity that enabled women to maintain their rural-bred economic independence. After all, the party ensured that jobs went primarily to men. Whatever the reason, UNIP served primarily male interests. An old story in the West, but does it have to happen here?

Back in my room, I found a letter from Professor Justin. I sat down and read it. His equanimity was calming.

April 29, 1973
Touson
Dear Karla:

I am delighted to have your letter of April 16, of course, and to learn that you are settled in the field. Your choice of Nzubuka seems reasonable; under present conditions in Africa, I can think of nothing more important than having the support of local government officials.

In the long run, the isolation of Lenda should be an advantage to you, unless officials in the area change too rapidly. You need to expect a lot of apparently waste motion in the initial stage of research, but if you keep a full daily record, you will find it invaluable later on when you are likely to forget the impact of initial impressions.

It seems to me that you are progressing quite well in view of all the problems you face. Your acquisition in the loss of privacy is wise; isolation would have been a poor choice. If the government people do provide accommodation you may be able to work out a fairly regular schedule eventually—but don't count on it. The main thing is to somehow get your field notes down. You should send copies to me, not merely for review but for safekeeping.

I wish I could give you definitive advice on the language learning vs. data gathering dilemma. If you could be certain that you would be able to remain in the field for an extensive period, concentration on Lenda would provide the real pay-off. Does everyone—women and men—speak Lenda? If so, control of the language would be highly desirable, of course. You already studied it before you went to the field. But you also need to take account of your relative skill in acquiring the language; how much time would you need to become fairly fluent? To what extent could you count on English-speaking assistants who could be trained for data collection? The counsel of perfection is to learn Lenda thoroughly, but this may not be the most practical counsel. In Kumozi, we tried to spend about half time on language initially, but this did not work very well. However, the procedure may be worth trying.

I will pass your letter on to Len; perhaps he will have some comments.

Again, I'm happy that you are beginning research, and hope that all will go well. Keep us informed and we'll try to maintain regular correspondence.

All the best.
Ralph Justin

Professor Justin had confidence in "his students," those who chose him as their advisor and those whom he accepted. His confidence in us spurred us on.

Then I read Bob's letter. It shook me to the core. It was a letter that reminded me of his kindness and a love that I did not expect. I mean a love that binds when that is the one thing I did not understand because all bonds in my life were torn up by war and the wrongdoing of my country of birth that had to be defeated for it. The only bond that remained was the peculiar one with my mother. And now this letter. It informed me that engine mounts were on the way and so were books and articles. The expression of love and of a future *together*—when that future was already gone—broke my heart.

It also filled me with pathos for us, for any couple, and for the human condition. I remembered Stephen Crane's short story *The Open Boat*, where one of the four survivors, contemplating the questionability of reaching shore safely says:

If I am going to be drowned—if I am going to be drowned—if I am going to be drowned, why, in the name of the seven mad gods who rule the sea, was I allowed to come thus far and contemplate sand and trees?

We agreed to my leap into the field. But now, no doubt, reading my growing alienation and facing a new job, he ended the letter with those few desperate words, "Please love me too." It was painful. I was unfair. To have to think about us did not help. So, I separated him from me and contemplated our differences.

There wasn't a thing on which we agreed. Whenever we started one of our eternal anthropological debates, we started poles apart. Bob started from the perspective of the system, I started from that of the individual. He talked about materialism, I countered with cognition. He talked about systemic constraints, I argued they were ideological. He was American, I was German history. "But we always meet in the middle, my sweet," he'd say.

Paul spoke rarely. He weighed things. In his presence, my past did not exist as final judgement. Importantly, there was no WWII, no complicated relationships, no defeated mother remarried to a man I could not stand. There was nothing but this moment, and I was at peace. He carried the valley inside of him, its stubborn women, its sudden flare-ups of vengeance and just as sudden returns to calm. Perhaps there was not much to say once one lived here year after year. One showed comradery, one drank beer, sometimes one fantasized, and then fell silent again. What dreams did these people have? When I asked some people what work they do, they would look at me irritably or surprised and say, *"Twikala fye, we sit, that's all,"* as if from now to eternity, as if time stood still. Were they angry at the monotony, the lack of change, the endless waiting?

My thoughts shifted from one man to the other, from one situation to the other until I recognized that the two situations were incommensurable and I had to accept that. I chose to do field work alone because I had to, and neither reason nor logic could guarantee the correctness of my choice. The decision was rooted in my distant past with its own logic. It simply remained to finish my task.

Suddenly, it became worthwhile to examine what data I had. I even enjoyed writing the report. It is what those 25 pages did not say that was important to me.

Still in Lusaka, I placed a long-distance call to mother. I was desperate for money. She promised to bail me out with $1000. I followed the call with a letter.

May 11, 1973
Liebe Mutti:

I am in Lusaka. The task of writing the report, which I just finished, has a calming effect: a rational context, a rational task, a rational human being.

Long skirts and tops sound beautiful. I cannot wait to have them, for I wear long skirts in villages. The women like that, and it is important I get along with them. Some of them are quite cynical, you know. Said one of them when I passed, "I must tell my 'husband' a musungu *(European) is here, maybe he'll return if for no other reason than to look at her." "Not much to look at," I returned in Lenda. That made her grin at least. In short, long skirts are important to me. To date I have but one such skirt which I made by hand. Do not send anything else, though, I am all right. By the way, some women here think that my flat stomach is most unbecoming. They much prefer a slightly rounded belly, firm, but rounded, sort of jutting out right below the breasts and then curving in only near the pubic area. I must say, it makes them look rather earthy, strong, and proud, especially, since their straight backs stand out by contrast. Most rural men seem to prefer these somewhat plump women, and when young, usually ones with warm round faces.*

Since I sent my first report to CAIU, I shall receive my next installment in five or so weeks. However, in future, I think you will have to ask the Bank of Montreal to CABLE my money for direct deposit into my COMBANK account here. That should simplify and speed up transfer problems.

Before I left Lusaka, Paul arrived. He was simply at the Institute one day. The next two evenings he showed me most of the bars in Lusaka. We started from the top down. At times, I felt as if I were looking at a painting by Toulouse Lautrec. A touch of decadence, an illusion here and there.

Paul felt uncomfortable in the exclusive bars with their ultra-modern men in ultra-modern suits. We sat quietly, gazing at them. Once we had come down from the Intercontinental and the Regency to below Rock Gardens, Paul was at home. Buddies from Lenda greeted us, as did those who speak the same language from Niassa Province.

Teachers Dancing

Sometimes I was the only white in the bar. I acknowledged my initial fear. It disappeared quickly. My pleasure mounted as I chatted with tipsy women and danced with tipsy men. Outside, vendors roasted cassava and meat over charcoal fires and the latrines, once again holes in the ground, were flooded with evidence of beery misses. I blessed the invention of platform shoes.

The time came to leave Lusaka. I asked that Paul not visit before my leaving. I disliked partings that compressed feelings artificially like steam in a pressure cooker. We had parted in Lenda.

I could not sleep that night. My mind pre-traveled the trip. It took 13 hours to drive down from Nzubuka. I gave a University student a lift. He could not drive and so the trip was painfully long. There was that long sweaty wait near the pontoon and mean-faced customs officials from Angara.

Near dawn, light sleep brushed away my thoughts. I dreamt a peculiar dream. Paul and I were in a crowd. In the shadow of my view stood another woman. Her ebony skin reflected his eyes. I heard the crowd whisper how he preferred that woman to me. They just stood there and looked at one another: she wrapped in red cloth with ivory beads in her hair. Then he moved away from me and I woke up.

It was six a.m. My heart ached and felt raw. I left Lusaka. On the Great East Road, I slowed the car to throw a glance at the university and saw Paul drive through the gate having returned from a night in the city. I took this scene as confirmation of my dream. I smiled, saluted, and then broke into laughter quite against my will. Suddenly I felt free as if released from a thousand clutches. Something big had happened and I was certain that the world would never quite look the same. Elation carried me along dusty roads. I felt like shouting, "I have broken free at last." At that instant, I was certain that where relationships with men were concerned, I had crossed a Rubicon.

Hours later, I drove onto the pontoon. Sweat shimmied on my skin. The moment of joy gone, I stared at the water.

The road was dusty and red. My nose bled. There we stood in a row looking ugly with dust, while nasty customs officials stammered French and fussed, and a memory stirred and transported me back.

My aunt and I stood together and I asked her what all those people were doing over there. The woman with the belly, what happened to her?

"Hush," she said, "the Russians have rounded them up, women with children, and a pregnant one about to bear."

"And where are they taking them," I asked.

"To Siberia," she said, "but hush child, hush."

A Russian yelled and exploded his gun, and they marched them off one by one. I felt their terror in my bones, as we stood there in dread and awe.

We would have continued to wait, I think, had it not been for a German soldier. He sat on a stone, his shoulders humped over.

"You have your passports, take to your feet and run; the French sector is just over there."

"Come with us," we begged.

"They took my papers," he replied. Aunt Luzi pulled me along. I heard a shot and, turning around as we ran, saw him cave in.

Comment 2018

During the difficult first weeks in Lenda Province with the anxiety about potential isolation or dangers in an environment that was at once familiar and strange, I experienced both flashbacks and nightmarish dreams. Often, they had something to do with ambivalent relationships with men. For example, there was my dying father who nevertheless took me, for the sake of my health, from the Russian to the British sector as my aunt would do later. There was the German soldier who, although held by the Russians and knowing that helping us would mean his certain death, nevertheless guided us to escape deportation to Siberia. Finally, there was my husband who, although he encouraged my efforts, would reap our separation.

I took my dreams to mean that I must free myself of being a burden. How to gain this freedom from burdensomeness and what it would look like was not clear. So far it consisted primarily of rupture. Distant past relationships ended in deaths and more recent ones were beginning to look suspect. What was missing was affirmation and, before that, acceptance that "the world is cockeyed" (James Welch, 1974, p.68). Sometimes one had "to lean into the wind to stand straight" (p.69). The notion that one could be free "toward" the inevitabilities of life, and that our capacity for responsibility might be the very foundation of humanity, was foreign to me. Freedom meant freedom from ... not also freedom toward ... Since my past would not go away, however, I would have to learn what freedom toward my past, and from there forward toward my future, could mean.

Returning from Germany July 2016, I did what the then President of the Federal Republic of Germany told me to do, read his little book *Freiheit* (*Freedom* 2012). Before reunification, he had studied theology and was a pastor for a while, but with reunification he decided to enter public service. Like many of us, he had experienced "freedom from something," but now wanted to practice "freedom for" the sake of something else (2012:24). He understood this latter sense of freedom as genuine yielding of himself toward serving democracy, which meant putting concern centered on one's self on the back burner (ibid:26). Joachim Gauck interpreted the peculiar Christian metaphor that "man is made in the image of God" as meaning that the human being was created with "the wonderful capacity to assume responsibility" (ibid:33). Furthermore, he sees that "faculty for responsibility" as holding "a promise, one that applies both to the individual and the entire world, namely: We are not condemned to fail" (ibid: 34, my translation).

When they felt strong, Lenda women often said to me that they had *amaka* (power). But did that power also include having the authority to shape freely their life, family, business, public office and other spheres of private and public life? Did they understand that the Christianity, which they and their men took up, promised that they were not condemned to fail? And did they realize that promise? Those who answered, "*Twikala fye,* we sit, that's all," answered "no."

PART III

IMMERSION

I realize once again how materialistic my sense reactions are: my desire for the bottle of ginger beer is acutely tempting; the concealed eagerness with which I fetch a bottle of brandy and am waiting for the bottles from Samarai; and finally I succumb to the temptation of smoking again. There is nothing really bad in all this. Sensual enjoyment of the world is merely a lower form of artistic enjoyment.

This morning (1.6.18) it occurred to me that the purpose in keeping a diary and trying to control one's life and thoughts at every moment must be to consolidate life, to integrate one's thinking, to avoid fragmenting themes.

Bronislaw Malinowski
A Diary in the Strict Sense of the Term

11

RETURN TO LENDA

At Mboua Inn, I washed, took my notes, sat comfortably in the gazebo and wrote.

"My name is Eneke," he said. "Have you finished that book?" He pointed to *The Beautiful Ones Are Not Yet Born*.

I looked up surprised. "Not yet," I said, noting his lively and intelligent eyes.

"I'll tell you about it then," he said, and so started a four-hour conversation about life, African literature and politics and, of course, Zambian women. He lamented the latter's preoccupation with materialism. He complained that he could not have exciting conversations with them and then inquired whether I had good conversations with Zambian men. I had to admit that any conversations with Lenda men or women fascinated me. How could it be otherwise?

What he said reminded me, however, of a comment made by Margaret Mead, namely, that:

> … One does not go to a primitive community to satisfy one's demands for sophisticated twentieth-century conversation or to find personal relationships missed among one's peers. Those who would do the first are fatuous; those who would do the second risk

endangering the reputations and work of their more disciplined colleagues (Mead, 1970, p.324).

Margaret Mead could be as maternal as men were paternal and as judgmental as moralists were self-righteous—something many of us become in our diaries. Existentialism meant nothing to her. Did she not also risk the reputation and work of the discipline? Furthermore, are not risks of one kind or another part of field work, indeed, of life itself? But my reflections are beside the point.

When Eneke asked to see me in future, I declined. He was looking for companionship. I was not. As well, I was clear that my research would color all my thoughts and actions. If my relationship with Paul came out of the blue and was an utter surprise, it was a happening that now, as it were, asked for caution and choice. Fear of isolation and loneliness might still plague me but, like heavy objects in water, they had now nicely settled on the bottom. Their days of prominence were gone.

I fetched my new letter of introduction, this time correctly addressed, and walked to the administrative offices. A secretary asked me to wait while she walked off to enquire about my visit.

In contrast with the sweaty bodies dressed in tatters of those outside, she looked pleasant and well groomed. The office too was cool, clean and removed from the valley's sweat, disease, hunger and pain.

The P.S., Mr. Kata, greeted me and asked that I sit down. While he read the letter, I studied the fold across his nose and heard him swallow his breath. When he finished, he simply looked at me for some time. "That is what you wanted?" I asked, a little worried by his long silence. He agreed. "Don't get up," he added and nodded toward the chair, "tell me a little more about this research of yours." Our talk seemed endless. The report was fresh in my mind and since all the data were of an economic nature, there was no need to hold back. My enthusiasm soon swept him along. He dropped his bureaucratic stance. His index finger slipped between the collar of his shirt and tie, as if to loosen it. I left feeling certain that he had no difficulty with any facet of my research. We talked about a common interest and it was gratifying.

By the time I arrived in Nzubuka, the glow of these last two days had worn off. Fatigue and despondency returned. It was hard to hold back tears. There was the heat and the dust. The people looked poor, as they always did upon arrival. The courthouse stood empty, and life continued covering in memory those few who touched my existence. Zambia was a land of stark contrasts. I remembered the cool corner and good whiskey at the Intercontinental Hotel and looked at the mud house and weak tea here.

At the rest house in Nzubuka, I lay back under the mosquito net and reflected about all the things that I did not include in the conversation with Eneke. For example, that the anthropologist's dilemma in the field was that of being simultaneously a practicing existentialist and a practitioner of social science. He cannot escape distress, and yet he is not able to record it in his main work, except in a preface or introduction. He cannot escape passion, and yet he is not able to claim it as relevant to his knowledge. When pain floods his mind, when he succumbs to affection, when his spirit runs dry, when he torments himself with anguish because he necessarily must live as a human being among those whom he studies, he cannot escape. There is no magic formula to prevent the arrival of these feelings nor to soothe them once they are there. Indeed, to avoid feeling is to avoid life; it is to be unable to assign it meaning and to interpret their meaning to us. The anthropologist must live daringly, she must combat fear tenaciously; she must demand of herself that she continue; she must overcome and create. She does this knowing that even logical research plans require faith if she wants to realize them, even when we must stretch and shrink them in unusual ways.

While it seems that scholars of the natural sciences need only bring to their study the desire to gain knowledge and leave dormant all other aspects of their personality, an anthropologist needs all aspects of his personality, not merely his drive to know. Furthermore, he needs to manage them to produce decent work. He is simultaneously an apprentice researcher and an apprentice human being until he has mastered his task.

It amused me to remember that I was not the only one who had these thoughts in the field. Margaret Mead too wrote:

> ... field work is a rather appalling thing to undertake. Nowhere else is a scientist asked to be vis-a-vis, and also a part of, a total human society and to conduct his studies in vivo, continually aware of such a complex whole. Perhaps the task of the psychiatrist is comparably difficult—as the psychiatrist is asked to take in, hold in mind, respond to, and respond to his responses to, whole individuals including those parts that are normally veiled from other eyes ... (Mead, 1970, p.304).

Reflection renewed my energy. I delivered various letters and gifts from Paul to people in Kakuso. There were several pairs of socks to be distributed and Grace would receive a dress. Then I settled down and worked out a new strategy to get at the data. It was easy enough to adjust my plan but without one, nothing happened in this valley.

In Lusaka, I had started work on a questionnaire. Now with the help of Yambana, Banachile, and Komeko we translated it. Komeko was my first male assistant. We met outside of the unemployment office. I met Yambana while delivering Paul's gifts and letters. Our meeting was memorable. I was about to stop and bring a parcel from Paul's roommate at the university to Yambana's sister when my car slid into a sand bank. The wheels spun wildly, raised dust, and then settled immovably into the sand. Hot and frustrated, I walked up to a man to ask for help. He was one of those poor men whose fawning had shaped the lines of his face and the posture of his body. He was bitter and he regarded me with pessimistic suspicion and refused to help. "Why should I help a white person who is so big and strong? Help yourself," he said. I looked at him with some astonishment. "You should help," I said, "because my car is stuck in the sand." He bent over his shovel and threw a hate-filled glance in my direction. I was angry but left.

A few paces into the village I found Yambana. She had just finished sweeping the yard and stood holding a grass broom gazing with some friendliness in my direction. It was good to see the comfort with which she bore her authority. Even more satisfying was her direct glance, her warm mannerisms and expressions, which she extended with the understanding that they were part of an act of communication between equals. When I asked her for help to push my car out of the sand, she came, bearing a big grin and on the way shamed the nasty little man into helping us as well. It amused me to see him trudging behind Yambana where her full strong body almost hid him from view.

Women's strength and sense of power varied. Some had it to the point of overflowing. Yambana was one of them. Every gesture told that she was confident and that she accepted her power, her tradition, and her domain. Where Grace communicated vulnerability, Yambana communicated self-possession. I was delighted with this chance meeting and enlisted her among my helpers. As primary school teacher, this robust and handsome mother of five healthy, well-bred children had little time to give me but every moment was a precious gift. Once she agreed to help with research, she called her five children to greet me. She delighted in being firm and decisive with them. Children must "fear" their mother she told me beaming with pride, and I could see their devotion and respect for her. Yambana headed her household and managed it well.

The afternoon of May 18, we tried questions on a select number of people, two women, a Seventh-day Adventist elder, and the principal of Kakuso primary school. Following their suggestions, we refined further. From the 19th to the 25th, we administered questionnaires in Booke and Kakuso. We noticed that some questions made people feel uncomfortable. A few were afraid when asked their names. Most were afraid when asked where they came from, and women stumbled over the question of marriage. Questions concerning cash, too, were sensitive. Much later, I discovered all kinds of ways to handle that problem independently of questionnaires.

In Booke village, people knew me. Now I was eager to learn about Kakuso and thought of strategies to gain entrance and rapport. Each weekend I attended services and asked church elders, preachers, or priests to introduce me to the congregation and inform them of my research. They not only cooperated, they also showed interest and goodwill.

May 23rd, Mr. Mukome, an elder of the Seventh-day Adventist Company announced my presence and purpose in Kakuso. He told people that I was from the University of Zambia and that I wanted to study and write about the life of men and women here. To reduce the reticence of women and, swept along by his explanation, he added that I wished to learn just where their life differed from that of urban ones. Indeed, someone should do that, I thought.

We discussed the questionnaires further after service. I asked Yambana what she thought women's feelings might be when I took along an assistant. We tried to anticipate anxieties of older as opposed to younger women. Since an unbiased sample was not feasible now, we decided to start with younger women who were also members of Seventh-day Adventists (SdA). In Kakuso Seventh-day Adventists and Jehovah's Witnesses had the largest number of adherents. Our visibility would soon reduce anxiety among the rest of the population and allow us to interview them too.

Yambana and I took a bamboo mat, found some shade, and continued our discussion of women. Generalities exhausted, I asked Yambana whether her "husband" gave her money? "No," came her forceful reply. "If I took money from my husband I would become his slave."

"Do other women feel as you do?" I asked.

"Oh yes," she said, "We women don't want to be enslaved. Therefore, we produce our own wealth. If I took from him," she explained, "his relatives would begin to see my possessions as theirs. They could come any time, especially his sisters, or any of his mother's people, and take things with them." She told how upon a husband's death his maternal relatives could take everything and redistribute it among themselves.

She explained that in Lenda people belonged to the clan of their mothers because those born of related women shared the same substance, blood.

As she discussed men, her tone became critical "Men move with many women whom they leave gifts. The money men earn they spend on gifts for other women and on beer. It is our custom. Husbands cannot possibly make wives happy. Our customs make that impossible. Nor are our marriages like yours, as you'll see." She assumed that our marriages were stable and men made wives happy. Two church elders joined us, and upon questioning them about the difference between their and our marriage they said much the same thing as Yambana, "marriage as you conceive of it is rare in Lenda."

Feeling the need for solitude, I had dinner at the rest house. Around 7.30 p.m. I returned to the home of Yambana in Kakuso. A villager told me that Yambana had gone to visit her grandmother, a cousin of her mother's mother. Yambana's children and I followed her there. It was dark when we arrived. Yambana had already taken the initiative to enlist the help of her grandfather, a Jehovah's Witness. He was willing to introduce me to that congregation.

In Kakuso, most women and children huddled near charcoal burners, while men and some women were busy visiting nearby villages and bars. Yambana and I sat and talked more about marriage and quarrels between men and women. She explained that men and women quarreled primarily over children. Children belong to their mothers whose substance they embody. Consequently, husbands worry that children will not look after them when they are old. She reminded me of the man who was mentally ill. We met him at the store in the afternoon. "You heard what he thought, that his wife's people want to kill him because he had fathered successful children." The implication was that his wife's kin resented any assistance he might receive from his children even when he had helped raise them. His children were primarily responsible to their matrikin.

"Are his children looking after him?"

"No," Yambana said. "He is alone. His children fear to help him. They help their mother and maternal kin."

"Shouldn't his maternal nephews help him?"

"They should and some do. However, today everything is confused. When children help their father, their maternal uncle is angry, when they help their maternal uncle their father feels neglected. The government and church want fathers to become heads of families and thus lead their wives and children, but overall people here do not like that. Women especially can't become men's slaves."

I began to recognize a dilemma in Lenda family life. Women in their childbearing years welcomed the support of husbands who were often willing to give it so that their children should know them. During that time women seemed even to agree with men's church activities. Once their children were grown up, however, women re-asserted an ideology, which they never abandoned in the first place. Their husbands were now free to leave and father offspring elsewhere. Children belonged to their mother's clan. Women had their fields, children, lovers, and kin. Even the mother of a man controlled his maternal nephews. Some men felt cheated and bitter. They felt neglected both as uncles and as fathers.

"Never mind," Yambana said, noting my sympathy for the condition of men, "UNIP is looking after men. Besides," she added, "no one is alone. There are always relatives. It is just that some men now want support from their sons."

Yesterday we practiced how we would conduct ourselves during interviews. We decided to hold interviews within the homes of respondents, not merely to ensure privacy, but also to assess "wealth" and well-being. Quite naturally, people were suspicious and often were unwilling to state what they owned. My assistants agreed, therefore, that initial interviews with SdA congregation members was sound procedure.

Even so, women inquired whether I was asking them these questions to report their husbands' laziness to the police. One amusing incident did occur. When visiting people, I took along refreshments, especially "Sprite" to drink as it was dry and hot. Upon offering a woman "Sprite," she asked whether I intended to kill her. The woman was only familiar with "Fanta." I assured her that I had no such intention since I wanted her answers. Nevertheless, the woman insisted that Yambana taste the drink first. Only one person refused to answer questions, probably because men surrounded her. There were certain questions men preferred not to answer in the presence of Lenda women and vice versa. However, contrary to Western men and women, Lenda men were more willing to answer, even matters concerning the most intimate aspects of their life, than were Lenda women. In the West, the reverse is often the case, women answer questions more willingly during interviews than do men.

Whatever the shortcomings of questionnaires, and there are many, they do force the researcher to go out and meet many people. It changes the picture. For example, in Booke's village all women had cassava gardens. In addition, they baked bread and scones and otherwise produced things for sale. By contrast, in Kakuso, when a husband earned money—some men were employed as maintenance personnel at the secondary school earning a mere 30 Zambian Kwacha or so per month—women adjusted their activities by giving up their cassava gardens. Instead of making their own gardens, some women bought them for 20 or 30 Zambian Kwacha. It also looked as if government personnel, who lived in low-income houses built of cement, were worse off than villagers living in houses built of mud-bricks. Kakuso had both kinds of accommodation.

Women brewed and sold beer on different days of the week. Those who didn't brew beer, wives of government employees, said that their money came from their husbands. In Kakuso, and among government employees, I observed the beginnings of wife-dependency on husbands. Among the rest of the population, if anything, men were dependent on women, although these women tended to be their sisters or mothers.

Each evening, we reviewed the questionnaires. We also revised questions when this became necessary and generally discussed the results. Certain answers puzzled me and we debated which ones might be lies.

I was under the impression that "marital" ties between men and women were largely casual and that both men and women had several spouses, sequential ones or multiple ones from other villages. However, on the questionnaire I found only sanctimonious replies protesting strict adherence to monogamous patterns.

"If this lying continues I shall have to throw out these questionnaires. Maybe the whole approach is useless," I said, feeling discouraged. Yambana looked up into the distance. Her mouth settled into a wry smile. "That may not be necessary," she said. "Look, there is a whole colony of women. They are coming to visit you."

Comfortably settled, the women told me that they had lied about their marriages. They claimed that they could not be expected to be honest when it came to their relations with men. They asked whether I was a religious sister. I assured them that I was not. Only then did they bemoan the fact that most Europeans, especially missionaries, expected Lenda marriages to be like European ones. In fact, they claimed, most women here have six to nine "husbands." Some have more. They find it advisable not to advertise this fact for several reasons. First, they claimed, relationships between the sexes are unstable and plagued by jealousy. Secondly, they did not want to be judged by outsiders or by the church. Thirdly, women who have the same husband or lover—it was hard to distinguish between the two—tend to fight one another. All in all, then, it was best not to discuss marital relationships. Finally, they suggested that while they told the truth, I must expect to be lied to by other women upon questioning them about marriage.

That settled, they wanted to know how Europeans kept such lasting marriages with one man. I had to think about that. Our divorce rate is increasing. Still, by comparison, our marriages last long. A marital lifespan of ten years would be long by local standards. The question is rather amazing. In most Western families to have but one divorce is a major calamity. The important question is not how we manage lasting marriages, but why.

Most of us like our relationships with men and most marriages are based on love. Love is a great power in the West. The classicist and atheist turned Christian, C.S. Lewis (1960), distinguished eloquently between the love of Affection, Friendship, Eros, and Charity. He saw the distortions and potential tragedies of all of them, especially Eros, and did not presume any of them to be self-sufficient. What better drives this home than field work? Whatever the classifications of love, tradition, institutions, social practice, law and church encourage marriage and hold it in check; although all this is changing too. At home, it's been under attack since the 1960s, as if to reinforce that destroying is easier than maintaining. At any rate, I answered their question in jest. "I guess we talk a lot," I said.

"Mother!" a woman exclaimed and laughed, "When we talk we fight. Our men are only good 'in bed' not before, not after." General laughter followed. Attracted by the merriment, several men joined us. The two sexes exchanged jokes and teased one another. Gradually, most women left. Those who remained changed the topic. Men were visitors, after all.

The week went by. Tuesday May 26, we spent the morning once more reviewing, revising, and typing questionnaires. Since we had interviewed most members of the Seventh-day Adventist congregation, I arranged to meet with elders of the Jehovah's Witnesses. Word of my activities spread through the village and soon it was unnecessary to limit my questions to

Christians. Indeed, people would look me up and insist that I interview them.

Around 2 p.m., May 26, I picked up Kate Mulito who sometimes escorted me in lieu of her sister, Yambana. To allay any fears, which my questions might have generated, I thought it wise to visit with people who answered questions in the past. We simply walked through Kakuso greeting them. One of the women was very ill with malaria. We drove her to the hospital and waited two hours until she and two other women were treated. Then we drove them back.

I returned to the rest house, feeling rather sick myself. My head was dizzy and sore. My stomach was upset. Every bone of my body ached. I wondered whether I too had malaria, despite use of Primaquine.

Women in the Field

On occasion, I recorded expressions of strong personal feelings. These were not verbalized to the Lenda. I recorded them because I began to note that fundamental changes were taking place in my perceptions and attitudes. I simply wanted a record of these changes. It behooves me, therefore, to compare myself with other women ethnographers. According to Mead (1970, p.323):

> Women field workers may be divided into those with deeply feminine interests and abilities, who in the field will be interested in the affairs of women, and those who are, on the whole, identified with the main theoretical stream of anthropology in styles, that have been set by men. Women with feminine interests and especially an interest in children are also likely to marry and so are less likely to go into the field except when accompanying their husbands. In practice, therefore, we have tended to have women who are more oriented toward feminine concern working with their husbands or only temporarily deeply concerned with field work, or somewhat masculinely oriented women,

independent, bored by babies at home and abroad, working alone,
and using male informants.

Mead's dichotomy is, I think, rather superficial, even arrogant. But, it
contains a grain of truth about Mead herself. Since she states that she did
not intend to compete with men in their areas of interest, and since she
conducted some of her research in the presence of different husbands,
since, finally, she claimed to like babies, although she produced none, one
would assume that Mead placed herself in the category of "femininely
oriented" women. However, on her first field trip Mead left her husband
behind. On later trips, she often went alone or accompanied by student
couples. According to Mead, I would have to classify myself as a
"masculinely oriented" woman. I am independent, less interested in babies
than Margaret Mead claims to be, with a tendency to work alone but to use,
contrary to Mead's prediction, both male and female assistants. However,
I did identify with "the main theoretical stream of anthropology."

One could also distinguish the two kinds of women ethnographers based
on the differential emphasis they place on description versus theory, and
on empiricism versus introspection. Mead's "femininely oriented" woman
is inclined to favor description and empiricism; her "masculinely oriented"
woman is inclined to favor theory and introspection. However, these
dichotomies are nonsense.

In Lenda, Mead's distinction did not make sense. While I arrived in Zambia
with a working hypothesis derived from my theoretical interests in the
relationship between kinship, religion and economic development, in the
field a second theme began to interest me. I am referring to my increasing
awareness of the nature of interactions between men and women. Both
gender began to fascinate me for that reason. I began to play with the notion
of different male-female interaction patterns. Overall, however, my
theoretical interests, though undergoing some change, continued to
predominate. Consequently, I took the attitude that where necessary

researchers should question mainstream theories and, when justified, drop, disprove, or rectify them.

By contrast, Mead has a genius for describing in detail the children, youths, and adults that surrounded her in the field. Nor can one say that her letters about the field are introspective. Rarely does she reflect about the effects of diverse cultures on her. At most, she admits, in accordance with her empirical orientation, that:

> (I) adapted to the style of people with whom I was working. In photographs taken in Bali I look dissociated, sitting among a people each of whom was separated from the others. In Samoa, the pictures show me dressed up, sitting and standing to display my Samoan costumes and rank; in Manus, I am alert and tense, half strangled by a child clinging around my neck; in Arapesh I have become as soft and responsive as the people themselves (1970, p.320).

Ignoring existentialism, Mead does not create herself. She adapts. She does not experience herself through her feelings or states of mind; she observes herself through a mediating medium. Thus, when she looks at herself, she does not become introspective; she looks at herself in a photograph and describes what she sees. Anything Mead says about women researchers working alone in the field, therefore, applies at best only to women she types as having "feminine interests." To the extent that it does not apply to a woman of her own kind, Mead is wrong. She is wrong when she says that "field work is in most cases lonelier for women than for men" (p.323). She is wrong when she says, "where a male field worker can afford a night on the town in an outstation, a woman—especially a woman who is a stranger in an area—cannot" (p.323). She is wrong in her claim that "many women tend to feel somehow abused by the intractability of material things" (p.323). Finally, she is wrong when she writes, "women alone in the field are also more likely to be preoccupied with present or possible future personal relationships than are men" (p.325). Any of these experiences depend almost entirely on two factors: the type of society in which the woman ethnographer conducts her research, and her willingness to take risks and discover strategies to circumvent restrictions.

Instead of drawing an immediate contrast with myself, let me compare Mead's *observations* about *field* work with the *reflections* about field *experiences* of Ruth Landes. Like myself, Landes is more introspective and existentialist than is Mead. Says Landes (1970, p.121):

> Field work serves an idiosyncrasy of perception that *cannot* separate the *sensuousness* of life, from its *abstractions*, nor the researcher's *personality* from his *experiences*. The culture a field worker reports is the one he experiences, filtered through trained observations. Noted writers say that their craft cannot be taught, though it can be perfected. In the same sense, field work probably can only be perfected (my italics).

Talking about leaving her husband behind, Landes expressed my feelings perfectly. Says she, "in the end, I dreaded not going more than I feared to go" (p.122). Deeply preoccupied with the link between experience, self, and other cultures, Landes writes:

> But such a scholar must dip into earth's paint box of cultures; he needs the changes they light up and ring on the familiar, the *insights they release,* the sharp awareness they bring him of his *own self* (p.122, my italics).

Landes continues her theme with the observations that "It seems evident to me that the methods of an effective field worker are rooted in his personality." She argues that "the field worker brings to his novel culture field a special, perhaps aberrant personality ... (and) a mighty, even zestful intention to *yield* himself to the field and *ponder his and others' responses.*" Finally, she reveals her sensitivity when she says, "One's concept of self disintegrates because the accustomed responses have disappeared" (p.123 my italics).

Then she ends her reflections with an almost triumphant last paragraph:

> But does one lose? Or is it rather that one knows so much about
> the hardships of field work? However, the addicted field worker
> does not really care for ease any more than does the competitive
> athlete. The lure of another culture can never be discounted, for it
> is the lure of *self*, dressed otherwise. Moving among the world's
> people, one sees that personalities here may resemble
> personalities there, underneath and despite the culture differences
> … When the field worker recognizes personalities this way in the
> alien culture, he discovers his own. This gives the human depth
> to information he gathers and will interpret for scholars and
> others. Back at home he sees his own people afresh, himself
> among them. The stance of field work becomes a private
> philosophy of living. What counts in the field and after is that one
> glimpses, over and over, humanity *creating* (p.138, my italics).

Without acknowledging their influence, her statement resembles that of
many an existentialist. Did she develop this sense of existentialism in the
field or, being an individualist, did she bring it with her? And why is it that
some researchers recognize the unbreakable link between personality,
experience, and culture, while others are ignorant or oblivious of it and
even resentful?

In sum, the distinction that Mead made between "femininely oriented"
women and "masculinely oriented" ones turns out to be more profound
than even Mead might have intended it to be. The "femininely oriented"
woman, because she is an empiricist, experiences herself as object. The self
that Margaret Mead sought was an "actual" empirical self. In that sense,
the self of the empiricist is too arbitrary and too dependent upon
particularities. Mead's self was the self of photographs, films, tapes, and
books. Hers was a self that preferred external constraint. For example, her
tipped uterus decided her against having children early in her life. Mead's
self was a self that lost itself in the world of others; it was an object, often

inauthentic and unfree. By contrast, Mead's "masculinely oriented" woman, who is merely an existentialist, experiences the self as a free and authentic existent whose possibilities and actualities are meaningful. Hers is not merely a self, which thinks, as do all other "selves," as does a self as subject. Hers is a self with a history, a self that is guilty, a self that wants a conscience, and a self that is responsible. It is a self that lives *with* others *in* a world. The aim of that self is not to assimilate, not to escape human guilt and finitude, but to disclose itself as it discloses the other. It is a self that may grow from society's girl into a liberated, that is, responsible woman—responsible for who she is and might become despite her inability to determine her gender, her origin, or her skin color at birth.

Attitude Toward Lenda Children

No doubt, Margaret Mead would agree with me when I say that I was not a field worker with an interest in researching children. Being a child that grew up in the destruction left by war, it is society itself and the adults that shaped children that bothered me. It is a curiosity that is a direct product of the conditions into which I was born. Already as a child, I had my eyes and ears firmly fixed on the world of adults. It is they in the first instance, not children, who puzzled me. It is they, who messed up our lives—why did they do it?

Still, there were in Lenda three sorts of children that affected me deeply. First, there were the children whose mothers recently removed them from the safety of their backs. Suspended in cloth, they spent much of the day in close contact with their mother. When they were older and removed from this "nest," they struggled with their seeming "rejection." These children frequently found their way into my lap where I watched them cope with uneasy dreams and restless sleep during which they usually wetted.

Second, there were children, frequently young boys, who suffered extreme alienation from their fathers. They were so bitter that their fathers had abandoned them, that some little boys would face me, eyes feverish with hate, as they swore vengeance upon their fathers. They knew that fathers ought to have an interest in young children even when the primary responsibility for their upkeep fell upon their mother and her kin. "When I am old," they would say, "though I see my father starve, he shall receive nothing." Their loneliness broke my heart. I would long to hold them and protect them but knew such brief emotional outburst would only turn into another betrayal. We would look at one another—that was all.

Finally, there were children plagued by chronic illness, especially falciparum malaria. It was endemic in the valley and often responsible for serious anemia. I watched these small children fighting against all odds, to experience life but a little longer. Always on the periphery of their herding peers, they seemed to carry within their whimpering being a wisdom far beyond their years.

These childhood experiences of separation anxiety from their mothers, abandonment by their fathers, and chronic illnesses usually to do with malaria and sickle cell anemia were direct results of ecological, social, cultural, educational, and economic arrangements. The new politicians did not seem to notice them. They trained their eyes on recruiting lively youths.

How these children struggled with their misery surprised me. None of it resembled the idealization of African or indigenous child raising practices in older anthropological literature. It was a separate topic and could not be part of this research. Nevertheless, I communicated easily with these children. No doubt, my interest in them, who worked against great odds to overcome their handicaps, had to do with my own childhood experiences.

Comment 2018

Let me conclude this section with the following story. When a referee first read the unedited version of my personal journal, he or she was furious with my seemingly contradictory attitudes. However, had the referee reflected, she would have realized that an open account of a person's life in a difficult research situation is inevitably riddled with contradictions. The field is not the ordered universe of the academy. In the field, we quite literally sleep and wake among our living data that, however, are nothing other than our fellow human beings at once similar and different from us. We observed one another and ourselves simultaneously.

Our usual accounts and explanations published in professional journals are largely free of contradictions only because "reasoning" is integral to the method, topic, and structure provided by the journal. It is the literary profession's specific goals and rules that temporarily free us of contradictions and allow us to present ourselves in the rarefied atmosphere of pure reason. In the field, this is temporarily lost. Unanchored by spouse, dependents, servants, and in the presence of changing tasks as well as unfamiliar, sometimes cruel behavior, the field worker experiences him- or-her-self as emotion as much as reason, as anger as much as affection; in short, as voicing in one breath frustration with, and love of, one's fellow human beings (see also Kleinschmidt 2015).

In this loss of her world, in this intense moment of existing outside of familiar normative social ties, the researcher experiences the absurdity of many assumptions that she brought to the field. For once she realizes a total freedom from prejudice knowing, however, that the end of this world-less freedom will come and exact its price. Not only does she understand the meaning of paradox; the fact is, she is also living it (allusion to Hannah Arendt 1969; 2016).

12

FROM PROGRESS TO SETBACK

The morning of May 27, I still felt exhausted from headache, nausea, and aching bones. It was malaria, but I ignored it. Instead, I decided to start the day by reading yesterday's mail. Professor Justin's letter was a response to my first report. His questions were his reaction to those descriptions and informed by comparisons with his own previous research. Professor Rediens, by contrast, reminded me to look more systematically at kinship. These are their letters.

20 May 1973
Dear Karla,

I have your letter of 12 May and the copy of the research report. In addition, I received a letter from Mr. Paladin, who stated that he had authorized payment of your next installment in advance of formal approval of the report. This will, I hope, resolve your financial difficulties for the time being. I have sent Mr. Paladin a statement approving the report, so you should be in good standing.

With reference to your letter, is the concern with bettering standards an individual one, or does it apply to communities as wholes? If the latter, parallels with Igbo come to mind—at least, prior to Biafra. The twin themes of demanding work and Ujamaa *(African Humanism) are familiar from Tanzania, of course. Despite the very different situation in Kumozi, there is similarity in a kind of "entrepreneurial" orientation, which I wish I could document better.*

Your report was informative and useful, particularly in providing the background needed for perspective on Nzubuka District. I was mildly surprised at the range of items purchased by families, but more so by the amount expended per week. I do not have comparable data for Kumozi, but I am confident that ordinary families would purchase much less.

I am curious about the basis for distinguishing one village from another since there is a continuous distribution of homesteads. Are there recognized "boundaries" of some kind? Or, are communities situationally defined, with variables other than location per se important?

If you have any questions about cassava, by the way, Karl Schwerin is extremely well informed on it, as he is on many ethnobotanical questions. Exactly what is a dambo*? I have encountered the term in reading, know the dictionary definition, but am still a bit vague about it.*

Keep in touch and don't forget field notes. I'm delighted with your progress so far, and hope things will move along well.

All best wishes,
Ralph Justin

19 May 1973
Dear Karla,

In your letters to date, you have not written much about kinship. Yet your descriptions of Lenda behavior and thought to Bob and Ralph hint at some intriguing problems. For example, you seem to imply that mukowa, *clan, is somehow significant to the Lenda. It looks as if it is a more meaningful and lasting institution than is marriage or family. I believe Cunnison called the latter* ulupwa. *In what sense can the* mukowa *be spoken of as descent? Are there matrilineages? If so, are they cultural categories or are they groups of people engaged in some sort of activities?*

You argued quite cogently that you don't want to push the kinship question until you are first able to hear and observe it. That seems to be happening already. You said you wanted to take seriously Schneider's suggestion that kinship may be a Western folk cultural category which should not be given the status of scientific concept. That makes me doubly curious about the nature of kinship or relatedness in Lenda. Indeed, we should not assume that kinship exists universally or that it is the idiom in terms of which other institutions are expressed. When you do study kinship terms, therefore, remember to check "their" meaning.

Yours,
Len Rediens

Canoe Fishing in a Dambo

Dambos were shallow wetlands filled with grasses, rushes and the like and visited by crocodiles. Such wetlands were common in this lake and river valley, used especially for fishing from narrow wooden canoes owned by poorer fishers.

Several things became clear from reading the letters of Justin and Rediens. Justin confirmed what I felt was needed, namely, to clean up the regional perspective, village boundaries, economic activities, and political hierarchies. Village boundaries were easy enough to sort out. I decided, therefore, to concentrate especially on economic activities. For Rediens, by contrast, it became necessary to begin researching the Lenda mental universe. Culture, as David M. Schneider defined it, is a system of symbols and meaning. Kinship is a cultural phenomenon and, therefore, should be rich in symbols and meaning. It was beginning to look as if kinship was also the idiom used to express all kinds of human relationality and responsibilities. Inevitably, I would have to attempt to answer questions, such as, how do the Lenda see their universe? Into what categories do they divide it? Are our social science categories that we use to analyze their universe in fact adequate to the task? I was beginning to realize that I was climbing up many ropes, so to speak, or that the Lenda picture was falling together piece by piece like a complex jigsaw puzzle. I knew what was wanted; Sartre's model was still the guide. Indeed, in my wanting I could be very systematic. Where I had to be flexible, think continually about new strategies and tactics, was in the getting of it.

I decided to observe economic activities in the morning when they were done, administer questionnaires in the afternoons when people tended to sit around, and hold lengthy interviews directed to ascertain the nature of Lenda thoughts during evenings when minds were playful. Clearly, it was possible to deduce, abstract, and reconstruct much of Lenda thought from their behavior. However, such an approach is dangerous if for no other reason than that the researcher might impose his or her cultural categories onto the subjects' mental universe. By discovering into what cultural categories "they" divide "their" world, one not only gets the sense of what might be solely different or novel institutions, one also begins to take seriously problems of translation.

The morning was gone. I still felt feverish and chilled. The chance to just sit and chat with Mr. Cheta was, therefore, welcome. Mr. Cheta was a respected elder among Jehovah's Witnesses. I wanted his support. Jehovah's Witnesses were also known as Watchtowers and locally as Chitawala. Like most Watchtowers, BaCheta owned a large house by local standards. We sat in his living room, which looked somewhat run-down, but was comfortable. Three couches, five easy chairs, and a small table constituted its furniture. I found myself fascinated by one dilapidated sofa. Shadows played on it accentuating each hole and tear. The wear and tear of it, symbolized Lenda life.

Opposite me sat a kindly man. The lines on his face were gentle, not bitter or hard. He asked me whether I knew the bible well and my negative but honest reply was a disappointment. I explained that my intention was not to become a Christian or a member of any religious body; rather, I wanted to learn whether and how the teachings of Jehovah's Witnesses affected the philosophy and life of church members.

Stressing that I would not become a member was necessary because I would attend several different congregations and people would of course want to know why. I wanted to be sure people understood that I was studying not becoming. The difference between studying and becoming I emphasized in many conversations with the Lenda. It was part of the process of negotiating my need to collect data freely. Furthermore, "going native" when I was among fellow human beings did not make sense either.

Mr. Cheta worried whether the government would let me attend meetings at Kingdom Hall and mentioned that in the past UNIP youths had destroyed their gardens and generally harassed Jehovah's Witnesses. I assured him that there would be no difficulties.

Mr. Ngoma, Kakuso's headman, came by. He was elderly, tall and lean, and his grey eyes shone as did his skin. Those eyes alone suggested power. I wondered why they were grey rather than brown and puzzled what it was about him that created an aura of reverence. He stood as if giving off light, ever so slightly bent with age, smiling at me. I thought he knew who he was, that man. He possessed natural grace and nobility. We bantered a little.

"We like the questions you ask," he said. "Will you ask me?"

"Of course," I said. "I could sit all day and ask you questions. I could sit all day and interview men that would be easy and pleasant. It's the women who give me trouble."

"Then you are learning already. Our women are strong and not in our control."

"What bothers me is that women are secretive. They seem to feel it necessary to hide information when men don't," I said. I wondered whether there is a double standard at work in Lenda or whether the consequences of men's and women's actions are different. Maybe it is both. He gave me a long and unexpected explanation.

"The colonial government introduced payment of compensation and divorce. These laws have different consequences for men and women," he said, "if a lover is caught sleeping with someone's wife, he now must pay compensation to the husband, not to her. Therefore, women keep their affairs quiet. What he pays in compensation to her husband is of course lost to her. You see, don't you, why women don't want to marry. Those who married in the past when they were first excited about Christianity, are asking for divorce certificates. When a woman has a divorce certificate her husband cannot ask for compensation."

"Well, he is no longer her husband," I said.

"According to whom? He may believe he is still her husband," he said. "What, after all, is marriage and what is divorce?"

"You make marriage sound so fluid as if it had no boundaries," I said.

"But it has none. It does not exist here. We have family (*ulupwa*) before marriage and that family continues after it. A mate is added; a mate leaves. A woman throws her spouse (*muka*) out of the house and that is divorce. But he may also come back. Women ask for divorce certificates only when their men are troublesome."

I wondered what to ask next when he said, "have you seen a big wedding?"

"No," I said.

"That's because there are none. Have you seen a big funeral?"

"Yes, although I haven't attended one yet," I said.

"Funerals are family, indeed, clan and neighborhood events; weddings are not," he concluded.

Before he left, he promised to spread word about my research. He also welcomed me to go on the lake with his fishermen.

Malaria and conversation left me feeling weak and I retired to the rest house. While resting I felt a deep joy. Effort and persistence were paying off.

The following two days I put my strategies to work. The morning I spent observing fish transactions, the afternoon administering questionnaires. When I interviewed women, men would come by and insist that I interview them. Since several men were building houses, I asked about that, too. I filled pages with earnings, quarrels, and labor disputes. Men hired women and women hired men, and the chain of people hired to do one task grew and grew. No wonder there were many court cases and unfinished projects. Importantly, while most women cultivated and men fished, the sexes were not segregated.

Then it was June 2, and all this bliss reached a sudden end. The trouble came from Booke and Dukana where Banachile administered questionnaires. Banachile told me that women refused to answer questions because they thought I might be a spy. Some argued that during colonial time too they were asked where they came from and then they were sent back.

"How am I a spy, for the government?" I said with some irritation.

"I don't know. I don't think they know. They are just afraid. Some say they'll answer if UNIP says it's OK."

Unable to think of anything to do, I decided to discuss the whole business with the Regional Secretary. He had malaria, but the publicity officer received me and read my letter of introduction from the Cabinet Office. He was interested, took it to the Regional Secretary, who, dressed in pajamas, came to see me in the living room. "Don't worry, we'll sort it out. I'll send a circular to various headmen and ward councilors," he assured me.

June 3rd, I drove to Booke. I was eager to check on any further developments. Banachile met me.

"The publicity officer told me to tell you not to attend Watchtower Services," she said after I asked her about further developments. Now that made me mad. I paced back and forth, hissing, "Darn, darn, darn."

While busy dispelling the heat of my frustration, the publicity officer and other UNIP officials arrived.

"We can't allow you to attend Watchtower meetings," the publicity officer said.

"But why not, I attend all the churches for about equal time. I have to do so if I want to represent the views and life of all people living here." The thought of omitting Jehovah's Witnesses from my research really angered me. I simply could not ignore the changes, which they were introducing.

"We UNIP people don't like Watchtower. If you attend, they'll tell their people that President Kaunda approves of them and then Watchtower will increase in number." He said this with some feeling.

"But that is hardly possible, Jehovah's Witnesses don't proselytize. They know that I'm with the university not a representative of the President." I had to argue back, the issue was too important to me.

"No matter, more people will join, and once they join they have nothing to do with us. They won't cooperate with UNIP and our work does not get done," he said.

I looked at them then. There they sat disgruntled and bitter little men. Theirs was the dirtiest work of all. Uninformed, unenlightened, and discouraged, they were to mobilize people and no one quite knew for what or when. They watched people join churches rather than UNIP. Considering the circumstances under which they worked, I had to admit that their frustrations were more than justified.

"We also ask that you take Banachile everywhere you go," he said. I wondered whether he recognized my sympathy a moment ago. With this statement, I became angry again.

"Am I to be watched?" I asked.

I was frustrated. After all, I had been meticulous in my observance that Watchtower would get no more of my time than SdA or CMML. My back ached each weekend as I sat through three or four hours of diverse services and meetings, mornings, afternoons, and evenings. Religion was coming out of my ears, but Watchtower was different. They, more than any other group, affected the outlook, business behavior, and family life of the local population. I could not give this study up, and that was that.

Troubled, I visited Van Gella. There I sat and stared at the lake and sipped lemonade. I did not hear a word that was said. When my mind cleared, I left.

The D.S. and D.G. both agreed that I could continue to study Watchtower. The publicity officer's view was his own they told me. Nothing in the national policy forbids research of this sect.

"You do not object that I have different people assist me?" I said.

"No, why would you ask?" I told them of the publicity officer's suggestion. The D.S. laughed. Much later, I learned why; their Intelligence Officer, of course, watched me. The latter had long since reported that my questions were primarily economic in nature and that was OK. Had they been political, they would probably have booted me out.

I thought about Banachile. Somehow, she had not been central to my concern. I simply took the D.G. by his word when he suggested that Banachile would assist me "free of charge." It took time to assess local need. Only lately did it occur to me how very hard her lot was. She was vulnerable, if very bright, and so eager to work. I cursed myself for my naiveté. Initially, I thought that paying her outright would somehow break a rule of etiquette. I also feared that she might tell the D.G. and he might disapprove or question my motives. Therefore, I started by buying food and having some furniture made. I paid her father's sister rent to live in the house. Gradually, I noticed that Banachile really could use some money and I began to pay. It seemed that by taking other assistants I was threatening her livelihood. Yet, I had asked her to continue to work for me. I was simply too ignorant early on. Even her treatment of me, as if I were a head of household, sat uneasily with me. Now, perhaps, I should have handled matters differently. Then, however, I was not ready for it.

"Look," Banachile explained, "the trouble in Booke is not as simple as you thought. UNIP did not start it at all. My *mayosenge* (father's sister) started the alarm. She forbade women to answer questions and you know she has power. When she asks, they obey. To warn UNIP of your Watchtower attendance was just an excuse. She asked the men to tell you of her decision."

"But why, I don't understand a thing anymore."

"She doesn't like Watchtower that is true. She is CMML, but that too is not important. Whom she really does not like is UNIP and the government, even though she used UNIP as an excuse. In her dislike of UNIP, she is not alone. Most people here are angry with the government and its party. My father was a teacher before independence and now he is nothing. There are lots like him. They resent their fate and blame it on the government," she said.

"But I understand even less now. You are the ward secretary, after all." This business really was confusing.

"I was. She has made me stop. She expected pay, I think. I received nothing from UNIP and they took much of my time. I have three children and she has asked that I tend my fields instead. And there she is right."

"And I thought you shouldn't be paid somehow, that it would be insulting.

How stupid I was." It was obvious they all had expected regular employment and regular pay without mentioning it to me.

"No matter now," she said. "I'll help our neighbor in her store and there I'll be paid regularly. The rest of the time, I work in my fields. My *mayosenge* threw me out of the house, you know." She pointed to a wattle and daub hut, much smaller than the last. "That's where I live now." My heart sank. How could I have been so blind? Banachile, sensitive and vulnerable, was obviously not aggressive enough for her *mayosenge*. The dress and other things I gave her were taken by other maternal kin.

"By the way," she interrupted my thoughts, "some women came to me. They will not answer the questionnaire, but those who can write want the little booklets. They are recording what they buy, the gifts they give and receive. Some are recording what they and their family eat through the day."

I was astonished and relieved. This information is more important than the questionnaire. We visited several women and chatted with them, explained my research again, reviewed all items in the booklets, and explained some more.

I did not lose the village completely, but I was shaken. The illusion was shattered. I had felt for some time that things ran too smoothly. Life could not be without conflict, disagreement, and some tension. For the first time, I could glimpse below the surface. The trouble was worth it then, except for Banachile.

Nevertheless, the image of those men left me feeling sad. They were so frustrated in their task. Lines of poverty and bitterness left deep grooves on their faces, and some Jehovah's Witnesses were as uninformed as they were. They blindly resisted all political participation but were the first to claim any benefits. Too many were impoverished, their political hopes disappointed, and life itself was stagnant except for people using one another.

The silence at the rest house was welcome. It enabled me to sit and stare while thoughts turned in my head. The women again, I was not doing right by them. Every bit of resistance came from them. If I were at home and I wanted to know matters of importance where would I go, to men, of course. Whom would I ignore the most, women. And I was doing it here.

Evans-Pritchard, a rightly famous anthropologist, wrote a book about *Man and Woman Among the Azande*. In it, he had to state that all the texts in that collection were taken down from men. Yet it was a book about men and women. In addition, he confessed that during his stay in Zandeland, he felt overall on the side of men, rather than women. Since Zande men discriminated against women, as did Evans-Pritchard, in his defense, he asked us to remember that the Great Aristotle mentions women only to compare them with slaves.

Were Lenda women materialists as Eneke described them? Did their needs militate against having inward conversations and sharing a vision? Was appreciative love between men and women as friends impossible? Was Headman Ngoma right that the laws introduced by the Colonial government and Christianity worked against them? Several women told me too that they thought Christian teachings would "enslave" them. From their perspective, having long conversations with men made me servile, when in fact the men and I enjoyed a kind of friendship. The painful fact is that men are civilized—by which I mean engaged with the larger world—and many women here are not (Lewis 2012 [1960]:57-90, 74). Nevertheless, the complaint that I did not give women a fair hearing was right. What was I thinking? Evans-Pritchard had an excuse; he was a man taking the view of his own. What excuse had I?

The sadness of the women's condition and my inadequacy depressed me. What is it I do not see? What do women expect? Why has my research somehow become centered on men? Why do I assume their activities have more import than that of women? Are these even relevant questions? In the West too, many men hold positions, which they do not like, out of a sense of responsibility toward their dependents. Too many women stay in undesirable marriages for the sake of security or out of fear that they are not ready to support their dependents by themselves. In a sense, these are just variations of a basic pattern of interaction between men and women.

However, while women here are economically responsible, they receive less help from the government. Silently and stubbornly, they work their fields. They remain at the center, while men "buzz" from hut to hut like bees from stamen to stamen. Women let me talk to men and do not interfere, but while I do so they have nothing to do with me. I must join them then, it is the only way. Perhaps, too, it's time that I honor the dignity that they honor in themselves.

I see the faces of little men; sad and bitter lines traverse their countenance. And I see the faces of women with grooves of pain, but their bodies stand erect and their heads sit high. "Our women are proud," I hear men say. My mind is quiet again.

Comment 1982 and 2018

In retrospect, I realize that I managed to pull off a dangerous balancing act in Lenda. The "negotiation" process to obtain data is not one that takes place between the anthropologist and her "trained" research informants as described by Rabinow (1977, p.152–153). Even if an informant tried to figure out how to present information to the anthropologist, in my experience, he or she is rarely successful. Usually the anthropologist struggles to learn something about the thought patterns and presuppositions of her informants and especially of the people under study. I found that an effective way to test whether my thought patterns resembled those of my "subjects" was to participate in dispute settlements and court cases. I would frequently reason through a case with a headman, a counselor to the chief, a court clerk, or magistrate. And when I reasoned as they would, their eyes would light up with joy and all of them would spur me on with their rhetorical "aah's" and "eeh's" to a successful conclusion. Usually, I would end by telling them that they reasoned thus because of such and such a premise. Then they would be overjoyed and reply, "you understand us now!" However, since most cases were handled by men, they received more attention unintentionally.

To my mind, the real "negotiation" process takes place between the anthropologist and the various factions or interest groups of the communities he studies. I learned very early that if I wanted to research Jehovah's Witnesses I had also to research Seventh-day Adventists and CMML. Had I not done so, District politicians would not have come to my rescue when I was "oozed" out of Booke Village by its powerful women and their male henchmen. In fact, I had continually to balance my research activities between the people and government, SdAs and Jehovah's Witnesses, men and women, the poor and the rich, traditional elites and modern ones. Not just that, but I had to ask questions of such a nature that my assistants (I had five), who were frequently asked about my activities, and specifically what kinds of questions I asked people, could openly answer local intelligence officers about my work and remain innocent. My assistants often told me that intelligence officers even asked them for our questionnaires. It was not only my assistants who were questioned, the public was also asked about my activities. Finally, at all beer drinks one could find at least one UNIP youth. It was, as I said, an incredible balancing act. I could pull it off only because all my questions ultimately reflected my primary interest in the economic activities of the people, and because I continually moved from faction to faction explaining to each why I also had to study those whom they disliked.

And while colonialism was on the tongue of many, I avoided asking questions about it. It was clear that more than a few locals preferred colonialism to Zambia's de facto one-Party state. But neither my colleagues back home nor Party officials would have appreciated the topic. Well intentioned, it is a problem. It avoids truths that the "correct" consider to be ideologically inconvenient and the "committed" consider to be dangerous.

The task of explaining was by no means easy. It is most naïve that we avidly record how "scientific neutrality" is a ruse used to hide ethnographic loopholes or how researchers affect informants and people among whom we do research, without also recording how the people, their varied views and factions, and their culture, affect the ethnographer and research. It is not only the case that we choose marginal informants or that we drive "mainstream" informants to the edge of their cultural boundaries so that they may critically assess for us aspects of their world about which we are curious (Jules-Rosette, 1980). Rather, it is as much the case that the anthropologist is marginal to his own society or, if he is not, that those, among whom he conducts research, may drive him to the very edge of his own cultural boundaries where he "hangs" in isolation and frustration until he redefines for himself new premises for an expanded universe.

13

LETTERS AND REACTIONS

It was late. Weary, I picked up my body, so to speak, and took myself in. Several letters had arrived. The letter from Bob reminded me that I hadn't written since I left Lusaka. I had forgotten to write too much was happening. I wondered whether he would understand that I was finally experiencing the immersion in research and Lenda life that I had desired some time back. He sent several Xeroxed papers and the Code from the *Ethnographic Atlas*, and he advised that I order my data accordingly. He wrote about dinners and dances back home. Funny that I wrote regularly when Paul was with me but forgot to write when I was free of any man. Usually, it's the other way around; it is assumed that men, not work, make us lose our head.

One letter aroused some astonishment. It was a love letter from someone named "John." Straining my memory, I finally recalled that a young Zambian passed through Nzubuka last Saturday. He was selling cosmetics and non-prescription drugs. We had a lively conversation about skin-toners and laxatives. It rather surprised me that people should need laxatives here, but apparently many people alternate between diarrhea and constipation. There is not much fiber in local foods.

This was simply field work information. Yet here was a love letter from him. If I reproduce his letter it is only to show the ease with which men and women respond to one another here and the sense of romance that the Lenda convey even when their English is still somewhat clumsy.

June 2, 1973
Box 999, Nanyuki
Dear Karla,

Glad to have this chance of writing you this letter. How are you? My journey back to Nanyuki was okay.

Karla, from that time I saw you my heart still has that memory of you, and I am very interested in meeting again, if at all possible. Will you come to Nanyuki? I would be glad if you could bring yourself to say that you will come. I should be glad to receive a telegram telling me of your coming.

Karla I long to see you again. I think of you every hour of the day. We will meet in Nanyuki, if only you will come.

Loads of love from
John

It puzzled me that I received so much uninvited and unwelcome attention from Zambian men. I de-emphasized those physical features for which I usually received complements at home. What I could never resist was conversation and, of course, I explored every topic under the sun. No doubt, these lively conversations charmed some men. They also admired that which they recognized in their own women, namely, "courage" and "energy." Men frequently commented on my "courage" and "energy." That still did not answer my question. Why this open and relaxed expression of their romantic feelings? What was I missing?

My first explanation was that there were no solidly bounded marriages here. The boundaries were fluid. Loyalty as established between couples in the West was simply absent, absent too were all expressions of intimate dependency. A man was not restricted to only one woman any more than a woman was restricted to only one man. It meant, therefore, that men and women felt quite free to express their interest in the other in any context.

If I told a Western man that I was married he would either stop his interest in me, turn it into humor, or come out with something like, yes but you're here and he's there. The point is he would mentally acknowledge a boundary and decide how to deal with it. In the process, the whole encounter would become a moral issue, and the innocence, the simple joy of conversing with another human being would be taken out of it. But in Lenda, if a boundary existed at all, it was vague and indeterminate. Certainly, the mental block wasn't there. In conversation, most Lenda men related toward Lenda women with easy warmth—and I guess this was extended to me. Where at home men usually found me forbidding or unapproachable, or where they displayed uneasiness while talking with me, here both they and I enjoyed talk. We "enjoyed" the Lenda say. Truth is, however, what I enjoyed was "data."

A better answer to the question of "romantic letters" from "the heart" came from primary school teachers. One told me that Zambians enjoy writing love letters. Another mused that the easiest way to teach young men how to write was to let them write love letters. Maybe that's why I received several before leaving Zambia. I was their chance to practice English.

Wednesday, June 3, we administered questionnaires again. Following his encouragements, we covered Mr. Ngoma's section of Kakuso. It was no longer necessary to restrict ourselves to congregational members. Only one woman refused to answer the questions; another one required Mr. Ngoma's persuasion. She feared to take the Fanta I offered, and insisted that she would only take a Fanta from an *umuntu wafita*, a black person. Contrary to us, by the way, the Lenda do not talk about men when they mean human beings. They use the word *umuntu* or *abantu*, human being or human beings. Translations into "he" or "man" were dependent on contexts so that in some of them, they are first human beings and then men or women.

Screaming interrupted one interview. A blind woman beat her child with a stick. The child screamed at the top of his lungs. This was the first time that I saw a child being beaten in Lenda. Children were treated with great affection, and were usually reprimanded verbally followed by hand gestures that ordered them to leave. Every muscle in my body twitched to jump up and stop the beating. I looked around nervously to check how others were reacting. Yambana held my arm, the woman is desperate; her hitting is not that hard; they must be left alone. It was painful to see this blind woman hit her child, sometimes missing it because she could not see. And what did the child feel, knowing that if only it ran away its blind "mother" could not find him; she would slash at air.

As we walked through the village, I observed some men sitting about drinking beer brewed by women. While it was morning, this was their after-work drink. In this section, more women were brewing and selling beer than in Mr. Matafwali's section. Even a Seventh-day Adventist woman brewed beer.

We shared lunch with the headmaster of the Primary School. He was on the church board of SdA, and I was curious about the procedures of settling disputes brought before the board. As well, I asked him if I could possibly observe such proceedings. He was dubious about that, but not final.

He explained the procedure as follows. When a person steals something, for example, and it is brought to the attention of the deacon, he sends a church elder to investigate. The parties involved are brought before the church board which deliberates, decides which commandment has been broken and, if the person is judged guilty, bans him or her from the church. The person is then no longer considered a "Christian." He or she is watched for one year and if he or she improves he can start baptismal classes again, become baptized and a church member.

The following afternoon until 4 p.m., we asked questions again. Feeling tired, I chatted with Mr. Muteta, one of the two big businessmen here. He was a short man, slight, alert, and animated by nervous gestures. Muteta remembered colonial times and commented that he might have been shot for lounging in conversation with me. He told me that I was becoming quickly popular. "You're liked," he said.

Muteta explained that he started his career as a houseboy for Europeans. Lendan by birth, he was educated and lived most of his life in the Industrial Belt. He claimed to like it in the rural area. "The crime rate is too high in the Industrial Belt. Here at least, I feel safe." But not without a night guard, a burglar alarm, and a reputation for being a powerful witch doctor.

On June 4th, a telegram and on June 5th a letter arrived from Bob. I was learning so much and so quickly of late, that I had forgotten to write him. Lenda life was beginning to fall together like pieces of a difficult jigsaw puzzle. I was experiencing a constant tension of joyful anticipation. Each day until the 10th, I administered questionnaires. Finally, June 11th, I took a break and wrote Professor Justin.

June 11, 1973
P.O. Box 1, Nzubuka
Dear Professor Justin:

Let me briefly reply to your letter of 20 May. At this point in my research I would say that the concern with bettering standards is an individual one, and is coming about mainly through the acquisition of money. And here many problems arise, but I'll come to that later. There would appear to be differences in this concern among men, women, and the government. The government would prefer "betterment" to apply to communities. It would be interesting to see whether the way loans and other aid are distributed might further or contradict UNIP ideology. As for the women, those who were asked questions about the future (for example, what would they like their children to become, or what would they like to improve about their own condition), most answered "twikala fye"—we merely sit. Women seem genuinely puzzled by specifically these questions (typical Western ones) and take an inordinate amount of time to answer. Now, these questions were asked along with many others in the form of a questionnaire. Women were uneasy about some questions, not others. Some questions are systematically answered with lies.

In Booke's and Dukana's village, the use of questionnaires has essentially terminated my research. Older people, especially women, were worried. Their concern and the resulting conflicts provided the first real look below the surface, so to speak. I was told that some questions, especially one asking where they came from, reminded them of colonialism. The intent of the question was quite innocent. It was intended to establish that the influx of population was a recent one. Unfortunately, in the past, following colonial labor policy, people were asked comparable questions and then sent back to where they came from. I should have remembered this point from the District Notebooks. It looked so minor.

I have learned with some astonishment that people are rather confused about what this government wants of them. Repayment of loans is a major irritation and so are the recent educational requirements, which leave many capable people who lack them stranded. Finally, the mention of money—and I didn't even dare ask how much they or their husbands might earn in some form or other—is understandably a real threat. It must be related to the nature of taxation and to various contributions which UNIP asks of them, though these appear to be small.

One more point about the bettering of standards. I believe that not just is it not a community concern, but it is not even a family concern, that is, family in the sense of nuclear family (husband, wife, and children). Yet the government insists upon community and nuclear family co-operation. You can imagine the lack of communication between government and people. As for the rest of the family, the mukowa, they seem to be there more to buffer a member from meeting complete disaster than to work positively for his or her advancement, although the latter does occur among those who can afford it. The above generalization must be qualified, however, because women do seem to set up in business, offspring, and sometimes even brothers-in-law.

The questionnaire was useful in one sense; it enabled me a glance below the surface. Many answers are lies. I have determined, therefore, to conduct lengthy, individual interviews and to record extensive life *histories. Each life history will gradually be supplemented with indirect data about earnings and so on. I am certain that questionnaires are next to useless unless they are augmented by direct observation, life histories, and other records. Without additional means of gaining data, too much is too easily hidden. As it is, each life is a beautiful mystery and I am finding means upon means to unlock it.*

I am now concentrating my research in Kakuso itself. The headman will rent me an old house which I am having improved. In the meantime, I sleep part of the time in the home of Yambana.

There are recognized village boundaries, though don't ask yet what they all mean. Interestingly, the headman and villagers see Kakuso as having three firm boundaries with potential to expand eastward into what they see as unlimited bush country. Again, the people see it as an unlimited amount of land. The government does not. Land increasingly belongs to the state and the Lenda will feel it some years from now. To the north a palm tree and narrow path "separate" Kakuso from Chandwe's village; to the south a forked road separates Kakuso from Nzubuka; to the west it's the lake; and to the east and across the main north-south roads are the cassava gardens and beyond bush. The old gardens along the road will eventually become sites for new houses with newer gardens beyond. I intend to consider boundaries further and check what they mean to villagers, headmen, and government.

I shall answer the dambo *(wetlands) question later. What I have seen so far can be described as low areas in the valley adjacent to a lagoon or what people call a river (note, it's the dry season now). The soil is dark and fertile. In the wet season, it is covered with water, and even now it is somewhat muddy. It is apparently prime land for rice fields.*

As for the field notes, I am typing them with copies but prefer to send them when I am next in Lusaka. My personal journal is kept separate. The earlier notes are too personal to be any good to you. What is of use in them, I have put into the report.

This will have to do for an answer to your letter. Thank you for the questions, they are very helpful and I shall keep them in mind and work them out as I go along.

By the way, I have been going to several churches in the villages, and lately to SdA and Watchtower in Kakuso. Some local UNIP people do not like my going to the latter, though they have not forbidden me to do so. I have explained and explained my research to them. And I am grateful for their tolerance, especially since their lot is not easy.

From June 18 to 22 I received a letter from Bob each day. His questions told me that my findings were on track as was the intellectual aspect of our relationship. The letters were filled with references to books, papers and engine mounts, which he had sent. And then came a wonderfully incongruent question:

P.S. By the way, should I sell the fridge and stove rather than move them?

I looked at the last question and it suddenly occurred to me that Bob was not clear who I was to him: wife or colleague, lover or friend. He called me these but it must have been difficult to get them fully integrated into one solid inseparable package. He obviously hadn't succeeded yet. By contrast, I considered everything coming from him as coming wholly from one person. Or did I? Did I not feel that he might for once dispense with being my teacher or playing a father in the abstract, and did I not thereby separate that aspect of him from his role as husband? Why couldn't we simply be two people focused on exploring the world? I was beginning to put our relationship under my analytical scalpel, and I didn't like what was happening to it.

Five further days of intensive interviewing passed without a hitch. Slowly the fog lifted, too slowly still. My notes were in order and I lay back. Candles flickered. Bob was a thousand miles away, yet we were tied to each other. I marveled at his letters and reflected that they were lucid and cerebral; no murky emotions. Like most of us, he had a way of splitting the two. During research, I remembered his ideas; at rest, I recalled my doubts.

Young women beheld his sexiness. In the nineteen sixties, that was a badge of honor. Perhaps their perceptions were right. I sighed. As the fog lifted from Lenda so it descended upon my own life. I would be unfair to him in my thoughts. Still, I let my thoughts ramble on as if to place them into space where I could look at them from a distance, judge them as irrelevant, and then blow them away like a wind dispersing unwelcome clouds.

We were part of the counter-culture of the 1960s. Was it liberating or destructive? Only the future would tell. One thing seemed certain to me, and I saw research in this valley confirming it: sex is not liberating. It may bring joy, or perhaps, it is, as van Gella said somewhat cynically, a form of procreative recreation. But liberation as in achieving "emancipation," or "democracy," or "freedom"—well, if it were these, then Africa would have democracies in abundance. To the extent that sex is an instrument of political correctness or justified by cultural fashions, it is banal.

I sat up disgusted with my thoughts and memories, until I remembered that I had promised myself to look at them as from a distance and feel relieved at their emergence. A Zambian witch doctor could not have done better when he willed pent-up resentments out of the bodies of his clients with a thousand gestures.

Even when its source has been lost, our morality of intent continues to police our innermost thoughts. Fact is, no matter how much I blamed Bob, I blamed myself more. Having dispelled these dark thoughts, the world looked beautiful again.

Mead, Emotion, and Breakthrough

One of my friends was deeply concerned that I should take the risk of conveying my state of mind in the field when I had just succeeded in publishing several well-reasoned papers and a book. Why would you want to take the dangerous route and tinker with emotions when what excited me most is your precise analytical mind? What do you hope to achieve by this tinkering?

These questions are hard to answer. Margaret Mead points out how troublesome Reo Fortune's passion was because it cast suspicion on his work. According to her, Radcliffe-Brown, for example, did not believe Fortune's account of the Dobuans because the passion with which Fortune wrote about his sorcerer-informant seemed somehow to match his own (1972, p.184). It seems perfectly natural to me, however, that a researcher should find himself in a society—often by choice for he will have read accounts about it before embarking on his research venture—whose people display a range of emotions and passions that do resemble his own. Mead, Fortune, and Bateson were very discontent in some cultures and made conscious efforts to find social settings in which the people's ethos or emotional tone was agreeable. I suspect that the rare accounts we get by anthropologists like Castaneda or Griaule, for example, who studied and even assimilated the philosophy of their informants, are the result of a unique harmony between the intellect and emotions of the informant and those of the anthropologist.

The answer to the question why one would wish to note emotional responses to field experiences can be made more profound yet. I take the reader back to Thomas Mann's question; how does one achieve the breakthrough? And to his answer that, for the artist, the breakthrough lies in achieving a new emotional freedom but one regained by the author on the level of utmost intellectual clarity. I suggest something similar happens to the anthropologist during times of intense experiences, especially, during periods of intensity in the field. At these times, an ethnographer, even one as little concerned with introspection as Margaret Mead, experiences a new emotional freedom that impels her to look simultaneously into herself and the other; and into her own culture as well as the culture she is studying. The result frequently consists of new theoretical insights and formulations. Margaret Mead (1972) describes the brief period in the field which she spent together with her husband, Reo Fortune, and fellow researcher, Gregory Bateson, as follows:

> The intensity of our discussions was heightened by the triangular situation. Gregory and I were falling in love, but this was kept firmly under control while all three of us tried to translate the intensity of our feelings into better and more perceptive field work (p.217).

And then she notes:

> As we discussed the problem, cooped up together in the tiny eight-foot-by-eight-foot mosquito room, we moved back and forth between analyzing ourselves and each other, as individuals, and the cultures that we knew and were studying, as anthropologists must (ibid).

It is from this emotionally charged period that her ideas about temperament and sex developed. Indeed, as one reads Mead's account of her surprisingly normal, although she considers it privileged, upbringing, one soon learns that most of her theoretical breakthroughs are the direct result of relatively "intense" experiences. For example, her unpleasant experiences at DePauw led her to observe that "in the setting of this co-educational college, it became perfectly clear both that bright girls could do better than bright boys and that they would suffer for it" (p.99–100). She developed this thesis in her work *Male and Female*. Finding co-education unattractive, she observes, "This preference foreshadowed, I suppose, my anthropological field choices—not to compete with men in male fields, but instead to concentrate on the kinds of work that are better done by women" (1972:100). Finally, upon discovering with considerable disappointment that she could not have children because of a tipped uterus, Mead remarks that the whole picture of her future changed: "if there was to be no motherhood, then a professional partnership of field work with Reo, who was actively interested in the problems I cared about, made more sense than cooperation with Luther in his career of teaching sociology" (p.164).

These experiences, which in the more chaotic lives of others might have gone unnoticed, are highlighted by Mead herself from her otherwise tranquil existence because through them she achieved remarkable insights. And these, certainly, had to do with her changing relationships with men, intimacy, ideas, and field work.

Faithful to her North American tradition, Mead avoids revealing herself through introspection. We never really know how she felt, only that she felt. And that she felt is almost consistently revealed to us through a mediating medium, a selected letter, a carefully chosen poem, and her frequent descriptions of herself from photographs. Believing that an ethnographer could, indeed must, free herself of all presuppositions, and that she must adhere to the subject-object distinction even when she talked about herself; believing, further, that members of privileged groups who had never suffered oppression themselves could yet initiate movements to improve the rights of the downcast, Mead, nevertheless, wrote:

> Certainly, positions of privilege can breed a kind of hardened insensitivity, an utter inability to imagine what it is to be an outsider, an individual who is treated with contempt or repulsion for reasons of skin color, or sex, or religion, or nationality, or the occupation of his parents and grandparents. A defining experience is necessary to open one's eyes and so to loosen the ties of unimaginative conformity (1972:93).

I suspect, however, that Mead is a liberal, as maternal toward the unprivileged as men have been paternalistic. And with Steven Biko, I must believe that while victims are as likely to flee from their fate as they are to stand up against it, in the end it is sufferers of great injustice who must also find the means to overcome their condition of suffering. And the difference between those who run and those who "lean into the wind" is the belief of the individual that joy will come when one embraces freedom, responsibility, and courage.

In the end, and from my perspective, the miracle of Margaret Mead is that so normal a person should have become so prominent. What Mead calls privilege, I call normal. The millions of people who live in poverty are not normal even when they are the majority in many nations. Not normal, too, are the millions of recent immigrants into the United States, or those among the middle classes who live with uneducated parents many of whom remain anchored to fundamentalist religions. Yet out of this morass of human misery arise those whose lucid minds grasp their situation and succeed to reach beyond.

To sum up, Mead's professional excellence is rooted in the single-mindedness with which she defined and pursued her projects. According to the tenets of Sartrean existentialism, her projects should have infused every one of her actions with meaning. In the case of Margaret Mead, Sartre's formulation is proven right. Her projects determined her choice of spouses just as they determined the nature of her research. Likewise, just as her projects allowed her to assign meaning to her relationships, so these same projects would determine the tone and range of her emotional responses. In short, through her clearly defined projects she simultaneously harnessed *meanings* and *emotions*.

Margaret Mead claimed that she had expected to adjust her professional life to wifehood and motherhood (1972:164). The reversal of priorities, she ascribes to the fact that she was told by a gynecologist that her uterus was tipped which would cause constant early miscarriages (p.164). It is my opinion, following existentialist premises, that this conclusion is inauthentic. Many women had tipped uteri, but those whose priority was to have a child would risk multiple miscarriages; indeed, they would do anything to carry their pregnancy to term. If the news of her tipped uterus had any effect at all, it was not to persuade her to switch her priorities from motherhood to anthropology. Rather, it would merely have added decisiveness to the project she had already defined for herself, just as her home environment, consisting of determined women, allowed her to formulate clear goals. Most women of similar intellect who grow up in more chaotic family settings are at a disadvantage only in the sense that it takes them longer to sort out authentic from inauthentic goals.

Comment 1982 and 2018

I am now able to answer a question that I was asked upon return from the field, namely: "If you were so immersed in Lenda culture, why did you not treat your husband with the same humor and mischief with which Lenda women treated theirs?" My answer is simple. First, I was immersed in Lenda culture to understand it and, unexpectedly, to understand myself. Empathizing with Lenda women, however, did not mean assimilating their customs.

Second, many marriages of ethnographers "fell apart" during or following field work. Usually unrecorded, the process of alienation from one's spouse, nevertheless, takes place during field work. I thought it worthwhile to document part of this alienation.

Third, learning another culture leads inevitably to comparisons. Even during states of despair, implied comparisons are evident, but adopting solutions of the culture being studied when it too might be wrong is not an option.

Even now, more than forty years later, my answer remains a *cliché*: two wrongs don't make a right. But perhaps I can offer more. It will be remembered that my early life was engulfed by the great disaster of war and dislocation. The loss of any natural sense of belonging made me aware of being a burden. And with the death of my father, just when his return promised hope, I also lost trust. The only thing I remember about my first boyfriend, for example, is his saying to me "oh ye of little faith." Without trust and faith, but with a deep aversion to being a burden, I was left with but one determination: to pick myself up and get on with the task that brought me to Zambia.

14

MURDER, THEFT, AND
OTHER DISCOVERIES

I wanted to see village night life and accepted Sichota's and the A.D.S.'s invitation to go bar hopping, rural style. Sichota was Nzubuka's chief of police whose profession was written all over his firm, chiseled face. Yet he was young without a spare ounce of flesh. His major trade mark was that he rarely wore his uniform. He hoped, he said, that this would help him gain rapport with the local population. Police techniques were so crude he claimed that without people's cooperation crime would go unsolved. Stealing was rampant in Kakuso and people feared thieves and murderers incessantly. But in the presence of the police, they fell silent. Sichota's explanation was that the police were still fighting their colonial image. I wondered whether they were fighting anything at all, whether it wasn't rather the case that people continued to settle crime their own way.

The night started innocently enough. We walked through villages which were extremely dark. I was always amazed by this. It was the absence of electricity that made nights appear to look darker than back home. Here and there the wind raised gentle flames from burning charcoal. Some miles away would stand a bar lit by candles or Tilley lamps. My worry, that being seen with the chief of police might have an adverse effect on my research, was soon forgotten. The conversation was too good for that.

Sichota explained various poisons. Fear of being poisoned was common and waitresses were instructed to open bottled beer only once it stood directly in front of the customer. Our conversation was being drowned by a noisy argument among secondary school teachers. A fight threatened to erupt between a white and black colleague. The latter accused the former of being unable to teach Zambian history and invited him, with his fists, to leave the country. Sichota walked over slowly, said a few calming words, and reduced the struggle to a comfortable simmer. Someone played music from a gramophone and a few men started to dance. We wandered off to another bar where the atmosphere was more pleasant.

I was musing about the sensuality of Zambian dance when one of Sichota's officers came over and whispered something into his ear. "Let's go," Sichota said and motioned us to follow him. A guard has been murdered he explained as we rushed in the direction of Chipili's store.

It was a gruesome murder. The guard was apparently strangled. His head was pulled back and the cord around his neck was tied to his legs and arms. The body was twisted rearward as if his back had been broken. Someone had tried to stick him into a sack. I turned stone cold and felt my breathing stop. The A.D.S. pulled me away. The store was robbed he explained.

Sichota questioned everyone around. No one had heard or seen a sound and yet some huts were but 15 to 20 feet away. The night was giving up its blackness to a hesitant grey with the arrival of early morning. We were chilled to the bone from the rain and still no wiser. As usual it was believed that the murderer must have come from and returned to Zangava. Every crime committed was blamed on someone from the opposite side of the Zambian border, which remained as "fluid" as the water of its wide river.

Kakuso had not been peaceful for several weeks. Someone had systematically searched out houses inhabited solely by women and robbed them of their pots and blankets. Apparently, the thief loosened several mud bricks on the bottom of highly placed windows. This business was conducted in the early morning while women were in their fields. At night he returned, removed the loose bricks, crawled through the widened space and stole what he wanted. Women indicated that they were afraid, but absolutely refused to talk to the police.

Yambana insisted more and more that I stay at her house, otherwise she would have to move in with her mother. Our nerves were frayed. The next few nights following the murder none of us slept well, yet no one would really talk about it. The police discovered nothing. Neither the murder nor the stealing was solved. Only houses of compounds to the east in the bush were left without locks.

I had slept in Yambana's house for over a week when Kakuso was agitated again, this time over a rumor that an unnatural lion, an evil spirit, was about. Yambana explained that it was a matter of unresolved resentment, someone bore a grudge against someone else. Seemingly, the offended individual marshaled the help of superhuman powers to catch the offender. The fear pervading Kakuso arose following the death of a sixteen-year-old girl during childbirth. Yambana suspected that her husband had gone into hiding because her kinsmen would accuse him of her death and beat him up. The evil spirit was presumably in pursuit of him. I didn't know what was easier to understand, this phenomenon or stealing. Since this was not the first time that I heard about husbands running away during a wife's difficult childbirth, I decided to ask some questions.

Yambana clarified that a man is required to be faithful to his wife when she is with child. This one was not. He confessed as much to his mother-in-law. When I asked about the nature of this confession, she explained that whenever a wife has a difficult childbirth her husband is summoned by his mother-in-law to confess his transgressions. Indeed, it is assumed that he must have been unfaithful.

According to local belief at the time, a fetus is formed from the blood of a woman. A man who copulates with someone else while his wife is pregnant will mix the blood of the stranger with that of his wife. Implied is that the husband continues to have sexual intercourse with his wife during her pregnancy because his activity helps mold the fetus.

Mixed blood interferes with the development of the fetus and the health of the mother. It causes difficult childbirth or death. The theory of blood and its relationship to the discreteness of clans was fascinating. Clearly Lenda theory of reproduction was different from ours. Later that evening we discussed reproduction further with one of the female elders.

Uneasy fantasies about imminent danger interrupted my sleep. Yambana could not have slept well either, for both of us felt disoriented and tired the following day. I decided, therefore, to observe the procedure of selling fish to Lakes Fisheries. Intensive interviewing was left for another day. Fishermen sold their produce on a cash or credit basis. Each transaction was recorded on a sales slip a copy of which was kept by Lakes Fisheries. Fish guards were meticulous about recording the fisherman's name, weight of his produce, distinct species caught, and the cash value of the catch. By god, here was a way to estimate fisherman's earnings.

The manager of Lakes Fisheries, Mr. Muera, willingly granted me permission to go through all sales slips from the beginning of the company's operation in 1970. I planned to start this task around the beginning of August following many intensive interviews with local fishermen. Earnings from Lakes Fisheries are only part of a man's income. Considerable amounts of fish were disposed of in other ways. I hoped that intensive interviews would lead me to them. How fish were distributed was not advertised because the government insisted not only that records be kept of catches but also that they be sold to Lakes Fisheries.

I now worked on a means to discover production costs. This was easier. It was in the interest of fishermen to explain how high these were. My problem was accuracy. I arranged to study the sales slips of Nkwazi Co. which sold nets, lines, and yarn for repair. I would check the amount of petrol used per trip for motors of different horse power. Banana boats were often built by carpenters living along the valley. I planned to check the cost of boat production and of finished boats with them. Gradually, I spent a lot of time with fishermen on the lake to observe what happened to the fish and to measure the yardage of nets. It was also necessary to check that fishermen used the same name repeatedly. The Lenda have several names.

As trivial as these discoveries may look, they were necessary pieces in the Lenda puzzle. And while it looks fantastic, not only did I vary my routine in accordance with frequent unexpected events, but I kept in mind, always, the need to collect three kinds of data, religious, kinship and economic ones. I "sensed" the pattern; missing pieces had to be filled in. Knowing that this episode of data gathering would come to an end with the Nzubuka Agricultural Show July 20th, I wrote some of my kinship insights to Len.

July 19, 1973
P.O. Box 1 Nzubuka
Dear Len:

I am becoming really excited about kinship. Clearly it orders the Lenda universe. Whenever I enter a new village, the first question I am asked is what my mukowa *is. The other day a man became quite angry with me when I said I had none. You are a human being are you not, he asked, and if you are, you must be of a* mukowa. *A* mukowa *is one's blood and origin.*

We had a lengthy discussion with one of the female elders about reproduction and this blood business. It turns out that these people believe a fetus is made solely from the blood of its mother. It is only the blood of women that can be passed on from generation to generation. The father's contribution to reproduction is not heritable. He seems to help the blood coagulate, shape the fetus or such. His contribution is congenital in nature, while the substance of women is shared across generations and is hereditary in kind.

There is here no sense, in other words, that genetic material of both parents makes up the fetus. The material that is handed on from generation to generation is blood of woman. This is Lenda biology, Len, just as Fortes said of the Ashanti.

If I am right, it is a real discovery. It blows Scheffler's most fundamental assumption, namely, that elementary relationships are always those of genitor-offspring, and genitrix-offspring. In Lenda, it is the latter alone, genitrix-offspring, that is at the core of their system.

Upon asking about the meaning of clan, people answer that it refers to those of one blood, mulopa, *or of one womb,* ifumu. *If the* mukowa *is in any sense descent, Len, then descent here means those of one blood, i.e., of one substance. Maybe this is the reason why Cunnison never drew a neat genealogical grid. If all are one and the same substance, zap, then one would not be inclined to trace descent from person to person as if to check each person's genetic contribution. Fortes says that the Ashanti do NOT trace descent from person to person in our sense. This would mean that "our" descent and Lenda descent or "their" descent are different.*

Let me end here. Please show this letter to Professor Justin. Also tell him that I have discovered a way to begin calculating fishermen's earnings and production costs. Locally, we seem to discover almost everything, except who does the stealing. It is hard for me to make sense of theft in villages here, except to note that it is somehow related to Lenda's participation in a cash economy, the Province's location by the Zangavan border, and the quite idiosyncratic individualism of its people.

Mad Head Love

On her return from her first field trip, Margaret Mead fell in love with Reo Fortune. She soon divorced Luther Cressman and married Reo. While she was in the field with Reo, she fell in love with Gregory Bateson. She soon divorced Reo and married Gregory. All her romantic involvements started in the head with conversations centered on subject matters that were dear to her "professional heart." As if she obeyed the prevalent Western maxim, that sex was best within marriage, her romantic involvements resulted in marriage. Finally, while her sexual partners were closely linked to her theoretical, field work, or methodological interests, all of them were Westerners.

To my mind, this sequence of events, especially the sequence of divorces and remarriages which are closely tied to field experiences and, generally, intellectual interests, is a natural hazard of the discipline. It is not uncommon that anthropologists who, during their life, experience intellectual renewal as they shift to adopt different theoretical or topical priorities, change spouses. There is a clear logic, if not a clear morality, to the above series of events.

I am not the only one who has remarked about the relationship between a scholar's intellectual interests and his love life. Gouldner writes (1971:57):

> Like other men, sociologists also have sexual lives, and "even this" may be intellectually consequential. In loyalty tinged with bitterness, most stick it out to the end with the wives who saw them through graduate school, while others practice serial polygamy ... My point is not that this is especially important, but that even this remote sexual dimension of existence reaches into and is linked with the sociologist's world of work. For example, it is my strong but undocumented impression that when some sociologists change their work interests, problems, or styles, they also change mistresses or wives.

While the sequence, though personal and loaded with emotional content, is extremely logical, for some present-day anthropologists some of the premises or "domain assumptions" have changed. First, the principle, good sex belongs within marriage, is still a moral imperative for many Americans, but not for all. Second, the "native" of the non-Western world has become far more sophisticated and educated. He or she may make a good conversationalist. In the past, this craving for deep conversation drove many an anthropologist back into the fold of the white or Western community. Today, however, given these shifts in the content of premises, it should not be surprising that more anthropologists will have affairs with, or will marry, members of the society within which they conduct research. This does not mean, that anthropologists will ever involve themselves with "villagers," it does mean that they are likely to experience involvements with educated and like-minded members of the state or society within which they are conducting research.

Why involvement at all? Gregory Bateson answered that question well when he said, "it is not frustrated sex, it is frustrated gentleness that is so hard to bear when one is working for long months alone in the field" (1972, p.155). And while Margaret Mead would have us believe that babies soothed her frustrations, it is quite clear that the prospect of falling in love met even her needs more adequately.

Gentleness in a stark environment is balm for the soul. Its beginning is so unexpected that one stumbles and falls. It is so clumsy, even humorous, that I shall do what few researchers ever do, relate some of it as I recorded events in my personal journal.

… In the Lenda context, the small discoveries of which I spoke earlier, created such euphoria that I have decided to participate and enjoy the Nzubuka Agricultural Show. It will start tomorrow. Nzubukans have been busy with preparations all week. We halted the usual research and followed the rhythm of the festivities.

Rural Development Officers (RDO), Permanent Secretaries (PS) and Cabinet Ministers (CM) arrived the evening of the 19th. As usual they teased me about "my home" and about expecting me to prepare them *nshima*.

Nshima was a thick cassava, maize, or millet porridge expertly prepared by Lenda women who know how to prevent it from clotting. It is also associated with intimacy.

I was the first to rise that next morning. My intention was to avoid the line-up for the bath. While preparing camera and film I could already smell the familiar scent of *Imperial Leather*. It was the favorite soap of government ministers. Together they created the momentary illusion of luxury and high culture.

Yambana recorded speeches; I took photos. VIPs were a motley crew and included as said, people from Cabinet in Lusaka down the hierarchy to District Governors and District Secretaries from Mboua, Zongwe, and Nzubuka. UNIP officials were out in record numbers. Chiefs Kikombo and Kanye decorated the stage and Mr. Ngoma, Kakuso's headman, sat between them. He always looked a bit uncomfortable at these festivities. Despite Ngoma's demur about the government, he and the other two locals stood for progressiveness among the traditional elite.

Minister, Agricultural Show

The national anthem was sung, speeches followed. "Back to the land" was stressed a lot. If only the land was not so hot, and dry, and prone to causing disease. I photographed Ministers inspecting agricultural products and then followed them back to the platform.

Traditional dancers arrived. Their feet raised glistening dust. Hips moved back and forth. Drumming approached a climax whenever man and woman danced together imitating the rhythm of copulation. How peculiar this democratic ritual of letting tradition follow modern suggestions.

I turned toward the platform and saw Mwewa look at me. How devastatingly sensuous rural life is, I reflected, looking at him. Our eyes locked, so I threatened to catch his eyes on camera. That persuaded him to don his official airs. I laughed and turned to watch the dance again.

As we walked back to the rest house Mwewa asked what we should do for excitement that evening. I swallowed my surprise and maintained an air of formality. "There is nothing one can do in Nzubuka," I said, "except, perhaps, drink beer and talk." I guessed he might have seen me return from a beer drink with several young men. I was proud of my non-sexually motivated comrades and hoped he hadn't misunderstood.

Toward evening he knocked on my door. My head started to throb as I wondered what to do. It was not appropriate for him to visit local bars. He was also aware that everyone knew me here. That could only mean one of two things, the lounge or my room. I insisted upon beer in the lounge. These feelings, half facetious, half serious, found their way into a letter to mother.

July 20, 1973
Darling Mother:

What is the nature of woman's love? Have you ever thought about that? Do you remember when I conducted research about gender roles and sexuality and I received that freakish letter from a prairie woman who argued that women were by nature frigid? According to her, women were unwilling to admit their frigidity owing to the new sexual morality which pressured them to enjoy sex. She felt that I ought to have cross-cultural evidence to support her hypothesis. I had none. We need only remember the Marquesans whose women were famed for their love making.

So, what is the nature of woman's love? In Lenda, if anything, society discourages intimate dependency of one woman on one man. Kin pressure, peer pressure, reproduction pressure, all work to encourage relatively frequent change of partners. It's not promiscuity. But it is a distinct way of relating to the opposite sex. In other words, men and women here seem to learn to enjoy, relate to, and be affectionate with several of the opposite sex. It seems so easy, so relaxed, so natural, not at all possessive and grasping. Van Gella's explanation is that "procreation is the only form of recreation in the village." Most peculiar to me is their concern that my sex life be healthy. To them, sexually deprived persons become erratic and are likely to go mad. To be facetious, they have an erotic apologetics.

I suspect, dear Mam, that sexuality is a very cultural sort of phenomenon. It has an overall logic or frame that seems to be culturally specific if not static.

By the way, Lenda women use techniques to increase vaginal constriction. It emerged from incidental conversations that girls lengthen their labia minora from age three. They are very proud of it. Men, even Christianized ones, claim these lengthened labia increase their pleasure. To think that this society does as ours did, namely, concentrate primarily on the sexual pleasure of men, would be wrong. Before their first "marriage" young men are taught ways to enhance a woman's sexual pleasure. I am told, that a young man is advised by elders to drop everything and engage in sexual intercourse with his wife when the latter desires it, no matter what time of day. One of the young men, currently a university student, told me he was surprised when he was taught "this" before his wedding. So am I.

It's the Agricultural Show here and one of the honorable guests is intent on stepping into my life. This time, however, I am amused at the incongruence of it. Imagine your daughter, mother, energetic, curious, restless, and inclined to occasional mischief and daring. And now imagine the man, bureaucratic, staid, cautious, and correct. Frankly, I don't understand the man's interest in me. I don't even understand how, in the name of heaven, one undressed in front of such a man? He must have read my thoughts, for he said; "Look Karla, we must begin somewhere." In response, my head nearly burst—and I headed for the lounge.

Luckily for me he is well educated, with a Ph.D. in social science. He spent many years in Europe. He is, perhaps because of his education, quite tame if also calmly sure of himself. Perhaps his profession dictates a calm approach. Most of all, he cannot do, what Paul could, rob me of a clear mind and good humor. And speaking of freedom, my sense of it is becoming transformed. It is much less based on breaking rules as in freedom from something. Instead, it is increasingly based on what Lenda women call "power," but which I see as freedom toward accepting my past and my present life centered on my task.

The following two days I was busy. When we met, Mwewa asked me to drive to Chalona with him where he had to give a speech gracing the opening of a new government rest house. This scheme did not fit into my research plans for I had to spend the day with Seventh-day Adventists who were beginning to organize their annual camp meeting in August. Then he asked me to spend the evening with him following his return, but my stomach urged me to sample the cooking of my C.U.S.O. friends. Not only would I be able to eat beef, but more importantly, I would eat "real" vegetables. The food here is atrocious.

We finally ran into one another Sunday morning before he and one of the Ministers returned to Mboua and I to Kingdom Hall. It was a glorious morning—the sky was blue, the air fresh, and my local knowledge was crowned with a little success. I had managed to procure eggs from a villager for the D.G. when his cook was unable to do so. It saved the D.G. some embarrassment since he was responsible for feeding the guests. And when the C.M.'s driver returned complaining that no one at Mechanical Services (a Government-vehicle repair center) would mend the tube and change the tire, I asked permission to find a man who would. This little mission was also successful. Since I saw little tasks of this nature as tests of my positive involvement in the community, their success filled me with joy.

When Mwewa and I met in the lounge we spent almost an hour in animated conversation. And when he suggested that he reserve a room for me in Katumba during the paramount chief's annual celebration of his years in office I agreed. Yes, we liked one another. But more importantly, those celebrations were important for my research.

Comment 1982 Modified 2018

In short, during my year of field work I became a relativist with respect to man-woman interaction patterns. Indeed, the 1960s counter-culture in America was a pre-adaptation. Going through that restless time, and observing American ways from the margin, I noticed that Western women of my age and younger followed the fashion of frankness about sex. But according to Schofield (1980, p.118), this frankness did not reflect "basic" changes in sexual behavior. Instead, where behavioral changes did occur, the women were confused, guilt-ridden, or self-punishing. Let us remember that:

> Less than ten years ago (during the 1970s) the Assistant Secretary of the British Medical Association declared: "As a doctor I can tell you that premarital intercourse is medically dangerous, morally degrading and nationally destructive" (Schofield, 1980:111).

And so, Schofield (ibid) observed that:

> The old question the teenage girl used to ask was: "How far should I go?" Now the question is more likely to be: "Does he really love me?" What she is really asking is: "Does he intend to marry me?"

> These young people continued to be subject to the established Western premise of "love and marriage," although the behavior informed by that premise was modified to read "that a licence for sex can only be obtained in exchange for a promise of marriage" (Schofield, 1980:111).

More recently, even that has changed.

Where my field work was concerned, I became more adept at negotiating my way around men, at least around those of them that showed an interest in this "European" female field worker. Local men and women were, at any rate, by habit or tradition or necessity or any combination thereof autonomous agents and, of course, so was I. Their notion of "romantic love" that was also learned in local schools as I showed earlier, did not seem to have the poetic depth and social underpinning of, for example, the world of Goethe. At least, I did not think it had. The deepest connection between local men and women seemed to be through offspring and even those relationships were under stress. Such a structural and affective foundation did not appeal to me. Herein it became essential to be honest, especially, with myself.

In this Zambian rural area, people voiced dissimilar cultural premises, ones that I certainly thought to be interesting. First, in accordance with their traditional theory of procreation, which postulated that the fetus is formed primarily from the blood of its mother, non-procreative sex was "somewhat" separated from sex for reproduction. I say "somewhat" because men were seen to play a role in shaping the fetus and, when expressing a deep sense of intimacy, imagined having a child with that woman. That image represented an "abstract" and unbreakable tie—or so it seemed to me. All the same, sex was principally pleasurable.

Second, because a child belonged automatically to the clan of its mother, there was here no issue of legitimacy. "Biological" fatherhood was "unimportant" because if one of the men with whom the woman copulated wished to be a father, he had only to "declare himself" as such. For example, in Nzubuka a young woman wanted me to admire her lovely baby. "And who is her father?" I asked innocently. "He has not declared himself yet," she answered to my astonishment. Such a happening was not infrequent locally.

Finally, although in the West we recognize the genetic contribution of both parents, today even traditional Lenda premises can be translated into ones applicable to ourselves. With birth control and increased scientific knowledge of sexual physiology, so Schofield, fun-sex has been separated from biological sex.

> If we agree that the human genitals are not designed solely for procreation, then all sorts of non-coital activities can be enjoyed; for example, it is no longer rational to maintain that homosexual activities are unnatural … Furthermore, it is no longer sensible to uphold the idealized version of women as being more interested in motherhood than sex, because girls want sex for enjoyment just as much as men (1980:122).

More recently we have moved beyond even that. In the process, we have lost some very important values, and it is the Lenda environment that has made me aware of it. I mean a love that grows because of grace, commitment, loyalty, and predictable responsibility for children. As well, it became quite clear to me that Lenda men and women too were conflicted about these issues, especially when they adopted one sort or other of Christianity or moved to Zambia's cities

15

THE MUTOMBOKO AND LOCAL ISSUES

My research followed local rhythms during the paramount chief's *mutomboko* festivities. Saturday noon, I checked in at the rest house in Katumba, near Catote, where the *mutomboko* would be held. A room had indeed been reserved.

Mwewa arrived shortly after six that evening. I was sitting in the lounge with a Cabinet Minister from Lusaka when Mwewa arrived. The Minister had invited me to eat watermelon with him. Mwewa looked over and smiled. Checked in, he came and bit off a piece of my melon. "A lovely greeting," I said.

He outlined his schedule. He wanted to see the District Governor first and then he would have to drive into Catote to check on the organization of things for the following day. I wondered how Mwata Catote would feel about these officious intrusions.

It was late in the evening. From the rest house verandah, one could hear wailing and watch a bonfire light up the sky. Mwewa walked over. We stood for a long time neither speaking a word. Finally, he suggested that we go to the funeral, "for in the beginning there was a funeral and god and humanity were one." Given the valley's frequent funerals, his words made sense. I would mention this funeral in a letter to Len later.

Next morning, I awoke to a busy atmosphere. Mercedes were driven back and forth between Katumba and Catote with last minute messages. By nine in the morning, several cars formed a stately colony. I was driven in the last car belonging to the Department of Tourism and Natural Resources. Incongruous and yet appropriate, I thought.

Being part of the official party paid off. I was never more than five to ten feet from Mwata Catote and his official entourage. I photographed and recorded continuously.

Ceremonial rituals took up most of the morning. Mwata Catote was carried to the river to sacrifice food to the ancestors. From there he was carried to the grave of the ancestor who conquered this area. Back at the school grounds, he was placed on his stool attended by his servants. Cabinet Ministers and government officials were seated to the right and left of him.

Paramount Chief

Mwata Catote's official speaker read the speech for him. It was custom. A chief did not address his people directly. The Cabinet Minister's speech took me by surprise and subdued my spirits. I had not been aware of the resentments against whites. Later I would notice that most political speeches voiced similar sentiments. Finally, I concluded that these resentments were mild, almost a formality.

The Cabinet Minister praised the chief and his people for perpetuating "this aspect of your traditions and culture." Shouldn't he have said *our* traditions and culture, I wondered. A trivial point. As he continued, however, my astonishment grew.

"Soon after achieving our hard-won independence," he said, "the party and Government thought seriously about reviving our lost culture, traditions and customs so that we could be ourselves and true Africans." What he said next surprised me even more.

"Although the Party and Government have decided to preserve our traditions and culture, it must be already understood that we cannot encourage and support bad customs and traditions. For example, the bad traditions regarding witchcraft and inheritance after the death of the husband and father must definitely be stopped and changed." As he talked about inheritance, I heard quiet but angry hissing from neighbors.

At the completion of his speech, there was complete and utter silence. An audience of more than two thousand people and not a sound.

I nudged my neighbor. I felt uncomfortable and almost sad, sad for the world and its misunderstandings. "Why is everyone silent?" I asked.

"They are protesting against the government's stance on inheritance. Inheritance goes from mother to daughter and from mother's brother to sister's son. The husband or father has nothing to do with this. He is a stranger, a guest, not part of the family," my neighbor said.

"Besides," he continued, "to do away with inheritance within our mother's house means changing the whole family and that, means further loss of the legal jurisdiction of chiefs and headmen. Loss of legal jurisdiction is a sore topic." I nodded and felt quite excited. What the Cabinet Minister said confirmed the continued importance, indeed centrality, of matrilineal beliefs and practices. "Most people are still in favor of traditional matrilineal justice and support matrilineal inheritance, which the government opposes. And to talk about changing it here at Mwata Catote

VI's ceremony, celebrating the completion of another year in office, is the utmost of ironies," he said.

I looked uneasily at the Cabinet Minister, at Mwata Catote, and at Mwewa. All wore blank expressions.

Then the ceremony continued. Every chief under Catote's jurisdiction presented himself by approaching the paramount in dance. Several prominent women of his kingdom danced next. The ceremony reached its climax when Mwata Catote danced himself. I was told that every gesture symbolized his power and control over his domain. Everyone understood the message of the dance.

Mutomboko Ceremony

The ceremonies were over, leaving us covered in dust. I was asked to follow Mwewa to Catote's rest house to cool down and wash up. We were to attend a reception at the palace but it was cancelled at the last minute. The officialdom was upset and Mwewa too grew restive. We returned to Katumba.

Mwewa acted subdued, as did all the ministers. Most of them left. "I've got to go too. Come to Mboua tomorrow, just for a day," he pleaded. He looked sad.

"I won't promise," I said. It was an honest answer, if also a "no" that both could accept. I watched him drive off. He turned his head and looked back. In the distance, red dust rose and slowly returned to the ground.

I guessed that perhaps the ministers would mull over today's events. None looked very happy when they left. Feeling tired, I returned to my room.

There was no water again. Towards evening the Information Officer came by to give me copies of the speeches. I queried him about the Cabinet Minister's speech. He confirmed that inheritance is a sore topic. Indeed, three issues anger the rural population, inheritance, crime and the increasing loss of chiefly power. He told me that at this year's meeting of the House of Chiefs, crime and justice were hotly debated. Chief Mashiba of Zongwe District who represented Mwata Catote advocated severe punishment of robbers. He showed me a newspaper clipping in which Chief Mashiba was to have said the following:

> We feel it is high time that the government listened to us for everywhere in Zambia today, we live in fear. We appeal to our government to act now by hanging armed bandits.

Following our discussion, the information officer asked whether I could give him a lift to Nzubuka. We drove off into the dark Zambian night.

At Nzubuka rest house, I scrubbed the tub with Dettol, took a long bath, looked over my notes, collected the films, and read the minister's speech again. Tomorrow I would talk to Mr. Ngoma and other villagers about the inheritance issue. Then it would be time to interview fishermen and start my scheme to calculate their earnings. Before going to bed, I wrote letters about my reflections on kinship to Len and Justin. Some of these observations came from the funeral that I attended with Mwewa.

July 30, 1973
Dear Len:

While most of my time of late was spent following local festivities, I have used every occasion to learn a little more about the nature of Lenda kinship. The use of the word KINSHIP is already a problem. Lendans have two categories. One is mukowa *(including* cikota*) which seems to mean descent. The idea of ancestor-focused is applicable as well as the business of one substance. The other category is* ulupwa, *which seems to mean kinship in the sense of a web of relatives. Ego-centeredness is, perhaps,* *applicable here, since* ulupwa *covers a wide number of kin types to whom ego refers by certain terms.* Ulupwa *is also the closest thing we get to a notion of family, that is, our type of family. The concept is often qualified by saying* ulupwa kuli mayo *which now approximates our idea of extended mother-centered (or matrifocal) family.*

Now then, to the next point. The other evening a friend and I listened to funeral songs. I hadn't attended a funeral yet so he took me to it. It was a funeral without a corpse. Apparently, the individual had died a year ago at the Industrial Belt and was being mourned here by his kinsmen. Relieved at the absence of a corpse I decided to ask how people were related.

*Here is an interesting sequence. Next to me sat two men who said that it was their brother who had died. Both referred to the deceased as their brother (*wesu*) and to one another as brother. Next day at the* mutomboko *(the celebration of the chief's tenth year in office), I saw them again. But now the younger man referred to the older as* yama *and the latter referred to the younger as* mwipwa*. After lengthy enquiry, they said that they refer to the deceased as brother because they can succeed (*ukupyana*) to his identity. By extension, they therefore call the deceased's children, own children and one another brother. Every day, however, they are* yama *(MB) and* mwipwa *(ZS) to one another.*

Now then, something goes on at a funeral that does not go on every day. More importantly, in the context of the funeral a Crow-type terminology (as Scheffler and Lounsbury classify it) seems to be indicated. The question is what does this alternative term business mean?

Again, at the funeral, everything was mukowa *business. For example, there were those of one* mukowa *who were in a joking relationship with the* mukowa *of the deceased. They literally clowned around; unfortunately, I couldn't understand all of it yet. However, one thing is clear, funerals have to do with* mukowa *and hence descent. Everyday life has mostly to do with* ulupwa *or kinship. Now, if these kin terms are context-dependent, can they be said to fall into types: A Crow-type in the descent context and another type in the kinship context?*

If Scheffler's and Lounsbury's typologies are, in last analysis, based on universal biological notions of reproduction and on universal elementary relationships, can the kin terms in the Lenda descent context, which is based on their own theory of relatedness, be a typology? In other words, isn't the Scheffler and Lounsbury typology based on etic categories and rules, and am I not saying the Lenda emic categories are different?

Yet, to identify the Lenda terminology as a Crow-type, if it were the case, would be so simple. Significantly, there is also the old association between Crow and matriliny, no? Finally, if I cannot use the formal approach to the analysis of kinship, I shall have to raise the question, what are kin terms? Indeed, what are they? Are they solely terms of reference? I look forward to your response.

July 30, 1973
Dear Professor Justin:

I just finished reading Keesing's Chapter 7 from his book Kin Groups and Social Structure, which you included in the material you sent. But before you continue reading this letter, read the enclosed copy of my letter to Len.

Keesing draws the following diagram:

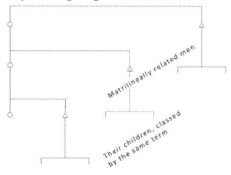

From Keesing (1975, p.115) – Crow Kin Classes

He then emphasizes (1975:114) that in a "Crow system a line of matrilineally related men are equated in reckoning kinship: usually it is the children of these men, who are actually classed by a single term."

There is something that is beginning to worry me. Why this emphasis on men? Why are men equated? What role do the women play in this whole business?

Allow me to be somewhat whimsical and ask you this? What does Lenda kinship mean? What are Lenda men and women all about? Why have we felt so certain, for so long, that there is something primary about men?

Does kinship, or does it not, have to do with reproduction? If kinship is about reproduction, if the Lenda believe that people ultimately originate from a common womb ifumu *and, finally, if they believe that those of one* mukowa *are of one blood (*mulopa*) or one substance that is inherited solely from one's mother, then does it not follow that women and not men are central to the Lenda system? If I am right, then the core relationship in the Lenda theory of relatedness (which terminologically resembles a Crow-type system) is centered on a woman, her siblings, and her offspring. Indeed, a woman equates her siblings with her offspring. Both are referred to as* mwaice *(perhaps best translated as the young of a womb). A woman, therefore, does not just equate men of a* mukowa; *she equates both sexes, as well as those of several generations, with one another.*

The elementary relationships of Lenda kinship might then be diagrammatically represented as follows:

Offspring are drawn under the female figure because children belong to their mother. Arrows indicate that a woman's offspring are equated with

her siblings. Squares are used for offspring and siblings to indicate indifference to gender distinctions in this context.

I have more questions than answers. If I am right, and I think I am, is succession more important than gender in certain contexts? Can we afford to ignore the role of women in kinship theory?

Frankly, I almost wish Len hadn't asked his kinship questions. As it is, I shall have to continue with this business, but for the next while I had better gather more economic data as CAIU will begin to wonder why they awarded me the grant.

For the next two weeks, I followed a rigorous routine. I rummaged through boxes of sales slips at Lakes Fisheries. Each morning I'd take a break and watch fishermen sell their fish. One had to be sure that they used the same name consistently. Then I'd return to the office and record the sales again. Toward evening we conducted intensive interviews. One interview per evening, each took so long.

At the end of this intense stretch of interviewing, Eneke arrived. He was simply there one day still trying to persuade me to spend more time with him. I refused.

"Why do you try?" I asked.

"Well," he said with some humor, "since we must know European ways, it is much more pleasant to learn them from a woman." We laughed.

Nevertheless, we sat for a while looking at the lake, the villages, and the houses. He was familiar with them. Through his eyes, and this is what I valued, I saw the starkness of the valley. It made me feel hollow inside. I realized that I saw the valley differently with each of these three friends. Paul showed me the valley's beauty, Mwewa its need for work, and Eneke its barrenness: illusion, reality, and deprivation. All were real, but I preferred Mwewa's view; he saw the work to be done. Nothing was ready for him. The valley and we were blind, struggling for vision, for realization of dreams of prosperity and wellbeing, for grace in living. In his recognition, he was closer to what I thought was real.

Miss Oddy's Painting

PART IV

WINDING UP

His biographers will tell how he went to draw water for the porter, but no one will know how he never gave his wife one moment's rest or one drop of water to his sick child …

This people accepted poverty, hunger, ill-treatment, disease, suffering and death with tranquil resignation. Some, in the direst circumstances, even looked happy. And few, in any event, thought of hanging themselves. Was it reason that helped them to bear the burden of their existence? Assuredly not.

Henri Troyat Tolstoy

Published in Stuttgart on the fifth of August 1950, the "Charter of German Refugees" states in conclusion: "We call upon human beings of goodwill to put their hands and minds to work so that from our guilt, affliction, suffering, poverty, and misery we may forge a better future."

Gunter Boddeker
Die Flüchtlinge

Copper sun sinking low
Scatterlings and fugitives
Hooded eyes and weary brows
Seek refuge in the night

Johnny Clegg
Scatterlings of Africa

16

THE SEVENTH-DAY
ADVENTIST MEETING

It was a week into August. The Seventh-day Adventist Camp meeting was upon us. Once again, the usual research was put aside as we concentrated on the meeting.

Mr. Chisaka was part of the festivities. He had lent members his truck to collect grass for the construction of a "grass tent." Now all grass shelters were in place, a big one for the general meeting and small ones for visitors from other villages. They expected 700–900 people.

I liked Chisaka more than many in the valley. His daring entrepreneurial spirit was admirable. He symbolized the right to one's individuality even in a traditional setting. When I handed Chisaka my gift for his wife and newborn baby he was very proud and commented that he was honored because it is better to receive than to give. His response sounded incongruent and I asked whether he had not muddled the saying which was, it is better to give than to receive? Now he was astonished and remarked that I was wrong. Giving is an everyday occurrence, so is receiving because of this giving. But to receive a gift, is to be honored.

He told me a story about an expatriate schoolteacher who had impregnated a Lenda woman and then left Zambia quite suddenly just before she gave birth. (I knew the man and remembered that he had been too ridden with fear to consider rational behavior, least of all any that might accord with

Lenda custom.) Chisaka commented that this teacher had not even left her a little money or any gift, nothing to honor her, no token of respect, and yet she was so proud of her child. Lenda men approached women with gifts to honor them.

We puzzled what shape the giving of gifts would take between men and women of different ethnic backgrounds. Would Zambian women ask for gifts and would they not look like crass materialists to those unfamiliar with Lenda custom? The Lenda seemed to spiritualize coitus through gift giving, just as we legitimize it through love and marriage.

When the conversation was exhausted, Mr. Chisaka mentioned that he had filmed me during the *mutomboko* ceremony. As he put it, he had "my energy on film." Apparently, my absorption in work and the rapidity with which I moved was a major source of local amusement.

Baptism

I was ready with my camera next morning. The colony of Seventh-day Adventists walked to Lake Tana where they would be baptized by immersion. I was in the water with the rest of them to take better photos. On the beach the crowd sang while evangelists repeated their incantations whenever initiates were immersed. As they emerged, novices were wrapped in blankets and led ashore. The most exciting events occurred on the Friday afternoon. A meeting to discuss marriage and family was on the agenda. The meeting was led by men who complained about disrespect of women towards husbands. (Conversations are transcribed from the tape).

"Women don't respect their husbands, that has to change," the evangelist said.

A woman stood up to talk. "You have your problem mixed up. Women respect persons who deserve respect. It is the behavior of men that must change."

She had barely finished when another woman rose to speak. "My husband has chosen to drink, to sit, and to sleep around. I look after my children. Do you think I can respect such a man? Change your men first and then ask us for respect."

The evangelist's face became serious. Perspiration dripped from his forehead. He wiped it off and said, "Yes, we sympathize with the complaints you women have against men. But women run off to their mothers and leave their husbands behind. They divorce quickly. You'll have to admit there are too many divorces."

Another woman stood up. She looked agitated. "We admit no such thing. To reduce divorce would be to enslave us. And you want to enslave us, admit it. But we will not be enslaved, not by the church, nor any man."

When the meeting was over women looked dejected. Yambana's mother told us that it was time to disjoin the church. I was surprised. Strong feelings from Yambana's mother, who seemed to live a peaceful life with her current husband, was unexpected. Reduced divorce meant becoming men's slaves because women would be unable to "throw out useless husbands," she explained.

She stood up and proudly walked away. In this instance, by being seemingly traditional, these older women were more modern than some of the young women. They valued their autonomy and individual freedom. They held fast to their position of non-dependence on men, a position which younger women were abandoning. Yambana elaborated that her mother is sending her father away because "he contributes nothing." She reminded me that her mother was strong because so far, she has persuaded both Yambana and her sister, though married, to stay with her.

I reflected that where Lenda women were concerned I was forever blind and surprised. Something is at stake here that I am missing.

Then there was the church. Its policies originated in the West. Although the local church hierarchy was black, the nature of the churches was hardly influenced by black fact. One had to admire local leaders for daring to debate which customs they would consider worthy of continuation and which not. And always the congregation was part of the debate.

It was ironic too that these women, by being aware of their interests, recognized the narrowness of the church. If they only knew it, if they could only articulate it, they were sowing the seeds of "black" theology. [As Steve Biko, the South African leader of the all-black South African Students' Organization (SASO) said, "a black theology does not challenge Christianity itself, but its Western package. It was necessary to discover what Christianity could mean for black Africa" (Woods, 1978). By 1970, Steve Biko was at the forefront of black politics in South Africa. I heard about him before I left for Zambia and heard even more of him in Zambia. He became popular news with his trial and death in 1977, two years after my last trip to Zambia.]

I could not but like these women. They have strength of conviction and the spunk to speak what they feel. They point to injustice openly. Indeed, women dare to protest more than men do.

There were other things to amaze even an anthropologist. First, there was in Lenda the combination of a strong individualism with yet an equally keen sense of communalism, a sharing to give everyone a chance to live with a sense of dignity. Some modern African leaders emphasize only the communal aspect in their doctrines of political liberation. And South African whites, or any whites threatened by black independence then, use these communalistic claims as evidence of black association with Communism. But there they are wrong. They forgot the other ingredient of communalism, which is lived in every African village, the keen sense of individualism, enterprise, and a sense of autonomy.

Secondly, in Lenda, kin ties did not suffocate individualism. In activities relating to production, trade, improvement of well-being, kinship furthered individualism, an individualism, however, that would benefit many others; not individualism for its own sake, but individualism for the sake of a community of people. It is as if the Lenda practiced what Sartre, unknown to them, preached; namely, when an individual chooses he chooses for the world. It is this latter aspect that has been lost in Western individualism, although Adam Smith thought it an unexpected consequence of competition and free enterprise. The African version of individualism, a pragmatic feature of everyday village life, sounds to us idealistic. Looking at the life cycle of some individual Western men, one sees an individualism largely lived for his own sake, although he likes to include his wife and children in his realm. Are we endangering our sense of responsibility?

Even here I have not properly grasped the individualism of the Lenda. Too much Western individualism is merely a matter of security realized through property; otherwise it has lost its sense of self. We do something to earn, to be praised by others, to be accepted by others, to be valued in the opinion of others. In our individualism, we flow with the tide. By contrast, a Lenda individualist goes against the stream, at least now. He knows that he will not get the praise from his kin, not, at least, in his daily work or his accomplishments. He will need the inner strength to ignore their witchcraft accusations, their accusations that his management of wealth is harming others. He will have to be a mountain of strength to resist their frequent begging. He will have to convince them with his very demeanor that he is immune to their clawing and threats. He will have learned to stand alone. No observer can miss him. What is surprising in the end is that he survives it all.

I remembered Mwewa's comments about his trips to Peking and Tokyo. He said that he truly admired what communism had done for China but he couldn't deny that his heart was with the freedom, even the decadence, which he experienced in Tokyo. He argued that Chinese type communism would be impossible in most parts of Africa because Africans are too individualistic within their forms of communalism. Perhaps that is why, when political coercion does take hold of an independent African country, it tends to assume the form of a military dictatorship. But my thoughts have taken me far from religion.

How would I ever adjust to life back home? Yet life is hard here and even monotonous.

It was the last evening of the camp meeting. My health was beginning to suffer. It was pointed out to me that I looked pale and tired. Yet I felt content. The tape recorder ran to record the last meeting.

A Malawian evangelist was being introduced. We sat up to listen more intently. His sermons were enjoyed by all. I heard his melodious voice read, "Enter ye in at the straight gate. For wide is the gate and broad is the way that leadeth to destruction. And many there be which enter by it. For straight is the gate and narrow is the way which leadeth unto life and few there be that find it. This is Jesus, pleading to his people," he said. My mind wandered momentarily and then I heard him repeat slowly: "There are two gates. Two ways. A wide gate and a narrow gate. A wide and straight road and a narrow road. This wide gate, this wide road, leadeth to destruction. But this narrow gate, this narrow road, leadeth to life."

His voice became more emphatic. The words were drawn out. The melody in his tone sounded enticing. And he repeated. "Narrow is the gate which leadeth to life. Each one has the privilege to choose to walk in the narrow way. But many choose the wide road. They like to choose easy things. I have trouble myself to walk in the narrow way." "Narrow way!" "*Ishila iyatota.*" "Leads to life!" "*Itungulula umweo.*"

The Lenda translation embraced his sermon with a cloak of splendor and magnificence. I looked at the sea of black faces and warm brown eyes. My glance took in the shelter and relaxed in the soft glow of Tilley lamps. An aura of spirituality, greater than that of any sect, pervaded the atmosphere. And all felt it. I heard nothing for a long time.

And then the sermon was over. Someone else spoke. The Malawian evangelist stood up again and signaled his desire to speak.

"Before I leave, ehh, I must also remember to, ehh, to show my appreciation for our European sister." He spoke haltingly. The laughter of the audience recalled me to the present. Someone explained that I was a researcher, no appreciation was necessary. But he smiled and said "No, no, no, I understand all that."

He continued, "I have enjoyed very much, you see, her presence. She has attended most of all the meetings. It is a very wonderful thing. I know that we have several missionaries here and several other Europeans here at the secondary school, but she is the only one who has offered herself to come and meet with us. And her life," "*Umweo uakwe*," "the way she has presented herself in this meeting. I hope to say that she must be a Christian of another denomination." He paused and said emphatically, "I don't know! But she shows that she's a Christian. There is really a wonderful life in her." The audience laughed gently as did I. "I don't know how long you are going to stay here. But before you leave Zambia to go home, we ask you to visit Malawi."

I was touched. I stood up, tried to prevent my emotions from running over, and could not. "I would like to say something." My voice shook and words were not completed. "I would like to say that it's not you who should th . . ., should thank me, but rather that I should thank you, for having made me feel welcome at this camp meeting."

My neighbor said, "Mm, mm, nice."

"Thank you very much." The evangelist raised his voice above the murmurs of the audience.

"Amen," the membership responded.

"I like, you see, the special attitude you have about Africans," the evangelist ended haltingly.

I smiled at that remark, and the congregation broke into delightful laughter. A kind of merriment ensued for some minutes until the meeting was ended with a prayer.

The experience left me with a sense of paradox. It felt as if the very spirituality of these people was generated by their sensuality, as if their sensual existence produced it. Indeed, it is the very sensual life in this valley that is the power behind this transfiguration into mind and spirit. It is not suppression of the senses that creates cerebration. It is rather one's receptivity that transfigures a happening into pure thought. It seemed to me that no denial of sex, no abhorrence of it, no abstinence from it, could possibly create the ascetic atmosphere pervading this setting. The reverse is the case, the very presence of an all too physical world powered this spirituality, as if the senses directed worshippers to heed transcendence.

For the first time, I became fully aware of these people and of my own being. It was humbling. My knees felt weak. Physical exhaustion contributed to my feeling emotional. The Lenda noted my preoccupation and obvious feeling. I was overwhelmed simultaneously by a deep sadness and extraordinary joy.

Next morning, I stood in front of Van Gella's office, this time as a patient. It did not take long to discover that I was indeed suffering from malaria.

Upon completion of the examination, I described to Van Gella the irony of a researcher being thanked for her attendance at the camp meeting when some of the expatriate schoolteachers, who taught local children, might have appeared. I also admitted that, following the camp meeting, I was compelled to suspend my usual dislike of the spread of Christianity. I claimed that the Lenda were turning Christianity into something of their own, powered by their own experience of life. All this was said with tears in my eyes. When Hans showed concern, I assured him it was merely fever.

In the car, I leaned my head against the steering wheel. Tears rolled down my cheeks. "What the hell," I muttered, "sometimes women weep; we're stronger because of it." I laughed, wept, and laughed at myself. It occurred to me that I didn't know why I was crying. And then I thought, woman, stop that lie. You cry for the hurt of it, the pain of the world. Your body feels anguish. You've been overwhelmed.

My brain was beginning to fry. Water was needed, nothing else.

Comment 1982

By now, I already had a considerable amount of data about Lenda Christianity. These data consisted not only of many transcribed and described sermons and services. Questionnaires, especially, revealed the primary concern of the Lenda with salvation. In-depth interviews with leaders and members, as well as impromptu discussions, showed how effectively these Lenda were beginning to Africanize Christianity.

Two things stood out from the data and my experiences. First, I learned that Lenda preoccupation with salvation meant, in effect, that many of them rejected the present world and circumstances, which they saw as chaotic, and desired to participate in a better one. In other words, how they envisioned their future affected their behavior in the here and now, and it resulted in a selected and differentiated assignment of meaning to present and past times.

Second, while both men and women shared many Christian views, it was clearly the case that women were far more critical of church doctrine and practice than men were. Women knew that within the church many more advantages accrued to men. Their criticism of these advantages ensured that the status of husbands as heads of nuclear families would be precarious even under the protective umbrella of the church. While it appeared as if women shared the same interest in Protestant teachings as did men, in fact, most women did not give up their adherence to matrilineal ideology. Indeed, once they were past their child rearing years, many left the church altogether or attended only, in their words, "to leave all options open for a safe and better life after death." The assumption of life after death has its origin in their own kin-based ideology. Furthermore, when lives are short, as they were here, thinking about the beyond makes sense.

Given the Lenda attitude toward salvation and the frequently reiterated claim on the part of men that their women were out of control, I wondered whether my impression that many of them glorified the past was true.

Many recent researchers, like Schuster (1979) work uncritically with the assumption that relations between the sexes have deteriorated and that colonial practices have somehow contributed to the breakdown of more stable family units. Nothing could be further from the truth. I suspect that Lenda comments such as the women are out of control, or their habit of telling dismal stories about their marriages and idealizing the "supposed" stability of Western marriages, are attitudes they have adopted toward, and for the sake of, the European. As far back as the early 1800s when colonial officers were still flabbergasted by distinctive Lenda customs, they wrote into their District Notebooks such things as, I must remind the chief to remind his men to control their women. Colonial officers openly bemoaned the power of "mothers-in-law" and of women generally (for similar conclusions see Rattray, 1923; Lee, 1978; Okonjo, 1976; Van Allen, 1972, 1976; and so on).

No, Lenda attitudes toward, and conceptions of, past, present, and future are representations or folk theories that envision their own idiosyncratic engagement in the world. They are interpretations of their history. Just as Native Americans first reconstructed their history in which the past was glorious, the present disorganized, and the future acculturative, in just that manner have the Lenda reconstructed their history. Only the Native American now interprets his history differently. In accordance with his new projects or new vision of engagement in the world, he now reinterprets his past with the concept of "exploitation," his present with that of "resistance," and his future with that of "ethnic resurgence." In accordance with the precepts of existentialism, the future pervades both the present and the past. Once the Lenda drop the habit of idealizing the West, they too will envision a new future and thereby assign new meaning to their present and past—and so will their ethnographers.

Comment 2018

Many years later, starting with this experience but after my archival research on the development of National Socialism in Germany, I came to recognize the importance of the Christian faith and like C.S. Lewis was surprised by joy. In doing so, I followed in the footsteps of anthropologists like Evans-Pritchard, Mary Douglas, and Victor Turner. Later too, I discovered that Bob had followed a similar route.

17

ILLNESS AND INSIGHTS

At the rest house, I sank into bed. I had a high fever and heard continuous conversation. Yambana reconstructed part of our jabbering as follows. She said it started with my puzzlement about the strength of character of Lenda women but with their simultaneous sense of racial inferiority and the repetition of words like "suffering" and "slaves."

"You remember those women in the rice field, don't you? What did they say?" (Yambana)

"Has that to do with their strength?" (I)

"It has to do with their weakness." (Yambana)

"Why? What weakness?" (I)

"They are black." (Yambana)

"Strong as women, weak as blacks?" (I)

"Remember?" (Yambana)

"Yes. One said that God must have hated black people. He must have wanted them to be slaves. Why else would he make them work so hard?" Then the other one said, "It is true, blacks are truly the descendants of Ham. Do you ever see whites work?"

"Stop it," I told them. I remember now, that is the second time I lost my temper. "Stop it. You may not see whites work in Zambia, but, by heaven, they sure work at home."

"You lost your temper before?" Yambana asked.

"Yes. Remember? Those eyes. Fish eyes. I was so hungry, so hungry. We had six large breams. You cooked them and then you brought me the head. 'What is this?' I snapped. 'The head,' you said. 'Eyes, for heaven's sake. Take it all back. I want fish. Fish! The whole thing, not its head. What is there to eat of this ugly thing? For Heaven's sake take it back.'"

"The fish head was brought to honor you." (Yambana)

I sighed … "There can't be any honoring of me. Water. That's what I want. Water. My brain will fry and that is all I have."

"Are you feeling better?" Yambana asked during my more alert moments. "Oh, but this valley sickens and kills," she reminded me.

Feeling strong enough to read, but not strong enough to interview, I read field notes and reviewed some of our questionnaires. I had to address two problems: (1) the tension between men and women or, what amounts to the same thing, kinship and politics here; and (2) the conceptual issues of my mentors back home. So, I jotted down some thoughts.

I am beginning to feel that one cannot understand women without understanding men and vice versa. The sole focus on women by some ethnographers is political. Theoretically, it makes for a sterile pursuit. It is not women we need to understand, but the logic of male-female interaction. Like Mead, whose suggestions seem not to have been pursued seriously, I can conceive distinct cultural patterns of male-female interaction. For example, ours differs from that of Lenda. Like Schneider, however, I think that male-female interaction should be treated as a cultural system. One then asks of what cultural categories such a system consists? And how these categories inform behavior? The focus is on the relationality between men and women; the analysis is cultural or rather socio-cultural and the categories are theirs not ours.

Clearly, men and women are differently valued in diverse cultures. In some cultures, manhood or fatherhood may be the central symbol, in others it may be womanhood or motherhood. Other symbols fall into place according to some hierarchy of values the nature of which the researcher would somehow have to discover. It is undeniable that one of the symbols epitomizing Western cultures is man. It is noticeable in our languages, families, political and economic structures, in short, it is there in everyday behavior.

Yambana took me out of the world of ideas.

"About Lenda women," she said, "birth is our department. Usually women welcome pregnancy because we want children. It's children we welcome, pregnancy goes with it. Yet that pain gives us power: it is power. In addition, we women know how to abort when the pregnancy is unwelcome, and women help others give birth. Some die. You have seen for yourself that birth here is not easy. Some women try for days until they are exhausted. Finally, they are taken to the clinic or hospital. Often it is too late."

I remembered the lifts we gave pregnant women. It was after I observed one transported to a clinic on a platform suspended between four bicycles. She looked emaciated. Indeed, she seemed to consist solely of skin and bones but for the fetus in her womb. She died on arrival at the hospital. There was a happier case. She too was given a lift. Her husband begged for a ride. "The women have tried for seven days with this birth. My wife is exhausted, can you give us a lift?" he stammered. We rushed for the car. Kin held the woman in the back seat. I am still haunted by her moaning. In the hospital, she gave birth and both lived. How exhausted she looked. Birth is supposed to be easy; too frequently, it is not easy at all. Too many women die of it. Another romantic myth destroyed.

"But here is the point," Yambana said, "white doctors are taking over. Missionaries step in. You remember the storm those missionaries kicked up when they discovered a case of infanticide. The young girl was so desperate. Pregnant by the principal who, as a government employee, was to be a nuclear family man, he scared her into silence. She did not seek the advice of older women. She wanted her schooling, not a child. Then she committed a desperate act, but they discovered her bleeding. Giving birth by herself, she could not get the placenta expelled. She had already killed the infant. Poor child, she was hysterical when the wrath of those missionaries descended upon her. What business was it of theirs? Oh, we try to avoid the hospital as long as we can."

I remembered. She had given birth and killed the infant upon emission. Medical personnel found out it was infanticide. For them, it had probably something to do with the recent Termination of Pregnancy Act of 13 October 1972. But, of course, what the young student needed was compassion. Only, the law makes remaining silent illegal.

My focus was not infanticide; it was enough to research the struggle of survival in this valley. The promise that a father-to-be would assume responsibility for the child and, beyond that, for the mother carried no weight here.

Given my anthropological bias, I was inclined to blame missionaries. But of course, I was wrong. Whatever their belief, once in the hospital they had to treat the teen in accordance with Zambian law. Whatever human shortcomings missionaries might share with the rest of us, they did considerable good: they looked after the blind; many healed the sick medically; some women missionaries ran hospitals alone; others translated biblical stories not only into Lenda but also into Braille. Whatever their frustrations with local people and conditions, they ventured where most others would not go and helped where others did nothing.

Lenda women ought to become physicians. They are becoming nurses instead; a few lucky ones who get even that much support. The day will come, perhaps it is already there, when even birth is no longer a woman's domain.

Be that as it may, Lenda life centers on women. Lenda philosophy of procreation, the importance of womb as the symbol of their society, the economic strength of women, indicate that male-female relations in the valley are significantly different from ours.

Unlike some parts of Africa, the Lenda do not have "female" husbands because marriage is not primary. But they have a version of what one might call female father and male mother roles. A female "father" is a senior woman of a line of women who heads a household, which includes married brothers and sisters as well as their respective spouses. Although rare, this "powerful" woman controls the economic resources: field assignments, village houses, often fishing-gear, and bars. She frequently starts small trading ventures for her brothers, sisters, brother's children, and even for a sister's husband if their marriage is stable. When its declensions are studied, one sees the notion of "masculine mother" in the term *yama*, but to postulate a dual sexuality is going too far. Emphasis is on her position within clan and family and her functions *vis-à-vis* other kin.

For example, ego's maternal uncle is called *nalume*. *Na* means mother of, *lume* means male. It means that, in certain contexts, a young man's mother is in a similar relationship to her son as to her brother, making those two men brothers of one another. I became aware of two men calling one another "brother" in a matri-focal family situation, only to hear them calling one another "uncle, nephew" at the funeral in a matri-clan situation. Another example is the Lenda term, *mulume*, which is usually translated as husband. But as I soon learned, to translate *mulume* as husband is to insist upon the existence of a husband-like social role when the term is only used by a woman, for example, toward a human being of male anatomy. Instead of husband or wife the Lenda use the gender-neutral concept *muka*, spouse.

My musings were interrupted with the arrival of mail. Since Len Rediens' brief note is about the same topic, I reproduce it here.

August 21, 1973
Touson
Dear Karla:

A brief note in reply to your letter of July 30. It seems to me you are onto something. By definition, a typology cannot be context-dependent. If kin terms are dependent on context then you are dealing with one kind of meaning. It is, therefore, the meaning of kin terms that need exploration. Continue.

Yours with best wishes,
Len Rediens

Further Reflections About Kinship

Schneider has always argued that one must discover what the native cultural categories are of a cultural system. If kinship were a cultural system or an ideology, then why would we think that only terms like *mukowa*, *cikota*, and *ulupwa* are cultural categories? What exactly are cultural categories? They are the same thing as "their" ideas. Scheffler (1972) and Lounsbury (1964), for example, treated kin terms as if they were linguistic signs used to point to an object. This may be a caveman view of seeing things, e.g., "me mother, you father." Did kin terms originate because human beings needed a linguistic sign to point to a human object? Improbable. Human beings, living, dying, giving birth are simply not objects as stones are objects. Therefore, what if kin terms and terms like *mukowa*, and so on, are not signs but native concepts and, therefore, part of their theories about, or worldview constructions of, the origin and nature of human beings?

Let us assume that kin terms are their concepts, not universal categories. A concept cannot be understood apart from its theory. Hence, native concepts, which I just said kin terms are, must be understood in terms of native theory. That means that native theory of some sort (perhaps, in Lenda, it is their theory of procreation, heredity, and gestation) must tell us the significance, meaning, and use of kin terms. *Denotata*, what the philosopher Wittgenstein calls ostentatious meaning, would be of secondary importance, and to base *significata* on universal biological and genealogical variables (generation, sex, degree of collaterally etc.) would be wrong. The primary meaning of kin terms, I think, must be derived from native theories in which kin terms are the constituent concepts. Such native theories are probably ones about the production and reproduction of human beings. They will tell us something about their, not our, notions of relationality.

When researching kin terms, I remind myself to not merely ask "what do you call so and so?" Rather, I try to discover first how the Lenda themselves think people are related; how they think people originated; what their theory of reproduction is, and so on? What I did so far, by contrast, is more like the following: I arrived in the villages and wanted to know (implicitly, if not explicitly), who is ego's father, mother, brother, and so on. In other words, I assumed a mother, father, brother, sister, for example, when none need have been there or when they might have meant something quite different from what they mean to us. We look for families and therefore find them. But need one exist at all?

What I am saying is, to some extent, old hat. For example, Griaule and Dieterlen, writing in 1954, recorded how, among the Dogon, owing to their theory of human origin, a son is identified with is mother; he is his mother. But each human soul has two spiritual principles of opposite sex. Hence, this son may be the mother herself or he may be her brother and therefore a substitute for the maternal uncle. All this theorizing is reflected in the kinship terms the Dogon used. Funny how these old works have become ignored under the flourish of American theorizing and our assumption of being a science.

Excited by my thoughts, I did what I always do. I wrote mother. Whether she would understand everything, did not matter. These letters were an extension of my Diary. I used them to express spontaneously frustrations, joys, or intuitions—anything informal and immediate to be used or discarded later.

August 31, 1973
Darling Mama:

I am quite excited about something. It's like a discovery. What's exciting is that Lenda kinship appears to be filled with female symbols. I can hardly believe it and maybe none of the men on my committee will either. But there it is. Listen to this:

The overarching Lenda symbol, it seems to me, is ifumu *or womb. It seems to stand for the Lenda universe. Under it is the* mukowa, *which we translate as clan, but which means "all those of one blood." The Lenda universe is made up of several clans.* Mukowa *is also always associated with a distant place of origin. Then there is the* cikota *which literally means big female. Cunnison took the term to mean matrilineage. The term is associated with all the descendants of one woman of a nearby place.*

Finally, we come to individuals. I was blind to some of the meanings of kin terms because they change depending on the declension used and on social context; for example, my mother is mayo, *thy mother is* noko *and so on.*

Working with this material, I find that I can best make my point by using the pronoun thy (your sing.). It allows me to bring out the sexual symmetry, with, however, a slight bias in favor of women. Here it is. Look at the native term and its meaning which is here written in brackets.

thy grandmother nokokulu *(literally, mother of bigness)*	*thy grandfather* sokulu *(literally, father of bigness)*
thy mother noko	*thy father* wiso
thy maternal uncle or mother's brother nokolume *(mother of male anatomy or male mother)**	*thy paternal uncle or father's brother* wiso (mwaice) *(father of youngness or junior father)*

thy maternal aunt or mother's sister	*thy paternal aunt or father's sister*
noko (mwaice)	nokosenge
(mother of youngness or junior mother)	*(mother of courting or courting mother)**

*Maternal uncle (to whom the Lenda refer as male mother), and father's sister (to whom Lendans refer as courting mother), are asterisked because here the symbolic bias toward women is greatest. Oberg (1938) who studied the Bairu and Bahima of Uganda back in the nineteen-thirties found a very balanced (bilateral) system among the cultivating Bairu and a male biased system among the pastoral Bahima. Among the Bairu, mother's brother is male mother and father's sister is female father. Notice, by the way, the implied separation between anatomical sex and social role. You know, Mama, anthropologists talk about sex being part of kin terms but perhaps, do not distinguish adequately biology from social status. Thus the term "male mother" (*nokolume*) simply indicates that in this case, a man assumes the social position or responsibilities of "mother." In other words, both biology and social status are subsumed under one word.*

In Lenda another fascinating thing occurs. Offspring of a woman become, for certain purposes, identified with her siblings because they are all the same blood or the same "biological" make up. It means that a boy could call his maternal uncle, "male mother", respecting generational difference when circumstances require it or, alternatively, he could call him wesu *(brother or ours as in same blood), ignoring generational difference when these are unnecessary during meetings or transactions. In Lenda, instead of genes one talks about heritable substance. Thus, in some contexts, a mother is also a sibling to her children.*

Didn't I always say that you were more a sister to me? Well, the Lenda would understand my feeling.

The reason, by the way, that I say, "mother of" is because, in Lenda, people are always mother of someone, owner of something, and so on. I am still a little puzzled about the term nokosenge, *courting mother. All I can say about* nokosenge *is what Banachile taught me. She said that to her face she called her father's sister,* mayo. Mayo *is endearing; it implies a warm, healthy relationship.* Mayosenge *implies distance and authority. To be funny, one reason for calling father's sister courting mother (*senga *means to court, flatter, cajole) is because she frequently heads the household and has considerable say over her brother's wife and children when the latter live, as they sometimes do, within her compound. In the case of Banachile, it was the* mayosenge *(FZ) who headed the compound, parceled out land and houses. One had to flatter her or else. You remember, this is the woman who threw me out of the village. I'm a poor flatterer. Seriously, at the time I did not give that woman the respect she deserved. I was too ignorant.*

I've just overcome a malaria attack, which has put me into a somewhat reflective mood. Let me, therefore, pass on a few rather personal, perhaps confused thoughts.

You see, Mam, I have just re-read some of Bob's letters. Something about them bothers me, perhaps because everything about the West looks suspect from this part of the globe.

Didn't you once tell me that Bob exercised an "unseemly control" over me? I know now that his letters, while I genuinely needed them Mam, were part of what caged me in back there in Lusaka, as if his grip extended across the ocean. Maybe it was the fever, but just lately, every time I see the words "love you" they turn into "own you." Does Bob want me to succeed for myself or for him? What I'm really saying is, does he understand that I am this work? I doubt that I would have ever asked this question had I not come to Zambia. Do married women ever succeed for themselves back home or just for their husbands? Do women succeed the way men succeed, simply because success is good, involvement in one's work is good not only for the family but also and especially for the broader society. I'm beginning to feel that Bob would only let me succeed to the extent that my success would bring "glory" to him. And I fear it won't you see. It would make that marriage conditional on my continuous success. How could I possibly live up to that?

You always disliked what you called his commanding nature. Back home his "commands" rolled off my back, as it were. Now I'm wondering whether his need to command others and my need to be in command of my life aren't contradictory. In the past, all this wasn't important. Maybe I even felt a bit flattered that he would possess me, as it were. After all, he was for the most part unobtrusive about it, and the whole business was part of the logic of our, as of our friends, relationship. In short, I am full of doubt. It seems that the more I understand the Lenda, the less satisfied I become with the West.

Perhaps my only worry is that I may want the content of our love to change; question is, will this be possible? It all depends on whether Bob accepted our separation because he valued my wholeness and because he did not want a wife to whom he would be the only reason for her existence. But I suspect neither he nor I were that clear about everything. It was purely a matter of our knowing that I had to go, which means, perhaps, that our future will witness marital problems or dissolution. In the meantime, I'm still here.

Comment 1982

I said that the purpose of my research was to examine the nature of the relationships among religion, kinship, and economic activities. Despite seeming confusions and many interruptions the goal that was taken to the field never relinquished its control over my research actions. What the exact nature of the interrelationship between religion, kinship and economy was and meant, I could not know in the field. It required analysis back home after the data were ordered and distance was restored. Important is that in Lenda nature is what it is in an obvious sense. Words are rooted in it. Which is not to say that they are not also rooted in mental scheming, action, and relational contexts adding to the realm of nature that of ideas and society.

The following month, September, I would organize my assistants so that we could gather, as systematically as possible, quantitative data about Lenda economic activities.

Comment 2018

At the time of my research, rural Zambian behavior and thought was still guided noticeably by kin-based relationship structures. Laura Bohannan's (1966) article, "Shakespeare in the Bush" underlines this point and two others that we in the West have tried to water down or make fluid: I mean, specific cultural notions of relationships between generations and between men and women. Although intellectuals and susceptible politicians as well as the fashion-conscious media, including myself at the time, worked hard to minimize them, there were, and still are, significant cultural differences in these matters across the world and within our own societies. It would take, I think, a painful structural cognitive break-down to change this.

For example, to work me into the matrifocal family structure of my assistants in Zambia did not work for me. Among other things, it would have seriously limited the scope of my research. It would also have given more leeway to subject my behavior to interpretations from the perspective of their worldview, and that would have led inevitably to frequent, I dare say repeated, disappoints on their part.

Furthermore, reviewing what happened more than forty years ago from the vantage point of hindsight and given my strategy based on Sartre's philosophy, I recognize that, despite the importance of women, without some sort of relationship with men in that specific field situation, nothing would have been possible. In other words, research that requires reason, as well as the heart, imagination, and affection of the researcher—his or her whole person—will *also* involve affective ties. And that may include romantic ones, although many people outside of the situation will regard it as wrong or sinful.

Indeed, that too is my *moral* judgement now of my behavior then. Where I differ, is that I cannot deny the reality of such happenings nor, where they are based on the surprise of love, their positive consequences of opening a view of the immediate world around and beyond oneself. As Kulick points out, these experiences too are "epistemologically productive" (1995:20); further, more than one person matures in the process. And yes, as human beings we must be allowed to make mistakes, admit them, learn from them, gain some wisdom, and record them for future generations. Let him that is without sin cast the first stone (John 8:7).

18

FROM ECONOMIC DATA TO A FUNERARY EXPERIENCE

August came to an end and September slipped by almost unnoticed. I worked every day including weekends. Every sales slip for the last three and a half years had been examined and recorded. Efforts to calculate production costs were succeeding. Finally, with each intensive interview I came to see more clearly the cognitive maps, which guided the behavior of Lendans.

I moved with ease among the people. First, there was the long greeting. It started with "*Muapoleeni, mukwai.*" The *eeni* and *mukwai* were drawn out, slow and melodious, with a lowered voice. I'd curtsey and clap three times and so would they. Respect was established and conversation began. And then we'd walk off in different directions.

Sometimes older men, or poor men would seek me out and insist that I interview them. They knew the history of the fish trade, or the history of certain customs, or they wanted their poverty recorded. The poor were most troublesome. I'd have to coax them not to exaggerate their poverty, for I could not save them from it.

I discovered that several middle-aged men lived alone. They cooked for themselves. Sometimes sisters would cook for them. Men who were Jehovah's Witnesses, especially, tended toward bachelorhood. Women couldn't be controlled, some felt, and would break men's Christian habits and beliefs. Some male Jehovah's Witnesses feared women's adultery.

Sometimes we would walk through the fields and casually discuss various affairs of life and work with those we met. Twice now, I came upon a male and female pair clearing a field together. It was hot, and men and women's bodies from the waist up were bare. Upon seeing me, the women would cover themselves and explain that the men with them were their brothers. It didn't occur to them that it was not their partial nudity, but their nudity in the presence of their brothers, that interested me. It was I, not their brother that made them shy. In front of whites one dressed, you see. What pleased me was the comradery between these men and women.

And then my research would become regimented again as I organized four assistants to record what people bought from various stores and how much money was taken in. One couldn't very well go through the books of these "large" business men and women, although one of them showed me his. But they agreed to have assistants in their stores all day to record what people bought and how much they paid. Four assistants spent a week each in different stores. Then they changed stores among themselves. This circulation continued for two months. Off and on, they'd do it throughout my time in the valley. Assistants changed stores not only to break possible boredom but also to enhance accuracy.

In the meantime, I learned the various arrangements fishermen made to store and sell their fish independently of Lakes Fisheries. Some things were learned through conversation. The arrangements to transfer fish from boat to home, to middlemen, to various district capitals of Lenda and even to Niassa Province would then be checked empirically. Here too the car was useful. I followed fishermen on their tours, hence my frequent travel.

The hardest things to record were the casual transactions. A fisherman's workers would take a few bundles of fish and hide them among the reeds before landing. The owner of the operation would usually meet his men some distance from the water. Some fish would be given away as presents, some as rations to workers who had already taken a few, some sold to friends, the rest sold to Indeco, or taken home to be stored and sold in other parts of the valley. There were the peddling traders who sold a few fish from door to door in one village. Then there were bicycle traders who sold fish among different villages 15 to 30 km apart. Finally, there were lorry traders who bought substantial amounts of fish to be sold in Niassa Province, or at the Industrial Belt. Some fish and cassava was sold in Zangava. Bicycle traders bought and sold fresh fish. Lorry traders bought and sold both fresh and sun-dried or smoked fish. Further south along the river valley, fish was both sold and bartered for firewood and cassava.

Fishing in the lagoons and river required different adjustments of fishermen. They too had dual homes; grass huts on islands from which they fished and where they lived several months of the year, and mud brick huts in villages along the shore. Wives spent most of the time in the villages tending their fields to the east of them. Husbands remained on islands catching, drying, and selling fish. In the river valley, malaria and bilharzia occurred more frequently, and I became aware of several deaths.

Each morning an assistant and I stood on selected spots near the river. First, we interviewed traders who came to buy. We usually had to wait between one and two hours before the fishermen's boats arrived, which gave us ample time for interviews. Then, we would be terribly busy checking loads and change of money, firewood, and cassava. Following these maneuvers, we'd interview the fishermen, especially those who lived on islands in the river. Finally, we'd canoe to the islands with fishermen to see with our own eyes and to record how much fish was caught, sun-dried, and sold to traders who were frequently women. In other words, we recorded how much fish never reached the shores because their prices were controlled and relatively low. The amount of fish sold on the east river shore was strictly commensurate with the amount of pocket money fishermen needed to buy immediate supplies in local stores. No doubt, they also intended these transactions to pacify UNIP officials who were to ensure that some fish was sold locally at controlled prices.

Voluminous field notes were collected covering everything; earnings, production costs, life histories, short interviews, kinship, sermons, church events, company charts and maps of housing arrangements. During September, I also prepared to understand the local schedule for beer brewing and selling. Preparation and fermentation took about 6 or 7 days. Women coordinated their various activities. One had to understand the labor coordination of brewers to calculate each woman's earnings.

Making the Coffin at a Funeral

Funerals became more obvious and I reminded myself to observe them. Women's wailing announced death. Sometimes a corpse might be transported from clinic to village, and the body is always returned to the village of birth. News spread quickly, relatives and kin arrive if they hadn't already. Men would collect wood for the night's bonfire and food preparation. Sometimes there would be several hundred mourners grieving the death. Throughout the night, the corpse would lie in full view among its last guests. Next morning it was taken into a hut. Hammering started. A coffin was made. Its preparation might take seven hours. Wood was hard in this part of the world.

On one occasion, a burial was delayed until the deceased woman's son arrived. The coffin lid was taken into the house. And then uproar spread through the crowd. The lid didn't fit. They had waited too long. The corpse had expanded. It was humid and hot, and the smell of putrefaction lay heavy in the air.

But usually nature was merciful. Lives were taken towards evening during the season when it was hot and dry. Women would wail and recite the deceased's history, and the deceased's identity was assumed by a person succeeding him or her. Only the body decomposed into nothing.

If I describe the following night in more detail than usual it is because it aroused painful memories. It was cool and peaceful. We were gathered around the bonfire. Its light played on the impassive face of a dead man. Each deliberate gesture of mourners engraved itself on my brain. The sound of their lamentations took me miles away. Sad tones of a dirge chilled my bones.

My mind wandered through the past to that house and those people gathered there to attend a wedding. I heard him say "I do," but couldn't decide whether it carried conviction. If only I knew why we married, my life might be so much clearer to me. We are living a lie, and I can't detect what it is. My eyes rest on the corpse where the flame creates the illusion of movement. Why did we marry? And who asked whom? It simply came about: that was our trouble right there. Perhaps, the emotional chaos was too great, and marriage was a convenient way to contain it. Perhaps, each fell in love with the other's anthropology.

Students arranged the wedding. The Dean of Arts and Science, who was also a chaplain, married us. I was "given away" by the department chairman. It was an abstract marriage. Abstracted from family, from our past, from any future. Lost in a haze was the name of the man in whose house we were married. I remembered, though, that he majored in anthropology. I hid in the den, listening to a funeral dirge, mourning my inability to know what I was doing or why. The chaplain came to fetch me. He looked anxious and urged that the ceremony commence. People were becoming intoxicated and might forget the purpose of this event. He expected, no doubt, imminent disintegration.

I remember marveling that Bob's ring fit his finger. He hadn't tried it before. A colleague of Bob's drove me to an Indian reserve where we had the rings made. When I placed Bob's ring on his finger a triangular piece of turquoise fell to the floor. The Indian had warned us this might happen, but I had insisted on a triangular pattern. And now the ring was broken, as if to confirm that the impossible couldn't last.

Flames licked the sky. I watched them desiccate and sear the air and then lose courage and cower and lurch near their logs. Wailing throbbed on and on until it blunted the hurt. And the corpse lay in our midst, more real than hundreds of people surrounding it. An eerie night it was, convincing enough to believe that the spirit left its body for another place. We sat, wrapped in blankets, in deep communion with eternity. And the bonfire threw long shadows across the ground, and the wailing of them, and the songs of them, lifted me out of myself. A Lenda funeral is a transition much greater than any wedding. That too was appropriate. Something substantial had happened. The change of that body was permanent. Their philosophy gave it meaning. A true transition it was, not at all like their wedding. But then the Lenda were wise. They knew a wedding couldn't be a transition. By contrast, a funeral was different; the transition was real not imagined.

Our wedding was based on self-deception. It was based on my assumption that I could somehow efface my past from memory. I believed that one could move mountains. Nothing was inevitable, nothing must be accepted. It could all be changed if only I applied myself.

But I remember those crippled men after the war, dismembered in body and mind, defeated in spirit, in life resigned. Their eloquence was diminished to the dull thud of canes, their beauty disfigured by dirty bandages and severed limbs. And part of their disfiguration was inside of me. It sat there, immobile, held in place by a heavy guilt, hidden behind an impenetrable silence.

Every American stereotypic conception of anything German was an accusation. Each stereotypic praise of the German character was an embarrassment, and more, an indictment: German efficiency was, German military prowess was, German intelligence was, German art was, German technology was, German ingenuity was, German rationality was. Anything seen as praiseworthy by Americans became an indictment. Worse still, I suffered from a sense of dissonance. Which child ever experienced its mother as efficient? Rubble in streets, feces in pails, thick moldy smells lingering in bunkers, shrapnel caught in steel foot mats, was this order? When we cleaned up the evidence of an all too familiar destruction and felt empathy for one another's aching muscles and read long stories from the pain written in our faces; when our mothers bathed us, and instilled in us the courage and caring to go on another day, and read us *Märchen* (fairy tales); were these behaviors mere manifestations of efficiency?

I was furious that I had to learn from Canadians and Americans who my countrymen were, who "Jews" were, what the magic was behind six million. I'd go through periods hating my mother for seemingly having deceived me, wishing she were dead. And then I would look at her and see that her suffering was worse than mine. At times, I would ask questions, first cautiously, not for her sake, but for mine, for the sake of one digestible answer—one answer at a time. Soon these sessions turned into interrogations. It was cruel and useless. I would always receive the same answer, "You don't know what it was like when it started. You don't know." Nor did I want to know, not from mother. What mother said was at any rate too different from what people said, what texts said, what Bob said. Can the guilty speak the truth or can they merely justify? And was her guilt handed to her second hand or was it the guilt of spineless women who fled with their children to refugee camps while men fought wars to make room for women's power of reproduction? And was all this inevitable?

I gave it up, immersed myself in my studies, and learned poetry and history of a new land. Much later, I married an American, not to produce children, not to form a family, but to escape my past and pursue a profession.

Comment 2018

In fact, far from escaping my past I confronted it. But that would happen two decades later when I determined to end field work in Africa and start archival research in Germany. But that is another story. Important here is to note one fact: the simple, natural fusion of *my* wedding with *their* funeral.

19

RETURN TO LUSAKA, RETURN TO NZUBUKA

It was mid-October and time to return to Lusaka. My second report was due and I wanted to write it in a sumptuous atmosphere offering steak and wine. This last stretch had been tiring if also gratifying. Research had gone well, but food remained a problem.

I drove through Mboua without stopping. Neither Eneke nor Mwewa were on my mind. Instead, I was puzzling about the incipient class differentiation in the valley. The mention of classes was not welcomed in Zambia, and yet differences in wealth and vested interests existed. Earnings from Lakes Fisheries seemed small. If fishermen did not have additional earnings, as they do, they would be in debt. Clearly, production costs often exceeded earnings from sales to Lake Fisheries, and this discrepancy inspired me to do a bit of detective work to discover how fish were sold privately. The imaginative ways in which fishermen augmented their earnings were admirable. It would be a mistake, in my opinion, to stamp out this individualism and initiative in the name of a socialism which seemed more appropriate for urban than rural workers. Before I arrived at the Zangavan border, I stopped, wrote down some of my thoughts, and continued my journey.

The Zangavan border looked deserted. I walked with considerable dread to the customs building. The official's face looked mean and wrinkled. Others quickly joined him. As usual, they took their time leafing through my passport. Twice I explained my research to them and finally they let me go.

The entrance to Zangava was barred. I asked the men to lift the gate explaining that I was cleared. They grinned at me. One of them carried a rifle.

"Please let me through, I am cleared," I shouted impatiently, although my shouting was tempered by fear.

"Not unless you give this man a lift." I looked at the man with the rifle. Horror filled my mind.

I explained that a woman alone who did not know the man could not possibly give him a lift. My firmness, however, only aroused their amusement. I remember debating with myself whether their amusement signified harm or sincerity.

"If you don't give this man a lift, you'll be here all day," said the one without a rifle. He turned to his friend and grinned at him. I could wait until other travelers arrived, I reasoned, but I knew they would not help. They were as helpless and scared as I. Zangava had a dreadful reputation. The pedicle was never free of guerrillas or disbanded army personnel.

"Alright, I'll give him a lift," I concluded and wondered whether the crook lock might serve as a weapon if one was needed. Cars were frequently stolen. Like most owners, I had bought a crook lock. It was made of heavy steel and was used to lock the steering wheel to the clutch. I fumbled to place it next to me, in case I had to hit him over the head. The thought did not appeal to me. How hard would one have to hit a man to knock him out without blood, too much pain, or death?

My hands shook on the wheel. I reflected that he could not know whether my shaking was from fear or bad roads. Zangavan roads were so rough, a car bounced more than drove along. No doubt, my pallor gave my fear away. My body was stiff from tension.

Two or three miles into Zangava, he gruffly shouted at me to stop. My fear was so great that I could not hear properly. "Stop here," he yelled, looking quite angry. I stopped and fumbled for the crook lock convinced that my luck had finally run out. He grasped his rifle and got up. My glance was glued to every move.

"Over there," he shouted gruffly. "Give that woman and her children a lift to Makombe." To my relief, his face broke into a grin. He had enjoyed scaring me, but now his intention was clear. Not trusting a man to give his woman a lift, he waited on the border for a woman, a sister, no doubt, when I happened along.

I helped the woman and children into the car. My hands shook and my feet felt ice cold. The car sank under the weight of a buxom mother and three children. The man with the rifle remained behind. Just north of Makombe, I let them out.

It was after eleven in the evening when I arrived in Lusaka. I was covered with dust and dirt. The Institute looked deserted: no one could find me a room. A caretaker was dead drunk and lay collapsed on the floor. The Regency Hotel was filled as well. I decided to try the Intercontinental. It was Lusaka's fanciest and most expensive hotel and therefore unlikely to be filled. There I stood, my clothes looked wrinkled, my hair hung clustered in sticky bundles cemented together by clayish sand. The receptionist looked me up and down with disapproval.

"We require a thirty Zambian pound deposit," she said dryly, keeping her eyes glued to the page. I wasn't worthy of further recognition. I rummaged through my purse, found nothing, and ran to the car. Money was hidden in several places, for I feared being robbed. I was so tired that it took a long time to remember where the Zambian pounds lay stashed away.

Both clerks looked up at my reappearance with money. I was sure they thought I got it from a man. Their sideways glance did not escape my notice. It is an absurd world. In my room, I fell on the bed exhausted. I had not even the strength to run a bath and yet I had fantasized about just that for at least a month.

But morning came, and the sun shone gloriously from a bright blue sky. I followed every ritual I could remember: a long soak in the bath, breakfast in bed, a pretentious hour by the pool. And then I packed my bag and left for the grimmer reality of the Institute and the writing of my second report.

Lusaka Spin

I was asked to share an apartment with Ruth who had just returned from her first excursion of field work in Eastern Province. Ruth was a frumpy young woman. Her mousey blonde hair was caught in a simple knot; her dress looked wrinkled and uneven in the hem. Behind her glasses, however, her bright blue eyes sparkled.

It was long past midnight. One bottle of wine stood empty and Ruth filled our glasses from another. She sank into the old sofa and deposited her legs on the coffee table.

"What I want to know," she said resuming our tipsy conversation, "is simply this, why do Lenda women have a positive image of themselves when women in many societies do not? Eastern Province women did not seem particularly favored. Why are things different in Lenda?"

"I hope you are ready for a long answer," I warned.

"Indeed, I am, I've talked all night. Take over. I'm curious about your answer." Ruth half-closed her eyes to indicate her willingness to relax and listen. We started a long discussion about Lenda women, specifically, and men and women, generally.

I argued that one reason why Lenda women have a positive image of themselves is because their emotional energy is largely devoted to their work, their kin, and other women. For many, intimacy with one man is not associated with the goal of marriage, and this has a major consequence for

Lenda women's self-evaluation. They do not suffer, as do we, from the view that a woman's overriding emotional commitment is, and ought to be, to a man, especially to one man: that men are, and ought to be, the most important people in a woman's life. In our view, finally, relationships between women are still largely unimportant and trivial. According to Lenda philosophy, women's overriding emotional commitment is, or ought to be, to maternal kin and children.

"But is love with more than one man a positive choice or an adaptation to necessity?" The question should have stopped me explaining—but the wine did not.

"Probably both given the ideological confusions in the valley. But there is a kinship pattern that still influences behavior. Lenda women are primarily and emotionally committed to matrikin, hence to women and woman-culture. They recognize that their interests are discrete from those of men. And as said, lovemaking is not restricted to one man."

"So, you think," said Ruth, "that sexual pleasure and reproduction, rather than commitment, is emphasized in the relationship between men and women and that sex is a form of recreation."

"Behaviorally that is so, but how much choice has to do with it is another matter. Whatever the reason ... and I don't know whether I shall find out ... sexual recreation seems to have won over commitment."

"Do you not think," Ruth went on, "that promiscuity has to do with stagnating economic conditions in the rural areas and that only its justification has to do with matrilineal kinship?"

"Pretty much," I said, "for where I have seen commitment of spouses to one another and their children, is among Jehovah's Witnesses. And their economic situation is better ..."

Ruth worried about promiscuity while I argued that promiscuity was not the issue; individuality was. I was thinking of Kwame Nkrumah's book

Consciencism where he argues that individualism does not mean giving to persons an equal right to dominate and exploit one another. Since promiscuity is exploitation, in his thinking, then understanding individualism correctly as its negation would solve the problem.

"Hm," said Ruth as she poured more wine into our glasses. "Hm indeed," I said.

We discussed social change for some time but generally felt that the discussion was fruitless. I admitted to Ruth that I no longer believe in massive changes: as in causes, rebellions, or revolutions. I don't see them working anywhere in the world. The human being is most recalcitrant about changes in the smallest things, which hinder everything else: in the perception of men that women can't do such and such; in the reality of child raising usually left to women; in the expectation that men should provide when that becomes a possibility; in the bitterness when it does not. With respect to these trivial things, we don't move forward as much as we move back and forth.

I suspect that I shocked Ruth with the argument that we stop our blind belief in inevitable progress and legal reforms, and that we forget the simplistic interpretation of the human being as good and liberty loving. I shocked myself with my emphasis on individualism. A woman who wants change, I asserted holding up my glass of wine, must get off her butt and struggle for change in her own being first. There is no other way, no matter how accommodating our society might become.

We stared into the candle and then at the shadows on the wall. The delicate movement of shadowy patterns filled me with a deep sense of satisfaction. There was peace in the gentleness and langur of that movement. We watched its change of pattern without fear.

The conversation ended, we walked to the window. In the distance, the gentle shimmer of the rising sun told of morning. It was as if my appreciation of its transcendence contradicted my stark atheism of the night. We basked in the luxury of our glorious freedom even as we knew it not to be of this world.

Having discussed individualism, I must admit to my irresponsibility. Apparently, my family had not received mail for some time. Did I forget to write or did letters get lost? At any rate, I spent the next two days apologizing for my family's inquiries at the German and Canadian embassies concerning my whereabouts. This done, the second report was written and sent off. My guilt lessened somewhat upon Professor Justin's praise of my research in his late October letter.

Following the completion of my report and before returning to Nzubuka, I met with Paul. He had become a friend and, it seemed to me, he had found his voice. Perhaps the city did that for him. He had new dreams which he wanted to share.

Return to Nzubuka

As soon as I passed Lusaka and the Industrial Belt, I was back on dirt roads. On the horizon rose into view the nightmarish pedicle. I saw it through the cloud of dust. The first border crossing was smooth. I breathed a sigh of relief. Once again, the car bounced over potholes in Zangava.

Suddenly, ahead of me, something moved and I felt the chilly hand of fear. I saw them waving their rifles, men in ragged clothes. The image transported me back.

"Don't go to the cemetery," my aunt pleaded with mother. "Hold on to your mother," she shouted at me. "Don't let her go. There is a Russian behind every stone. Your Dad is safe in his grave."

Now they were next to me those Zangavan men. I drove on. "Stop," I heard the voice of an irate man. I glanced at him briefly and stepped on the gas. Terror filled my chest. I heard a distant "stop" again. The insanity of Zangava.

It was inconceivable to stop. Worried, I looked in the rear-view mirror. My foot slammed on the brake. A rifle was pointed at the middle of my head. Then he came running to me, flailing it.

"Wait," he commanded, turned, stepped aside, undid his zipper and urinated. I groaned and turned away.

But the image stayed with me and I was back there again. My stomach contracted in pain.

"No!" I screamed and clung to my mother's skirt. I saw him nudge her ribs with his gun.

"Get in and find the accordion," the Russian said. My mother cried. She looked pale and worn.

"I can't," my mother said. "It's the last thing I have of him. Take anything, not that, not his accordion."

"Get it, or I'll shoot," he said. He pushed the gun into my mother's back. She stumbled forward. I cried and held her skirt.

We were inside. He flung her on the floor. "The child," my mother said.

"She's young," he said and pushed my mother down again. I clung to mother's skirt. His iron grip held me and flung me against the wall.

I felt the danger of the brute and charged and screamed and flailed and bit his hand. My nails scratched his neck. He tucked his flesh away and zipped his trouser up. My mother trembled. Vomit ran down her face. Her stomach heaved and vomit spread on the floor. The Russian spit on it and cursed.

"Get out you swine," someone screamed.

When I lifted my head, I stared at a man with brown skin and from the corner of my eyes I saw the Russian walk away, then turn and spit again.

"I'm American. American, do you understand?" the brown man said. He lifted mother up and sat her in a chair. I watched him look around, walk to the kitchen and return with a wet towel. He wiped my mother's face and pushed her curls aside. His hands cupped her cheeks. She looked so pale and he so brown.

"All right?" he asked and lifted her face. Her eyelids dropped in assent. He walked to the kitchen again and returned with a cloth and wiped the floor.

I stared at the man with brown skin and remembered that we were in Zangava.

"Your bonnet!" He grinned. "And stop staring at me! Here! Here!" He jerked his rifle up and kept repeating, "Your bonnet, your bonnet." I looked at the back seat in confusion wondering whether my sun hat was in view. I saw nothing. "Your bonnet," he screamed and hit his rifle on the hood.

"You want me to open the hood?" I asked still looking confused.

"Yes, yes," he sounded impatient, "Your bonnet first and then your boot."

I opened them.

"We are police," he said.

I looked carefully at him. "But you wear no uniform," I said. It was impossible to be serious. Suddenly I burst out laughing at my fear, memory, and misunderstanding. I hadn't recognized their choice of British words for "hood," and "trunk," and explained as much to him.

"Ah," he breathed "You are American?"

"Canadian," I said and watched him poke around the motor while his buddy checked the trunk.

"You can go. Next time you stop right away, you hear. We shoot to kill." My knees felt weak again. I slid onto the car seat and drove off.

Comment 1982

National borders terrify me. This is undeniably a hangover from my origins in a partitioned Germany. Between the ages of four and seven, owing to constant illness, I was shunted back and forth among relatives in three occupied zones, the temporary American Zone, which became Russian, and the British Zone. I witnessed people being herded together and sent off to Siberia, I also witnessed inhuman assaults. Not surprisingly, I relived some of these memories upon crossing the Zangavan pedicle. Fear has never stopped me from traveling across different countries, although I have never quite overcome it. The poverty, dryness, tattered people and armed men of Zangava were too much like my past, however, to go unnoticed. The horrors and human suffering created by men reaches beyond all understanding. If I refer obliquely to some of these horrors here, if I expose emotion, it is because understanding and reason cannot prevail on top of an active volcano.

Comment 2018

There is Germany, there is my guilt, there is my being a woman—there is, in short, my origin, conscience, and person. It is their inevitability that I rejected and that, therefore, held me captive. Instead of accepting these givens, I let them trap me. I tried to lose myself in Bob, assimilating, and realizing the American dream. Experiences in Zambia simply made me aware that I was unwilling or unable to love the history that shaped me. Hence the ambiguity and, at any rate, pre-analytical thinking over a glass of wine.

We are to use freedom to assume responsibilities toward improving the human condition, not to complain. One cannot be both responsible for who one has made of oneself out of what was made of him and blame others for it. Only much later would my being a person who was born to guilt, become the impetus of future possibilities. Thankfully, I had much to learn—and what could be more fulfilling.

20

REFLECTIONS THROUGH
FREE ASSOCIATION

November 17, 1973
Darling Mother,

Bob once commented that I have written my most exciting insights to you and not to him when he is the anthropologist. If I have done so, it is because I can more easily express to you the unity between the experience of field work and its being a craft as well as a social science. When we separate these, we do so in accordance with conventions of the humanistic and scientific communities. The latter, especially, have become laundered and sterilized of life. What happens to a man who sits outside his cage of rats and experiments on them? Does the interaction between these men and rats affect the scientist? I think it does. I think such a scientist's view of the human condition might become deterministic; in some instances, he loses all sense of the individual's integrity, freedom, responsibility, and dignity. It is not, however, that I would stop rat experiments, or any responsible experimentation for that matter. It's simply that I would want a more self-aware scientist. I would like to hear some of them, at least, ask themselves whether something of rat handling has rubbed off on them.

How can an anthropologist avoid such self-questioning? In the field, he is but one human being among others. He cannot avoid pain, anguish, and scorn. His perspiration, his faltering, his surprise gives him away. He hears their logic and reflects upon his own; one or the other may look better to him. Why not, there is no genetic barrier between him and the other person; there is only a barrier of thought. A scientist cannot breed with his rats, but there is no law of nature to prevent breeding between ethnographer and his subjects. When he feels an attraction, he must handle it. Whose conventions does he follow his or theirs? His thoughts may lose focus.

When something like a food or habit repulses him, he may feel nauseous or angry; he may incline to ignore or make a nasty remark. In the end, however, he must listen to all of them; he cannot escape feeling their suffering and frustration and some of it rubs off on him. The invisible wall between ethnographer and his subject has collapsed.

More and more I find myself conversing with imagined others, as if these were the only ones who could understand the immediate penetration of Lenda life and thought into my own: as if they and I, my thoughts and theirs, their concerns and mine, had come to form a magnificent kaleidoscope. Symmetrical patterns, strong to the sense, have become inseparably interfused with one another. What I feel has become thought even before I stopped feeling it, a warm touch has become humanity, and my philosophy has become a single act of love.

I write this because this is how I feel now, tonight. Tomorrow I will be asked to pull it all apart, and when I come home and write my dissertation, I shall barely be permitted space between the lines. The work will stand-alone, I will have absented myself from it. Convention triumphs again.

It is Sunday morning, November 18. The air is warm. Rain has left the leaves looking tender green. The searing sun has not yet burned all moisture from the air.

Yesterday I picked up a deodorant in Mboua. Its smell has strong associations. It reminds me of the time when I first fell in love with Bob, of the many jealousies and unbearable passions, of the little lies and deceptions. All that, so many years ago and the smell brings it back.

My mind wanders before it focusses on Jehovah's Witnesses. I wonder how Jehovah's Witnesses fit into the local scheme of things. It worries me that they preach exclusivism. Some encourage members to relate only to their own kind, to consider themselves so different as to make cooperation with outsiders impossible. Watchtower distinguishes their concerns from those of the outsider and nation. They seem to recognize no complementarity between themselves and the party. It shocks me to learn that they teach expectation of persecution. Were they persecuted first, therefore teaching members to expect it, or did they teach it first, thereby creating a self-fulfilling prophecy? I must find out.

Watchtower leaders read magazines written by Americans. These prepare them to recognize and expect behavior, especially persecution, before anyone personally experiences it. Is this foresight or deception? Whatever it is, it channels the perception of its membership. At first, Jehovah's Witnesses regard any "outsider" with suspicion. They move in pairs, meet quietly in the privacy of their homes and hide at the approach of strangers. The community adjusts its behavior to them. All goes well, until the party stages a rally or tries to raise funds and experiences their indifference. I shudder. Groupness bothers me. It seems to destroy the ability to recognize the universal in one human being. Is this my bias? I must find out.

True, the country is now a "democracy," it is a form of "capitalism," but two things are missing in this province and country. I mean what the West calls "the rule of law" applied systematically and "civil society" protected by it. In Zambia, or at least in its provinces, party politics remains a set of free-floating ideas used primarily to fight another set of ideas that political activists find threatening. At present, it is primarily ideas of different churches or of matrilineal kinship. What is missing are associations with legally recognized rules so that any schools, libraries, nurseries, loan associations, sports clubs, cassava-growing and processing clubs, and much more, may become established and be seen to benefit society. At present, ill-informed and insecure rural dwellers resist these as "colonial," or as "Party Political," or as "Jehovah's Witnesses," or as "capitalist and European."

As it is, many ideologies paint an unexpected picture. If UNIP is honest, it will have to admit that it has not yet given villagers a vision that they recognize, and that villagers are, therefore, busy filling a seeming void with diverse scriptural ideas that function in lieu of politics. Except, some local churches too are bankrupt of innovative ideas. Is it surprising that people cling to some of the old ideas, which at least have the effect of giving a person an element of control over self and circumstance? Villagers see others, who, without even these ideas, fall apart, or simply sit, or spend their energies on feelings of defeat and self-pity, or on blaming others, or on no feelings at all, because they anaesthetize their ills with alcohol like Katapa, Simba, or Castle.

There are no libraries in the rural areas, not enough dictionaries translating the vernacular to English and vice versa, not enough speakers with vigorous ideas and realizable goals to channel energies. Consequently, people have adopted what ideas they can to make their life at least bearable and to give them energy to spit at those few who succeed.

Villages have no organizational center, no systematic lines of communication with other villages and provinces, no regular meetings of inter-provincial leaders to exchange ideas and organize trade. Technical skills are lacking and where they exist are not concentrated to enable training.

It has not occurred to national politicians that many villagers are avid readers. What is available to them in the way of readable material? Moreover, when they have read it, to whom do they talk? Do national politicians and their advisors know what qualities go into the making of a successful rural dweller? Should not Zambian youths study the philosophy of indigenous daring men and women who have gone against the current of their own setting? Instead, they rush off to foreign lands, import more ideologies, and start more parties that are political.

I am a kaleidoscope, turning around and around in a sea of many colors, and many reflections peter off into nothing. But while I am turning, all is radiant.

False humility corrupts; poverty corrupts absolutely. According to the Lenda, the universe is like a womb of wombs, it gives birth eternally, century after century. It refuses none of its children food. So too is their attitude toward the land, a person works it and then it is her spot. Otherwise, there are no boundaries, no institutions.

And now a UNIP official comes along and he says that beyond those trees, the land belongs to the nation. We have no private property here. "Ah," says the villager, "I am of this nation, so I can make my field there." "No," says UNIP, "that land belongs to the state, village land ends here." "Then state land is private property, why did you lie to me?" "No," says UNIP, "how ignorant you are, you do not understand, that land belongs to all the people." "Then why have you taken it away from me?" And we sit in the village and UNIP youths visit. They carry big baskets.

And a youth says to my friend, "Give me some cassava we're on a fund-raising mission." And the villager says, "Get your cassava elsewhere. I need it to feed my children." "You are not a humanist?" the youth says threateningly. And the woman looks at him. "Show me your hands," she asks, and demands that he look at hers. "Do you not see on my hands the lines of work and age? And where are those lines on your hands? Go," she says, "we have paid our due. You took our land. Go and plant your own cassava and sell it for money. Make your own fields in the land you took from us, that is my charity and tax." And the youth looks threateningly at her. "Would you mock humanism," he asks, "you selfish woman, you'll see what will happen to you." And the woman retorts, "I am the self of many people, there, look around you at my children. I am the self of me and of them. Go beg for your party from someone else. Have you forgotten? I gave you life."

And they go with malice in their eyes. Next day her garden is destroyed. Months later, they come back again, and they ask, and she gives them cassava. Now they are happy. They have added another self-less soul to their party, and in time, they will have another beggar. Where is the self-sufficiency in this?

I am a kaleidoscope, turning around and around, radiating many colors.

I sat on a wooden bench with several grass roots UNIP officials. A Central Committee member had given me permission to attend this seminar on Humanism, which is the party's and country's official ideology. I usually attended only those political events that were open to the public. It was Institute policy not to conduct political research. The topic of discussion was how to know the enemy, and the aim seemed to be to persuade people to a better appreciation of the government. "When the white man was here," one official said, "we were asked to pay two pounds tax and you didn't complain, but because President Kaunda is not a white man, and he asks for tax, you complain. You say he himself does not pay tax. During colonial days, the European would go to every village collecting tax. We looked like fools—he would ask, 'come here' and you would say, '*Mukwai*, Sir,' and you were happy about it because you were answering a white man. Some people did not have money, and they pretended to be mad or abnormal so that they would not have to pay. These days, have you ever seen a person behave like this? No, for we are free."

To my right, several men were bending over some photographs, which were passed from hand to hand and created spirited responses. I nudged my neighbor and asked him to pass some my way. He was embarrassed and giggled a little, but finally handed me two. Staring from one photo was a big, fat white man. His upper body was bare, showed his bulging stomach, and freckled skin. He sat on the shoulders of a slight black man who was carrying him across a river. I took a deep breath and chortled with embarrassment. The second photo showed a white man lying on the ground, his belly up. Beside him stood a slight black man with one foot on the white man's belly. I looked up into expectant eyes, and then I laughed. "Ya," I said, "this white man is definitely overweight." They joined in. "You laugh," said Mr. Chisango pleasantly, "but we used to think the white man was weak because of the look of his skin."

And I remembered President Kaunda's speech on 4 November, the day of the burial of Mabel Shaw, a missionary, who died in England but wanted to be buried here. "*Ukutemwa kwacine inkunda ya muntu,*" he said, "True love chooses no color—true love is color blind."

I am a kaleidoscope.

There I stood in the sand down the hill from Van Gella's house. Looking up, I saw Michelle sunning herself in her Chinese underwear. She turned to me with some irritation. "Would you tell me why those damn villagers are staring at me?"

"Yes, Michelle, I can answer that, it's because you are sunning yourself in see-through underwear."

"Nonsense," she said, "they don't know what this is."

"They do, you see, you bought these at Chisaka's store."

"Ah, but they don't know anything about a woman's body."

"Are you implying that they are not human, or are not adult, and therefore do not appreciate the curves of a woman's anatomy?"

"Well, they aren't."

"And Paul, was he not human?"

"He was westernized, like us."

"Somewhat, but he was very much a man of this soil."

"Push the umbrella around, you make me feel naked."

"You admit then that they are men?"

"Do their women really wear this underwear?"

"They do, Michelle, they do."

I am a kaleidoscope, and so are you.

She wants a divorce from her husband. The court assessor asks why, "Because he is a leper," she says. "Has he provided for you?" "Yes," she says. "Has he hit you?" "No," she says. Her husband pleads, "don't give her a divorce. I can provide. She only wants a divorce because of my disease."

"No divorce," the court assessor says.

"I look to the past," the court assessor explains later, "the past was clean. In those days when a man committed adultery during his wife's pregnancy, he was afraid, so he'd get some medicine and rub it on her womb. His wife wakes up and knows his deed. When a woman committed adultery, she was afraid, she prepared medicine, rubbed it on her womb, and when he woke up, he knew her deed. Even if she were pregnant and not married, she would reveal the name of her lover to ensure his faithfulness and her easy birth. Nowadays, women sleep with many men. My sister is pregnant and I went to her and said, 'Tell me who your lover is so that I can get medicine for you'. And she slaps me on my back and says, 'how can I tell you brother, they were hundreds, wake up, brother, wake up'. No, the past was clean," he says.

"But you just said that people committed adultery even then." He looked up suddenly and stared at me. "Aah," I said, "you mean his fear showed that he knew he did wrong; rubbing medicine on the womb was also a confession or a ritual of forgiveness, to set things right."

In the past, so his explanation, there was an accepted practice of righting a wrong, of restoring a sense of order that made the past clean. Now, however, its future is lost, and thus obviously the present is chaotic. In other words, I thought, it is not what we call "philandering" that changed, what changed is the loss of social calibration.

I am bombarded by a kaleidoscopic jumble of colors, patterns, and noises; smells, pain, and taste without meaning. And yet out of these random images some sense emerges.

Indigenous Lenda philosophy can be reduced to a single principle, namely, that the human being is at the center of the universe and that in this human being existence and essence are one, flesh and spirit are one, thought and feeling are one, the dead and the living are one, the past and the present are one.

Like Greek Epicureans centuries ago, the Lenda place body and spirit upon a parity. From this union, several things follow. Body and spirit are both corporeal. Consequently, all reactions of the individual to his environment are total or psychosomatic. The greatest good is not something beyond men, it is in man, and in man is life that continues in the following generations. And the purpose of life is the pursuit of pleasure. The greatest pleasure unites spirit and body and is thus sexual union. The Lenda do not die of the flesh to live, they live in the flesh to replenish the earth with life coming from them.

Among the Lenda, "God" dwells within them, as do their ancestors. Like many African groups, the Lenda speak of the living dead. The past is lived in the present, except the present is in transition.

From the assumption that essence and existence are one, can be deduced the following: (1) That the Lenda man is simultaneously a living dead and himself. His ancestors and he are one substance. (2) That man is who he is by chance, because he is the outcome of several forces coming together; those of his ancestors, his matrikin, his community, and himself. He is a group in health and in illness. (3) Consequently, what he is, is the responsibility of these combined forces.

In recent times, many Lenda also resemble Western existentialists in their earth-directedness and individualism. Here, however, the resemblance ends. The difference lies in their assumption. For the Lenda, existence and essence are one; for the existentialist existence precedes essence. In fact, Lenda have more in common with Christianity, because for the Christian essence precedes existence, but that essence became flesh in Christ, and is immanent as the Holy Spirit and, finally, the core relationship is with the individual person.

For the uninitiated let me simply define existence as that which is, a person or an object; and essence as the plan, idea, or spirit behind that which is. The simplest example for the Western mind may be taken from production. We argue, for example, that the essence of the typewriter was first an idea, a plan, and then it was manufactured into what it is. Christians argue that the essence of man is God so that man is made in His image.

But I wanted to compare Lenda philosophy with that of existentialism. The assumption of Sartre's existentialism is that existence precedes essence. The idea that there is no plan or no transcendent God, has the following consequences: (1) that man is nothing else but what he makes of himself; (2) that man will be what he will have planned to be; and (3) that man is responsible for what he is. An impossible doctrine, and indeed, toward the end of his life Sartre himself saw the impossibility of his scheme. He changed it to "I am what I make of what is made of me." Somehow that too is not enough. But if I change the tense of the verb 'to make' so that it reads "I am what I made of what was made of me" it captures something of my apprenticeship.

Comment 2018

There were moments in the field when I indulged in the luxury of daydreaming. This free-flowing mental activity was so pleasant that I wrote down my thoughts just as they occurred. The results were usually a series of profiles described from different perspectives. My activity amounted to a lazy way of doing phenomenological reductions.

If I did not delete sentences that were written in a personal tone it is precisely because the intimacy and particularity of the tone made me aware not only of preoccupations, prejudices, fears, and fantasies, but also of a distinct longing for a better world. Worry about prejudice is, I admit it, the eternal search of many Germans for redemption. It came up, because Lenda Jehovah's Witnesses drew parallels between themselves and Jews, something they learned from reading American Watchtower magazines. In the later analysis of data (Poewe, 1978), these parallels played no role. They were sentimental and were replaced by subsequent historical research in German archives.

21

THE LAST STRETCH

Even meeting with Bob in London did not free me of a sense of alienation. Anthropologists call it reverse-culture shock. It means being bombarded with all too familiar and somehow petty Western worries. There were the usual divorces of friends. The Vietnam War had ended. I remember it only as morbid university student romanticism and seemingly exciting but useless protests. Ended too had the Yom Kippur War, although the "first oil shock" was still nagging at us. Somehow, one knew that all this would continue endlessly, when the end should have been World War II. Was World War II the end of Middle East conflict (or its beginning), the end to streams of refugees (or its beginning), the end of unstable marriages owing to war, flight and loss (or its beginning), the end of abandoned children, orphans, and fatherless families (or its beginning)?

As soon as the Christmas and New Year's celebrations were over, I returned to Lenda. From now on, my entries into the personal journal radically decrease in number. There are two simple reasons for this. First, the collection of data was smooth. Second, in the swampier south, my health suffered from a malaria attack. Consequently, I felt more pressed than ever to collect, transcribe when necessary, and record carefully my data, leaving little time for the personal journal.

This last stretch of research would be spent primarily in Kaduna and the river valley where it is hotter, swampier, and unhealthier. Billions of perpendicular mosquito abdomens crowd muddy waters. Buzzing flies form black clouds over sun-dried fish. Lagoon islands are barren and stingy with shade. There is grass but few trees. Even grass huts are hot. No breeze touches the water. Mid-river the air is deathly still and blazingly hot, as if we had neared the entrance of Hades, and here I am ferried back and forth between the abode of the damned and that of the wanton.

Mr. Chisaka a big businessman, responsible husband and father, took an interest in my research. He introduced me to Kaduna village. I traveled several hours with him up and down the valley to learn about his business arrangements. Kaduna was a chiefly capital under a sub-chief by that name. Here too were congregated many of Chisaka's matrikin. Mwansa Lukonde, Chisaka's brother, was running their business in Kaduna. He managed a store, rest house, bar, petrol station and brick house.

The rest house had long been invaded by matrikin; each room became a family dwelling. The brick house too was filled with kin and the bar saw few strangers. Mwansa, who complained of constant back pain and headaches, was convinced his kinsmen were trying to do him in and he negotiated with his big brother for a transfer to the Industrial Belt. I noted that several people, when they were better off and lived among their kin, complained of similar pain, aching backs and heads. To these Lenda, their disease was always psychosomatic. It was explained in kinship terms. When people were pressured by kin, they became ill, and when they were ill, they referred the source of their illness to kin pressure. It mattered little whether their illness was madness, leprosy, or a difficult birth.

Since my return from England, and noting my presence in the southern river valley, Chisaka begged me to take his daughter with me. He suggested she could assist me. I told him she was too young, and I had already found a man by the name of Kasonga Chabwe who would help with my research here. Kasonga was in his fifties, a Christian and well respected by the older population. He was dissatisfied with the accomplishments of the present regime. It hurt him to watch Zambian schoolteachers getting drunk. He was critical of the moral decay of the valley. However, he was respected, and he backed up every complaint with evidence. We interviewed his drunken chief, we talked to drunken schoolteachers, and we watched women negotiate the sale of their body.

Since my misfortunate handling of payment for Banachile's help, I now made it a point to pay each assistant a monthly wage that matched that of a boma government clerk. Kasonga was one of the most predictable and responsible assistants I could find. He had a wife some twenty to thirty years younger than he was, and he needed the money. As well he was moved by the problems of the valley. As deacon in his church, he was a Seventh-day Adventist, he took me to the source of many enigmas.

Chisaka persisted with his request to let Nawela, his daughter, accompany me. Just for a month, he said. He wanted to send her to England to become a nurse but feared that with nothing to do in the interim she might become pregnant. In exchange for this favor, he said, we could stay in a room of his Kaduna rest house.

My research was so systematic and time consuming now that I spent evenings reviewing notes of interviews. Entries into my personal journal became fewer each day. Since my return from England, Bob rarely wrote. I am not surprised. In England, I was unable to free myself of my Lenda obsessions. I began to limit my memory of him, convinced that he had already or would soon find other, more heedful ears.

Mwewa too was transferred to Lusaka. It was a big promotion for him and a quiet pain for me. For the valley, it was a major loss of talent, a hemorrhage it could not stop. Before he left for Lusaka, we spent a day in Wafema District. Wafema was a shallow lake and swampy region to the south. Its quiet waters stretched endlessly into the horizon. We walked its sandy beaches, or I stampeded through its shallows near the shore. Mwewa's mood vacillated between fretfulness and joy. He feared my demise by a crocodile, a not unlikely end, one met by a nun the month before.

Now it is the beginning of March. I can't sleep. Across the room, Chisaka's daughter had a bad dream. She is probably pregnant already. Nor could she handle the constant pressure from her father's kin. They wanted money or jobs.

I can't sleep and sit up in bed. On the floor, I search for the bag of roasted peanuts. I'm hoping that chewing on something will settle my stomach. It's hot. We can't relax. Noise keeps us awake. The walls that separate rooms are paper-thin. They are literally made of cardboard. Nawela cries. She's pregnant already, I think. She was pregnant before she came with me.

"I can't stand to hear them," she hisses. "Ah, child," I say, "Nawela, relax. They're just screwing behind that paper wall. Why don't you laugh at them?" I use the word "screwing" rather than "making love" because our sharers of the paper wall are quite drunk. One doubts the presence of refined sentiments under such conditions.

It's the first of the month. Lowly government officials buy their women here. Their money turns into beer, beer into urine, and urine covers the toilet seat and floods the floor.

Next door, the baby coos while her mother engages in procreative recreation with another man. It's payday, after all. Nawela holds her ears. "Nawela," I say, "relax! I want to talk to you." I sit up on my cot. "You're pregnant child. Don't look afraid. I won't tell your father." She admits that she's pregnant and adds, "I must go to the Industrial Belt where my mother lives. It's easy to abort there. But I must leave before my father finds out."

"This place is bad," I say. "You should have left already. Take the bus tomorrow."

I can't sleep. And I remember the woman giving birth on the road. When she was finished, I helped her into the car to drive her home. She claimed she no longer needed the clinic. Upon helping her out of the car, blood flowed across her feet. Her relatives collected the umbilical cord and deposited it into a plastic bag. The placenta had still not come out.

I can't sleep. And I remember that he took her to Lusaka and left her there while he spent the little money he earned on beer and other women. She thought that in the city she would be free of work. Instead, she died of malnutrition. In court, he demanded a successor for her. Someone had to succeed to her position. Without such succession, he should suffer ill health. "No successor," her kinsmen said.

No sleep touches my eyes. And I remember her die when she reaches Kaduna on the way to Cuito hospital. Eight months pregnant, she was. The husband would need protection for it was assumed that he had played with other women. "We merely play, *ukuangulafye*," men say.

In the adjacent room of the rest house the "recreation" continues. The baby is quiet while another one is being formed. "It excites him to fantasize that he's molding a child," Nawela whispers, "he'll forget it before it is born." I know the story; she will ask several men if they are the father of it. Not me, they'll say, I only slept with you once, so I could not have fathered your child. Nawela wails.

We walk outside to relax, but cannot. Young women sit in the bar with babies on their backs. "This will not be my life," Nawela asserts.

Back in the room, I try to sleep. Instead, I remember that anemic looking woman. Seven months pregnant, and no man is in sight.

She is fourteen years old. Yes, I remember her, the baby died after birth. It's not uncommon for babies to die when mothers are children themselves. Memories of these plights hound me.

She arrived at the hospital. The baby's feet were hanging out. She left it too late; one arm breaks on delivery. "Brain may be damaged," Van Gella says. He pushes his food aside and moans with disgust.

She was completely exhausted. Cheeks looked sunken. Her body was wasted away but for the little blob in her womb. She couldn't give birth. They died in the hospital. "I'm weary," Van Gella says.

The price of rooms is controlled by the government. Low paid employees flock to the rest house to practice their "procreative recreation" in style. Government rest houses, especially, are fine. "We can do it but once a month—on payday," he says and looks deprived.

I am to assign this meaning: emotionally hollow—a quick outcry; ethically meaningless—no commitment is made. No one assumes responsibility for the act nor its consequence. The act is empty. Thoughtless pleasure. Sex is indulged, matrilineal generosity abused.

How busy these men are, like bees fluttering from stamen to stamen in a wild search for honey. No commitment is made. "How can I reflect about myself when this valley is making me suffer? One struggle is enough," he says. Sex and survival, not sex and liberation go together.

"What has happened?" I ask. "Look at me," she says. "Look at my hands, my skin. Look at the sweat on my body. My livelihood comes from the land, his from shuffling papers. Smell his perfume. And you ask what happened?" she says.

I remember the little boy. He led the horde of children following me. "And who are you," I asked studying him. "I am the son of BanaMusanda," he says. "And who is your father," I asked. "Ask not about my father, I hate him," he says. "But why do you hate him?" I ask. "He left us thus," he points to his tattered clothes. "When I grow up he shall suffer, I promise you that. My father shall die for what he has done." I ask no more, just look at his wise and aching little face, for on it is written the Lenda law.

Then there was Mr. Ndaisa. I remember our interview. "I help only my mother, not my father," he said. He sat there fidgeting, awaiting my response. I asked him other questions. He didn't answer. Instead, he burst out, "why didn't you ask me why I don't help my father, you being European?" when I asked him, he answered, "Because my father returned to his first wife. He didn't think he needed to look after us young children because he had older ones. Now he is starving and I won't help." Mr. Ndaisa told me this as he sat with his first wife and her children. His other wife lived some miles away. Had he abandoned her?

"We are no Christians here," he says. "There are too many women. This is how it's done. *Asompola muitumba lupin lwandi, aya, namukonka twayalala pa ulupia lwandi.* She takes my money from my pocket and I follow her and we sleep for my money, I speak the truth," he adds, "for I am the father of twins."

What has happened? Behavior is the same, but their system of thought has lost its meaning. Actions have become exaggerated. A system of thought is vulnerable for all its coherence. It cannot be more than a purely pragmatic tool because each system rests on accepted but not proven propositions. Accepted propositions of the Lenda include that offspring are made from the blood of their mothers. This blood is the same for all those of one clan. The deceased are living because their essence continues with the blood of their successor. He who is now living is therefore not one but many, a group of the deceased he inherited and his matrikin. If those whose essence he inherited and those whose blood he becomes were strong, and if his matrikin are strong, then he is a formidable individual. Harmony is what he needed and pleasure gave him that. Only now, his pleasure too has become sordid.

Many Lenda no longer accept these propositions. Some have become conflicted individuals. Their spirits were torn away by visions of a jealous God. Their ancestors are now finally dead.

No sleep entered my eyes. I suspected that Lenda culture generated its own form of alienation. In many parts of Canada, to this day, strong women are still seen as ogres. By contrast, the Lenda ogre is the weak woman. There is little sympathy for her need to depend on men. When she is forced to bargain and trade with men, if she does not become cynical, she sits immobile in front of her house too petrified to move at all.

It was May when I became more seriously ill than I had been before. No one was around. Nawela had left for the Industrial Belt. Kasonga was on his deacon duties. Reality faded in and out. I could feel exhaustion overtaking me. There was nothing left to vomit anymore. I called one of Chisaka's kin, gave him a note, and asked him to take it to the Boma. He looked at me a long time. "The valley sickens and kills," he said.

He came back some hours later with the report that there was no nurse and that the D.S. did not have a lorry to fetch me. Afraid of losing consciousness, I sent him off again. He was to ask for a driver since I had a car. Some hours later, a driver arrived. He helped me into the car and, while I taught him how to shift gears, we drove stop and go to Limambo mission. I remembered that nurses took some tests and that I feared being put into the hospital. The missionaries considered their hospital to be very sanitary. It may have been, but it reminded me of a series of animal stalls.

When I awoke, I was in a spacious room. Its brightness struck me first. Soft white curtains moved in the breeze. I lay on a big four-poster bed, surrounded by a mosquito net. A cabinet, standing on the opposite side of the bed, was filled with several knick-knacks. They reminded me of my grandmother's home back in Prussia. On the edge of the bed sat a kindly missionary nurse with a bowl of soup. As she prodded me to eat, she explained that I had been in their home a week. Their test confirmed falciparum malaria. I was lucky, she told me, that it was not cerebral malaria.

It is perhaps somewhat ironic that it should be missionaries, about whom I had frequently complained, who should nurse me back to health. My morality was not so much Sartre's heroic "individualism" of utterly free choice as it was simply wrong—a kneejerk reaction to a deeply ingrained anthropological bias.

Each day I was offered a light breakfast and a lot of soup. One day I was prepared for the flying doctor who was to examine several hospital patients and would be asked to examine me as well. When the doctor arrived, he caused a flurry of activity, all to hide his completely drugged and drunken state. He was unable to see any patients. The nurses put him on the plane and sent him back.

Limambo hospital was run solely by women. All were missionaries of CMML. Some had been in Zambia over forty years. As I became better, I sat with them at tea, listening to their stories of their near demise during the independence struggle. As it was, only their school was closed, leaving male missionaries with nothing to do. It was male missionaries who had taught. The hospital could remain as if to confirm the unhealthfulness of the valley.

Three weeks had passed before they let me go. I was advised strongly to fly home. Not much persuasion was needed. I would stay two additional weeks to finish my research in Kaduna. Some court cases had yet to be recorded. Also, I wanted further information about the agricultural community to the east.

By the third week of June, I felt satisfied. The fourth report was written and sent off. I drove to Kakuso once more and held Mr. Ngoma's hand. I thought that would be my only good-bye for I was certain of a return. But, at the Lusaka airport Paul and Mwewa arrived with their cousins and colleagues. They were people who "took me out of myself." For a brief period, we built a bridge between continents. What remains is not sentimental, but the fact of a meeting of minds during the charged period of my apprenticeship.

Some years following my return from the field, anthropology changed. Various colleagues had guided the discipline to greater self-reflection. Others became postmodernists with a knack for inventing texts. The result was the proliferation of different ethnographic genres often based on skillful rhetoric that put into question the importance of empirical and evidence-based research.

The postmodernist turn meant treating anthropological classics, which are bound by rules of specific schools of thought and practice, as ideology. What went missing was a genre written by ethnographers who were willing to write up how they experienced the field and how it affected them during their time of coping with the unexpected and unanticipated. Both the personality and history of the researcher, as well as the "mechanics" of entering, living among, and researching people of the society, would be made transparent. While such a work too would not be a classical ethnography, it would remain a close cousin. It would be an account of a journey that showed how doing research affects the researcher while yet revealing something about the people being researched. Contrary to textualists who privilege representing cultural difference, field workers realize that personal experiences have as much to do with showing how we know what we know, as they make visible the research process and our common humanity.

In the mid-nineteen-nineties, I thought it worthwhile to distinguish between experimental and experiential genres and treat them as distinct approaches of doing and writing field work and culture. It would mean reclaiming experiential ethnographies from the textualist lock-in to which some experimental ethnographers led the discipline. More importantly, distinguishing between types of ethnographies invites us to puzzle about the role of rhetoric by examining, for example, the importance of metonym, the receptive imagination, empathy, and memory, as well as motivation and deception. The conclusion to this little book is the paper that was first published in the journal called *Ethnos*. It is a fitting conclusion, because it was the direct consequence of meeting Africans in Africa for the first time.

What I have described is a meeting of minds; an intellectual journey where ideas are rooted in the ground of experience, and where unexpected memories emerge to form bridges between continents and human conditions. And that is all it is and has to be.

22

WRITING CULTURE AND WRITING FIELD WORK

The Proliferation of Experimental and Experiential Ethnographies[1]

Prologue

In 1986 Clifford, Fischer, and Marcus published two books that were instrumental in shaping a new culture of anthropology (cf. Clifford and Marcus 1986; Marcus and Fischer 1986). For Clifford (1986:2), the cultural marker of a new anthropology was a photo of Malinowski in which he "recorded himself writing at a table." For Marcus and Fischer (1986:1–3) it was two publications. One was by Said (1979) who criticized western representations of Orientalism. The other was by Freeman (1983) who criticized Margaret Mead's poor research in Samoa. The consequences of Freeman's revelations shook public trust in the adequacy of using anthropological knowledge as a form of home critique. Rather than address methods, Marcus and Fischer addressed representation.

Ignoring the historical fact that Malinowski, at the time that the photo was taken, contemplated becoming a selling writer because "there was no career as an ethnologist" (Kramer 1986:10, citing Thornton 1985:7–14),

Clifford read the photo's appearance in a 1983 Stocking publication as "a sign of our times not his (Malinowski's)" (Clifford 1986:2). To Clifford, Fischer, and Marcus the photo and books signaled "a crisis of representation" which expressed a general "state of profound transition" within the West (Marcus and Fischer 1986:8, 9). This intuitive, sign-based, assessment required a radical response from the discipline, away from the focus on participant-observation and interpretation of cultures to text making and rhetoric (Clifford 1986:2). If participant-observation, the collection of data generally, and the process of "writing up" were regarded as central to what anthropologists did in the past, writing was to be central in the future.

According to Clifford (1986:2), an old "ideology" had "crumbled," a new one was born. This new ideology of the discipline, argued Clifford, sits on the following new assumptions: culture as a composition of "seriously contested codes and representations," poetics and politics as inseparable; science as part of a historical and linguistic process; written cultural descriptions as "properly experimental and ethical," authorial authority as a thing of the past; writing as invention of cultures (ibid).

Just as Afrikaner culture was constructed from Afrikaans the language, Afrikaans literature, a prescribed ethics, and a political will (Poewe 1996),[2] so the new culture of anthropology was constructed from postmodernist language, experimental literature, a politically committed and morally engaged ethics (Marcus and Fischer 1986:46, 167; Scheper-Hughes 1995:410),[3] and the dogma that politics is pervasive and inseparable from writing. This seemingly well-meaning new culture shares some of the discomfiting demands made by both Afrikaner nationalism and German national socialism, among them, individual subordination to the will of a self-defined new culture or state (Stapel 1933; Poewe 2000, 2008). Thus, in the new anthropological program, the individual anthropologist is to subordinate his or her authorial talent to the cooperative evolution of the text (Tyler 1986:125).

Like political radicals or anarchists who have a ready label for all they oppose, so too postmodernists label everything they oppose "ideology" and "privileged" (Clifford 1986:2; Tyler 1986:126). Thus privileged ideological categories include: monologue, "observer-observed," monophonic performance, "positivist rhetoric of political liberalism," power, and author (Tyler 1986:128). They must be done away with. Their substitutions include categories like: "mutual dialogical production of discourse, of a story of sorts," (p.126) "cooperative story making," "ethical discourse," even the Biblical model (p.127), and a specified ideological attitude toward the ethnographic other (p.127). Rather than being built from the rubble of South African townships (Scheper-Hughes 1995:417), postmodern ethnography is built from the "rubble" of the "deconstruction" of Walter Benjamin, Theodor Adorno, and Jacques Derrida (Tyler 1986:131): from the ravings, in other words, of Western *Querköpfe* (people who deliberately cultivate wrong-headed ideas). Nowhere is mention made of whether or not the fabulous world of experimentalism and postmodernism has anything whatsoever to do with the people we research. Like God in the beginning, the postmodernist "creates" the world with categories from his newly invented culture of anthropology. To question these categories is to be a "stooge" of hegemonic capitalism, as South African comrades loved to call anyone who disagreed with their politics.

Let us end this section by returning to Clifford's photo of Malinowski writing (1986:2). While Margaret Mead in the film, New Guinea Journals, is prominently shown writing, in the photo Malinowski is not. The photo in question appears on the cover of Stocking's (1992) collection of essays entitled, *The Ethnographer's Magic*. It shows a dark profile of Malinowski presumably writing at his table. He is in shadow because the camera is focussed on Trobrianders who appear in full light. The attention is, after all and against Clifford's reading, on the people whom Malinowski intends to understand. By contrast, the photo of Stephen Tyler on the cover of the Clifford and Marcus book (1986) is almost the inverse. The focus of the camera and the light is on Tyler and his paraphernalia in the foreground. Tyler has his back to the people among whom he conducts his research.

Like a horse wearing blinders, Tyler wears glasses with a cloth hanging over one arm of the frame, as if to prevent distraction or shying. He sits writing with his head bent over a clipboard while a man and child some distance behind him look on bored. It is a perfect image of postmodern or experimental ethnography: the anthropologist, his strong ego intact, sits dis-located on location, in the protective cocoon of a postmodernist program. As Probyn (1993:68) remarks about Clifford:

> ... in shifting the whole ethnographic activity to the level of writing ... he displaced attention away from local field work practices. In other words, he has turned the normal order of things upside down ... the text takes prominence.

Ethnographic Genre Proliferation

Experimentalists have generated,[4] or appropriated as "experimental," numerous ethnographies which they classified into several ethnographic genres. From my perspective their activities pose two problems. The first problem is that of blurring experimental and experiential ethnographies. The second problem follows from the first. We want to know whether the motivation for the proliferation of ethnographic genres is the same for experimental and experiential ethnographies. To gain insight into these problems of blurring and proliferation, we must de-blur three groups of ethnographic writing: ethnographic fiction, experimental ethnographies, and experiential ethnographies. In this paper, we want to focus only on experimental and experiential ethnographies. Ethnographic fiction or narrative anthropology is based on specific techniques that achieve blurring between fact and fiction. The goal of achieving just the right amount of blurring to arrange ethnographic facts into a story without denying the story's factual foundation, create such subtle problems for social science as to warrant writing a separate paper (Bohannan 1995:147–158; Richardson 1996:623; Bruner 1986, 1995; Jackson 1986; Reck 1984).

1. The problem of blurring experiential and experimental ethnographies

In a stimulating article, Olivier de Sardan (1992), criticizes the "ethno-ego-centrism" of some postmodern anthropologists. In the process, he raises a problem centred on blurring experimental and experiential ethnographies. The blurring results from the fact that postmodern ethnographers who concentrate primarily on text do at times make the claim that their personal involvement and their subjectivity as narrator bring "to light hidden facts which would not be revealed by a classical anthropological approach" (Olivier de Sardan 1992:6). At the same time, given their rhetoric, it is not clear whether this rhetoric corresponds to an actual illuminating experience or whether it is artifice and mystification. Therefore, our first point of distinction between experiential and experimental ethnographies is this: to experiential ethnographers the self and especially experiences in the field are "epistemologically productive" (Kulick 1995:20); to experimental ethnographers the self and especially rhetoric are textually productive.

To the experiential ethnographer facts, data, and real experiences are central because one's contact with their reality raises vital epistemological questions about how we know what we know. As Hastrup (1987:294) says, "The reality of anthropology is not text-bound but life-bound." By contrast, to the experimental ethnographer "facts and data are merely products of ethnographic construction" so that there is nothing to prevent the ethnographer from "attributing one's own aesthetic preoccupations to people of other cultures" (Olivier de Sardan 1992:7, 10). Rather than the self being epistemologically productive, it functions as a device for realism (p.10). Thus, Marcus and Fischer are not concerned with questions about the epistemological productiveness of experience. Nor do they subject the question of whether or not cultural difference exists or is significant to empirical and experiential research. Instead, they argue that one radical trend in their "new anthropology" is taken up with "ethnographies of experience" which are concerned "with how *cultural difference* is to be *represented* in ethnography" (1986:43, my emphasis). Cultural difference is not only assumed, it and its representation are, in their lingo, "privileged."

Enough is said to show that experiential ethnographies are distinct from experimental ones and should be removed from the textualist lock-in (Bohannan 1995). Indeed, as Clifford (1986:20) makes clear, the experiential approach of Cesara (1982), among others, was deliberately excluded from the "advanced seminar" on which the edited volume of Clifford and Marcus (1986) was based. In short, experiential ethnographies are part of a very different anthropological concern, attitude, and approach (Abrahams 1986). But about this, more will be said later. Let us turn now to the problem of motivation.

2. The problem of motivation and discursivity

Is textual invention the only thing that motivates ethnographers to generate ever more genres and, if so, what are the dangers and uses of these genres for the discipline? Are we in the presence of a new brand of scholarship that freely mixes personal experiences and research expertise, as Scott Heller (1992:A7–A9) suggests? Are experiments in ethnographic writing a response to increased pressure from the non-Western world or from feminists to understand and learn from another's perspective, as Marcus and Fischer imply (1986)? Is there, as Rao (1988) suggests, a shift away from a science of propositions and true description of a domain to a practical science of advocacy concerned to tell not only how things like sorcery, for example, are done, but advocating its doing? Is it possible that in addition to doing field work and writing ethnographies, (or even in lieu of these activities as Geertz (1988:24) suggests), anthropologists will have to remind students of, or teach them, literary styling and rhetoric, or schemes and tropes?

However one answers these questions, one thing is certain. Anthropologists no longer write only classical, general, or specialized ethnographies as they were first developed by the British School of Social Anthropology and carried forward by students of Boas (Gatewood 1984:8).

Barbara Tedlock pointed out, for example, that the nineteen seventies saw a "shift in emphasis from participant observation to the observation of participation" (1991:78). It brought with it new kinds of ethnographies, that were broadly experiential in nature (p.79). Having observed a "blurring of genres" in various disciplines and having tired of "author-saturated" accounts, Geertz argued that we should shift "part of our attention from the fascinations of field work" to the fascinations of "authoring" discursive fashions as was done by the "founders-of-discursivity" (Geertz 1988:6, 21, 24, 20).

Marcus and Fischer (1986) seem to have gone a step further. While their postmodernism is not as anarchistic nor as glib about the discourse of the ethnographic "other" as is that of Tyler (1986), they "want to elevate the ethnographer and his subjects into a realm of *pure discursivity*" (Probyn 1993:72, my emphasis). Consequently, they do not so much observe changes in the way anthropology is done (1986:45–76), as they specify the kind of anthropology and ethnographies that are wanted. The anthropology that is wanted is a politically and historically sensitive anthropology that takes account of a changing world order as it is perceived by those who belong to the inner circle of postmodernists (1986:vii). This anthropology of cultural critique would challenge established theories and research programs, question established ways of representing the world (p.9), and in the process, invent more genres.

But what has changed in the world order and what kind of anthropology would capture this change? To the last half of the question, Marcus and Fischer answer an anthropology that pays less attention to social action and more attention to the categories, metaphors, and rhetoric embodied in the accounts informants give of their culture. In other words, rather than researching the "theaters of language" that founders-of-discursivity built, as Geertz suggests (1988:21), we are to research conversations, idioms, and tropes of other peoples.

Marcus and Fischer's answer to the first part of the question is not easily discerned. What is changing is not the world per se as communicated to the public by politically indifferent or distanced scientists preoccupied with observing and measuring change. Rather, what is changing are discursive fashions and perspectives. Contrary to British social anthropology which placed its emphasis on observation and the sense of seeing, a politically sensitive anthropology places its emphasis on discourse and, in the research phase at least, on the sense of hearing or on other senses that act as correctives "to the metaphor of sight as the sense of reason" (Tyler 1996:617). The invention of politically and historically sensitive sound-and-smell genres of anthropology are a fascinating consequence (Feld 1982; Classen, Howes, and Synnott 1994). Taken to their logical extreme, however, even these politically and historically sensitive ethnographies require, before anything else, that we heed symbols of denigration and hierarchy. Because postmodernists maintain a political affinity for the Frankfurt version of Marxism, their sense of history is significantly biased or provincial rather than sensitive in the broad and basic sense of the term (cf. Tyler 1996; Bohannan 1995:181–185).

Furthermore, alternative senses-ethnographies may sit on poor research. For example, in a recent publication, Classen (1993) who was with the *Center for the Study of World Religions*, Harvard University, at the time of writing, made the following statement: "The Hausa of Nigeria divide the senses into two, with one term for sight and one for all the other senses" (p.2). Having never encountered such a phenomenon among Africans I researched, I checked her footnote expecting to find details about her field work or other field work on which this statement was based. Alas, none existed. The footnote refers to another general introductory book about "the diverse sensory systems of different societies" (p.139). Method is also not of concern in the Classen volume reviewed by Tyler (1996). The description of smells by the anthropologist, for example that of Radcliffe-Brown (cited in Classen, Howes, Synnott 1994:95–97), is not clearly distinguished from that of the people being researched. Nor are the concepts used to "constitute the olfactory landscape," for example, "smellscape," (p.97) those of the Andamanese. Footnotes refer one to other

Western scholars who did the classifying. And while ethnographic "others" are said to divide their world according to smell, observational materials about how these people pick up scent, what postures they take up during it, are entirely lacking. Indeed, the issue is not quality research, the issue is to right a wrong: "Our singling out of scent for attention serves to redress this long-standing imbalance" (p.9).

I have two further problems with the text making approach. First, being sensitive, in the sense of partial to symbols of denigration, frequently means reading denigration into things where it does not exist or does not necessarily exist (Olivier de Sardan 1992). More discomfiting, sensitivity of this political sort would mean that we must subject ourselves to the political judgements of ethnographic "others" and committed colleagues, rather than to the canons of science (see D'Andrade 1995 versus Scheper-Hughes 1995). But political judgement is based on commitment to an ideology,[5] a cause, or as in South Africa today, "service to the state" and its politically prescribed goal of inventing a "new South Africa" (Bekker 1995:7). In South Africa as among some American anthropologists, politically sensitive anthropology has led to "moral totalitarianism" which is, furthermore, "presented as an academic virtue" (Bekker 1995:7; Scheper-Hughes 1995). Given my research of Afrikaner and German nationalism, on one hand, and of national socialism in Germany of the nineteen twenties and thirties, on the other, I can only say that scholars of this ilk are limiting research to "ideological lock-ins" (Bohannan 1995:181). The favourite cause of the political left at the turn of the century was the small Afrikaner nation that fought to survive imperialism (Hobhouse 1901, 1984). The only problem is that the same small Afrikaner nation instituted legal apartheid that robbed millions of people of their basic human rights (Poewe 1993, 1994, 1996, 2000).

Ideally, experimental ethnographies concentrate on experimentation with style and rhetoric in order to transform into words data from **all** senses and faculties. And, indeed, Marcus and Fischer (1986) describe three major types of experimental ethnographies: psychodynamic ethnographies with their emphases on emotion and feeling (p.48–49); realist ethnographies with their emphases on sight, sound and analytical reason (p.54–63); and modernist texts with their emphases on word-based realities (p.67–73). It would appear that the last mentioned texts most closely approximate the discursive fashion of postmodernism and are subject to the dangers of deception that Olivier de Sardan analysed in his article on *Occultism and the Ethnographic 'I'* (1992:10). Since Marcus and Fischer argue, however, that all senses are mediated by indigenous discourse and commentaries, all ethnographies must become centred on problems of discourse (Olivier de Sardan 1992:7).

The Problem of Deception

Olivier de Sardan raises the problem that has haunted rhetoric through the ages. Does rhetoric encourage deception or does it increase the possibility of giving a faithful rendering of what is experienced and said?

Part of the problem of deception is linked to the insistence that ethnographic writing is dependent on cultural differences (Marcus and Cushmann 1982). At best, experimentalists argue, as stated above, that the feelings and experiences of the native are mediated by indigenous discourse and commentaries so that the ethnographer must capture these through innovative writing strategies. Research is therefore twice removed from action and experiences, first, by the indigenous discourse and, second, by the researcher's discursive rendering of the indigenous discourse. My research experience of African and New Independent Churches in South Africa leads me to question aspects of this approach. I wonder, for example, whether the idea of mediating indigenous discourse is not too convenient. It could, for example, protect experimental ethnographers from the charge that their discourse could have been written without their doing field work, a possibility first raised by the work of Castaneda (Fikes 1993). After all, it was thought that Castaneda described the most authentic mediating discourse to date when, in fact, his work was a hoax (Castaneda 1968, 1971; Fikes 1993).

Furthermore, research of African Independent Churches made me question whether all feelings and experiences are mediated by an indigenous culture. One might argue, for example, that there is such a thing as "pre-categorical" or "acategorical" feeling and experiencing when people use, for example, the receptive rather than the analytical imagination (Green 1989; Poewe 1989, 1994). Especially in the religious sphere, receptive imagination refers to sudden insights, revelations, visions, dreams, and voices which may confound existing indigenous categories or encourage adepts to borrow categories from a foreign discourse. The imagination is receptive in the sense that individuals in African Independent Churches, for example, described themselves as "receiving" visions from "ancestors," "the spirit," or the "Holy Spirit" (interview with Londa Shembe, Ekuphakameni 1987). Analysis of numerous interviews with black, white, "coloured," and Indian South African believers led me to conclude that ancestors, on one hand, and the Spirit (*umoya*), on the other, are part of a reality that is tacitly known but only partially revealed (Polanyi 1964; Poewe 1994). It is revealed in the above mentioned ways or in mundane events that were seen by interviewed believers as signs of something bigger. One could say, therefore, that African or white charismatic Christian thought is based on a realist ontology but a revelationist epistemology. As for the mediating discourse, it is indigenous or Biblical depending where on the spectrum of South African religiosity an individual is found. Of course, I realize that one might call all discourse of those we interview indigenous. But doing so, would be artificial and mystifying. It would omit the plain fact that much communication is direct, simple, and unmediated by cultural differences.

The question is, are works like that of Stoller and Olkes, one of several discussed by Olivier de Sardan, true to the above mentioned epistemological-cum-ontological assumptions on which African religious practices and beliefs seem to rest? It would appear that Olivier de Sardan's assessment is correct; they are not. First, the epistemology-cum-ontology of experimental ethnographers tends to be radical relativist, not revelationist and realist. Consequently, reality is what the ethnographer says it is; namely, a seemingly faithful rendering of the mediating indigenous discourse in terms of, however, a discourse based on the anthropologist's epistemology-cum-ontology. In other words, "realities" are discourse or word based; they can be anything a persuasive ethnographer says they are. Like Foucault (1972), this sort of work has not only taken leave of observation, it has also taken leave of the human being so that the human being is but an effect of specific language or discourse systems.

Second, if the epistemology of African religious practitioners and of African charismatic Christians is revelationist, as I found it to be, it is not metaphor that transforms their belief into "knowing," but metonym. Yet a discussion of rhetoric in general, and of metonym, is virtually ignored in these works.[6] Important exceptions to this claim are Ohnuki-Tierney (1991:175–178), Durham and Fernandez (1991:192), Friedrich (1989:306–307), and Jackson (1989). Ohnuki-Tierney discusses the uncomfortable shift in meaning when a metaphor may "bring to the fore an inherent metonymic relationship" (Ohnuki-Tierney 1991:176). Friedrich (1989:306) and Jackson (1989:138) discuss the power of synecdoche which may be used to substitute as easily a whole for a part (as when Goldhagen (1996) accuses "the Germans" for a crime committed by some "Germans"), as a part for a whole (as when Kakar (1982:156) interprets coitus as the ultimate state of "enlightenment"). Ohnuki-Tierney's focus is on the Janus-like ambiguity of symbols, including synecdoche. Thus "the Germans" may also refer to a small elite which, however, comes to be taken for the whole population with the subtle implication that "minorities" are excluded (Ohnuki-Tierney 1991:179). Likewise, "enlightenment" may refer to the illusion that the "simple pleasure of intercourse" is more than what it is literally, namely, coitus (Kakar 1982:156). While Ohnuki-Tierney and Jackson discuss these tropes in relationship to analogy, allegory, contiguity, and ambiguity, they seem to miss the characteristic of metonymy that was most important to the charismatics I interviewed, the characteristic that made their faith real. I mean, of course, causality: **their** assumption of an active link between an event and the reality that caused it. An assumption which the researcher is obligated to respect (Probyn 1993:77). Instead of continuing to play with symbolically based meanings of metaphor, metonym, and synecdoche, let us look at the existential reality of metonym.

Metonym and the Receptive Imagination

Metonym is a figure of speech (a way of saying something) which allows one to interpret an event or a happening as a sign that the whole, of which this event is a part, also caused it. It should be kept in mind that my empirically grounded definition is somewhat different from the textual one, which simply says that metonym "designates one thing by an object closely associated with it" (e.g., the "King" is called the "crown," Horner 1988:447). On one hand, my use of metonym is based on observed practices of, and interviews with, black and white charismatic Christians of African Independent Churches and New Independent Churches; on the other, it is based on a theory of rhetoric. This theory argues that rhetoric is most effective when it imitates life, nature, or when figures "*demonstrate* feeling" and are "signs of a state of mind in the speaker," not necessarily in the listening anthropologist (Vickers 1989:304, 303). As Cicero purportedly said: "For nature has assigned to every emotion a particular look and tone of voice and bearing of its own" (quoted in Vickers (1989:66)).

It is this theory of rhetoric that persuaded me to give figures another look in the context of my research of charismatic Christians. For example, charismatics are prayed over and fall down which is referred to as "resting in the spirit," this happening is experienced and interpreted by black, white, "coloured," and Indian believers as a sign that the Holy Spirit, who caused their falling, is working in their spirit and life. To their mind, this small event is therefore a part of and caused by a much larger whole, namely God's presence. Researchers usually miss the causal aspect. It is because of this oversight that I emphasized the importance of metonym (Poewe 1989, 1994), even though charismatics and Africans belonging to

Independent Churches otherwise symbolize like any other human being with all the ambiguity of meaning highlighted by Ohnuki-Tierney (1991).

What charismatic Christians told me in numerous interviews were things that happened to them, and that they experienced as coming from the Holy Spirit. Analysing these interviews persuaded me that the outstanding (but not sole) characteristic of this form of religiosity was what I called a metonymic pattern of thought (Poewe 1989; 1994). By metonymic pattern of thought is meant the habit of seeing a simple happening as an aspect of a whole that caused it, even when the whole itself is but tacitly known. A similar thing is argued by Hastrup 1987:294–5), except that she calls the larger whole "world" and refers to what I call happenings as "events." Furthermore, following Ardener (1982:6), but in disagreement with my findings, Hastrup too denies causality. To quote:

> We should be careful here not to imagine arrows of causation from symbols or categories to the material situation, including actual behaviour. Rather than causing each other, the material and the categorical realities form a simultaneity (Ardener 1982:6).

But the point is, interviewed charismatic Christians did imagine causation, except not from "symbols and categories" but from what they tacitly knew to be reality. The power of this kind of literalness was brought home to me by science students in Atlanta, Georgia, who were also charismatic Christians. Distinguishing "knowing" biology, algebra, or geometry from "knowing" chemistry, they said about the latter (Poewe 1994:246):

> "With chemistry you have to learn the way things happen. And you can only make things happen when you discover something in the formula that makes it happen." In chemistry, and matters related to chemistry, "things aren't just the way you observe them. What you do and what happens are separate. The teacher tells you, 'if you do this something will happen,' and you learn to expect it and believe it will happen."

What surprised these students was that even doing science involved faith, that if the teacher were taken literally, something would happen that was abstract. In this sense, metonymic thought is revelation and metonym a vehicle that makes known personally and experientially a reality that is otherwise invisible and independent (Poewe 1994:235).[7] Provided other researchers understand what I mean by metonym, my conclusion is testable, even falsifiable. Above all, there is nothing spectacular nor mystifying here. Human beings of any make up are simply using a faculty that is clearly available to anyone anywhere who wants to access it.

Given the above, and the fact that African ontology tends to be realist, by which is meant that Africans (certainly those who were interviewed) assumed, as many of us do, that there is one reality out there which is independent of them (although it may affect them), then it cannot be said that African belief systems support the postmodern belief in "multiple realities" (Stoller 1989:118, quoted in Olivier de Sardan 1992:21). While knowledge may be said to be personal for both experimental ethnographers and African religious practitioners, it is so in very different senses. For a postmodernist, knowledge is personal because it is interpreted by him or her from within the position of postmodernity which "is ... a culture of imitations and simulation where copies predominate over originals and images over substance" (Tyler 1996:619 agreeing with Classen, Howes, and Synnott 1994:619). Here the link to originals and substance is lost and "multiple realities" are multiple copies and images. Thus, in the example of a smell evoking "things that are not there" (ibid), a postmodernist puts the emphasis on an "absence," a seemingly disconnected image. By contrast, charismatics put the emphasis on the experience, not only because the experience is real, but also because the evoked images reveal something that was real or will be real: something rooted in personal history, past experience, memory, things, actions, or perceptions of past and future time. In short, to the African believer knowledge is personal because it is revealed in very specific personal experiences (Hastrup 1987).

Recent anthropological literature does not only research the use of the receptive imagination by the ethnographic other; it can also be said to sanction its use by anthropologists. It goes with the assumption of Kakar (1982:10, 24), for example, that common understandings or psychological universals are "masked by superficial idiomatic differences." In other words, if the ethnographic other experiences something, so can, indeed should, the anthropologist. This reciprocal experience is described eloquently by Jill Dubisch (1995). The context is an unexpected visit by Marcos, a man whom she had not previously met in a private setting or persona. Rather than assuming the role of researcher, Dubisch decided to let this meeting be simply one between herself and a friend. The dropping of her mask turned into a revelatory experience. In her words:

> To an outside observer, nothing happened in this brief visit. But for Marcos and myself, something had changed, for I had let myself be myself in a way which acknowledged our sameness and at least a small degree of attraction between a male and female friend. What was important was that by letting myself reveal what I experienced as my 'authentic' self to a degree I had not before, and by acknowledging, however subtly, that we were a man and a woman in a sexual way, I was treating Marcos more an equal, more as I would treat a man in my own society than I ever had before (1995:47).

Most striking is Dubisch's final conclusion:

> To the degree that the female anthropologist takes account of her own sexuality in the field, she may create or enable contexts in which a more 'authentic' self can be revealed, **and thus perhaps a more authentic 'other' as well** (1995:48, my emphasis; cf. Cesara 1982:60, 224; Newton 1993:8).

It is Don Kulick (1995:1–28), however, who makes most explicit the epistemological importance of reciprocal experiencing. He does so in the context of an edited volume where "anthropologists discuss desire, erotic relations, and sexual encounters" (p.1). Writes Kulick "erotic subjectivity in the field is a potentially useful source of insight" (p.5). And discussing the Cesara book, a personal account about the effect of doing research on the researcher, Kulick correctly concludes that "sexual relationships were illuminating ... (because they) compelled reflections on the nature of field work, relationships, and knowledge" (p.15).

It is precisely about matters of experience, and not only tabooed ones like sexuality, that experimental ethnographers are ambivalent. Let us look again at Stoller and Olkes' (1989) work dealing with sorcery. It is an important work, because we are left guessing whether its rich use of rhetoric has its source in experience or authorial artifice. Stoller and Olkes (1989) use such rhetorical devices as sign (for example, p.23–24), suggestion (p.32, 36, 38, 55, 57), literalness (p.32), and leading questions which they ask and answer themselves (anthypophora, p.37, 52–53). Olivier de Sardan (1992:8–9) mentions others. It is fair, therefore, to ask whether Stoller's and Olkes' use of tropes and schemes is a consequence of their determination to evoke as faithfully as possible the reality of Songhay sorcery which they and the Songhay experienced personally, or whether it is calculated to create belief in one of "multiple realities?" In fairness to Stoller (1989:xi), he does say in the *Prologue* that the book "is an account of my experiences in the Songhay world."[8] But who is the "my," Stoller or Olkes? And while narrative strategy is mentioned, it is not explained of what exactly it consists. Furthermore, Stoller talks about "my experiences" in one paragraph, only to belie them in another. Thus they or he or she write, *"In Sorcery's Shadow* is a memoir fashioned from the textures and voices of ethnographic situations" (p.xi). It leaves one with the interesting question of whether the book is about sorcery or whether sorcery is practised on the reader? Criticizing Tyler (1986:128), Östberg reached a similar conclusion: "If ethnographic particularism had put anthropologists at risk of becoming what Geertz (1984:275) called 'merchants of astonishment,' they now seem to have turned into magicians" (1995:15).

To be more explicit, is Stoller locking the reader into a discourse thus persuading him or her that this discourse is one of many distinct realities? Or is he trying to render an experience-near description? If it is the former, it is as Olivier de Sardan says, deception and the deception is broken when readers become aware of the rhetorical techniques or "charms" used to channel their perception. If it is the latter, there is more to be explored.

Unfortunately, Stoller's work does not point to an unambiguous answer of this question. By contrast, the work of Jackson (1986; 1989) does. *Barawa* (1986) is a clear example of an experimental (mixed genre) ethnographic novel, written in the third person, in which rhetoric is a deliberate methodological device used to create the reality which Jackson wants to create. But his claim, that writing *Barawa* was a "totally authentic" task (1986:3), is not self-evident.[9] More so than first person narratives, third person narratives in which the anthropologist makes himself the main character come across as contrived precisely because they are a purposefully constructed discourse (Wolcott 1995:206–7). A fascinating exception are Hastrup's (1992) reflections about the play *Talabot* which was based on her biography. Her account of its production and effect starts in the third person but then shifts to the first person in order to enhance reflexivity. It is the occasion of useful insights into vulnerability, being "field worked upon," concealment and revelation (1992:336, 337). As Cesara who in "writing herself" *chose no hiding place* as the subtitle of her book, so Hastrup in a section on "Writing Myself" comments:

> I felt naked when I entered the room and sat down in the circle of heteroglot actors. Normally, I could hide behind a paper or a prepared speech, but at this occasion I just had to be myself and to give the group a part in my life. There was no hiding place ... (1992:331).

If Jackson's *Barawa* is a questionable success, he does succeed with his method of "radical empiricism" (1989:4–5). This method requires that we treat both their and our experiences as primary data in order "to grasp the ways in which ideas and words are wedded to the world in which we live" (p.5). What is interesting about this approach is that it links the rhetoric used in the construction of an ethnography to the field work that preceded it.

It is not only an ethnographer's rhetorical skills that mediate feelings and experiences of the ethnographic other to us. Sometimes people use foreign cultural symbols to capture a deconstruction brought about by the use of the receptive imagination. Thus in my research of African charismatics in South Africa (1994), the concepts *umoya* or spirit and ancestors are given new meaning and the power to generate new experiences, precisely because they are mediated by foreign discourse.[10] For example, founders of African Independent Churches who invented new liturgies and styles of worship through their visions and dreams, (universal experiences expressed in a culturally specific discourse) claim that they are like those of the Old Testament (a foreign discourse). For similar concerns see Barnes (1989), Hackett (1989), and Hexham (1994).

At this point it is important to look more closely at the difference between experimental ethnographers and experiential writers. We can do this by asking the following question. Is the blurring and proliferation of ethnographic genres solely a consequence of deliberate experimentation with literary styles and discursive fashions, or is it also a consequence of heeding field experiences?

Participant-Observation and the Proliferation of Genres

In 1982, I published *Reflections of a Woman Anthropologist: no hiding place* under the pseudonym Cesara. The aim of this book was to **show** both, "the effects that a foreign culture might have on the researcher" (p.48) and, more generally, how doing research affects the researcher (p.vii). I was working with the oxymoron of "being field worked upon" while doing field work. It was done by highlighting several things: (1) experiences that were epistemologically productive, as Kulick (1995) observed; (2) understanding without undermining nor excluding science (Cesara 1982:216–221); and (3) discussing writing strategies that were integral to existentialism (Cesara 1982:33, 49; Gill and Sherman 1973:10, 16). For that matter, experimentation with writing was also part of German Romanticism going back to the seventeenth century (Kleßmann 1979; Poewe 2008). Furthermore, it was hotly debated among German missionaries to South Africa in the nineteen twenties (Poewe 2008). Finally, like Probyn (1993) and Kulick and Willson (1995), I highlighted the importance of considering the partiality of knowledge, not in the sense of being ideologically locked-in, but in the sense of being open to the disclosures, insights, and creativity that participation and diverse experiences would bring. This partiality was shown in the following: the metonymic and existential sense of part-whole relationships (Cesara 1982:10; Hastrup 1992:332–333); the temporality and intensity of field work (p.21); and my position in history and vis-a-vis gender (p.3–9). The history of my origins and its interplay with my anthropological interests was the most important theme of the book.[11] Consequently, before returning to the relationship between Cesara and genre proliferation, it is important to elaborate briefly on the partiality of knowledge and historicity.

From the first page of the *Introduction* to the Cesara book, and for several pages thereafter and throughout the book, I describe carefully the sense of my "self" before I entered the field. It was a self that would be changed by field experiences, but by no means destroyed, defined, nor limited by them. The self that I was and am has a long history of which I am not only acutely aware but which I deliberately research along with my other work (Poewe 1988, 1996a, b). It is from this history that I speak to and about the world I research; and it is to this history that my research speaks. I was no more defined by the field than was Rabinow whose field experience Probyn (1993:76–78) discusses eloquently and in some detail. For me, the field was set not only against the America that I left in the seventies, but importantly against Germany toward the end of the Second World War in which I first saw the light of day. Throughout the Cesara book I use this relationship between my historical self and field experiences, in order to throw light on those anthropological methods, assumptions, and theories that were for too long hidden in shadow. I wanted to show that it might be worthwhile to write, not only classical ethnographies that contribute to the accumulation of knowledge about the world's people, but also field work memoirs or autobiographies that contribute to the knowledge of the history of the discipline and its practitioners. Furthermore, it was clear to me that the method of participant-observation was an open invitation to write alternative ethnographies. One could say, participation compels participants to create new genres. Let me elaborate.

According to Rao, actualization of practical science consists of **doing** (controlling the action process as is done during empirical research) and **happening** (suffering or experiencing it) (1988:347). The division into doing and happening is important because it reminds us that a specific kind of ethnography is not merely the outcome of a deliberate choice of writing style. It is also the result of a deliberate choice of style of field work. More so than the collection of data, paying attention to happenings may lead to new disclosures, revelations, and insights about the people, discipline, and researcher. That was the main insight that I intended to convey in the Cesara book (1982) and that Hastrup (1987, 1992a, b) and Kulick (1995) have conveyed more effectively since.

Extrapolating from Rao, actualization is important here for two reasons. (1) It gives substance to our doing because it makes gestalting possible. Which is to say, we are structuring stories about the ethnographic self, other, or both from remembered happenings (Bohannan 1995). (2) It requires thinking about doing in order to attend to the happening aspects of actions in the process of doing them. Which is to say, we are exercising the metonymic faculties of thought (Poewe 1989).

Metonymic faculties are exercised when we take an experienced happening to be part of a whole that is tacitly known, and puzzle about how things, events, and people are reduced to parts and what this implies (Polanyi 1964, Hastrup 1987). The dialectic is not complete, however, until we also see the part as a sign illuminating the whole. From this angle, "thick description" of a happening may help elucidate the cultural whole or lead to a breakthrough of a major cultural theme.

Field work assumes a metonymic structure, when it is experienced by the anthropologist as the actualization of the cultural schema or "the world" of the other in the anthropologist's life and world view through a series of happenings (Hastrup 1987:294).[12] Alternatively, anthropologists' empirically collected data and their exploration of remembered happenings allow the researcher (whose epistemology or identity has become ambiguous in the field) to use the imagination to create a gestalt or story (Hastrup 1987:297). The story is illuminated by major, often newly discovered themes about the researched people, the ethnographer, and human beings generally.

According to Kant, it is a function of the imagination, without which we should have no knowledge, to complete the necessarily fragmentary data of the senses, just as it combines our remembered experiences into a single connected whole. Not unexpectedly, the researcher's life, world view, and theoretics can undergo significant change, which is a story as important for the history of the discipline, as is the story about the researched people important for the accumulation of ethnographic knowledge. Again, to show this was the purpose of the Cesara book (Kulick 1995:14–15). What might be called the "self-revelatory" aspect of that book was simply the means, or vehicle, to express epistemological changes (see Tedlock vis-a-vis other such writing, 1991:79).

It is not surprising, therefore, that the very nature of intense field work lends itself quite naturally to the creation of several different kinds of experiential ethnographies or genres even before the anthropologist deliberately experiments with styles of writing. The heuristic table below depicts the different ethnographic genres that are possible by simply working out the permutations of participant-observation or kinds of data with ethnographic foci. Participant-observation allows us to record empirical data (doing), experiential data (heeding happenings), or both.

Ethnographic focus means that we can focus solely on the ethnographic other, on the ethnographic self, or on both (Tedlock 1991:79, 82). Ethnographic self can refer to the ethnic group of the researcher or to the person of the researcher. Before we begin to write, sometimes prodded by a strong preference, we make a deliberate decision on which of these permutations to focus the book. The result will be different genres as indicated in each box of the table below.[13] Naturally, the permutation chosen will also affect our style of writing.

	FOCUS		
DATA	ethnographic other	ethnographic self	ethnographic self & other
empirical data (doing)	classical ethnography general ethnography	native ethnography auto-ethnography	comparative ethnography
experienced data (heeding happenings)	interpretive ethnography	field work memoir, diary	reciprocal illumination
both (doing & happening)	ethnographic case study	ethnographic autobiography	accommodative ethnography

According to the permutations shown in the above table, writing classical (or general) ethnographies, which were a specific invention of the British School of Social Anthropology (Langham 1981), was but one possibility among many. It was the specific predilection of that school of thought to place emphasis on observation and to produce works that were written in a clear and appropriate style for what was then considered to be science. Ornament by which is meant the "study of the figures of speech, language devices such as metaphor, that enhance or change meaning" (1981:12), were generally discouraged except where they were part of the experiential data of the "other."

None of the other permutations were attached to, or sanctioned by, schools of thought, although one could associate some permutations with specific approaches, for example, ethnographic case studies with Oscar Lewis's culture of poverty approach. The permutations in the last two boxes of the Table are associated with an old tradition. Thus the superb book, *Healers in the Night* (1985), by the Jesuit priest and scholar Eric de Rosny, is based on reciprocal illumination (above the last box in the Table).[14] Reciprocal illumination is associated with the Jesuit scholar Joseph François Lafitau (1670–1740). The accommodation method (last box), an extreme form of participant-observation, was developed by P. Matteo Ricci (1552–1610), a Jesuit and eminent missionary scientist to China (Mühlmann 1968 [1984]:44, 45; Poewe 1994:7–12). Coming out of a long and solid tradition of scholarship, these methods and the ethnographies based on them are fresh and innovative. Other examples of works falling into each permutation exist, but are differentially tolerated. For the sake of brevity, I shall leave the task of finding examples or rethinking the labels to the reader.

It is important to remember, however, that alternative anthropological writing always existed, but fell into other existing literary categories like: poetry (Sapir, Benedict (Handler 1986)), narrative and journalism (Herskovits 1934), novels (Laura Bohannon (Bowen 1964)), letters (Mead 1977), and diaries (Malinowski 1967). For excellent overviews of the history of alternative writing done by anthropologists in the past see Tedlock (1991), Reck (1984), Gatewood (1984), Schmidt (1984), Handler (1984), Swiderski (1984), Bruner (1995). Gatewood's paper discusses different ethnographic genres in terms of four "constraints on the form and content of the final product" (1984:5): (1) "what natives do and what they think," (2) "Ethnographer's own values, motives, life ambitions, theoretical prejudices, and so on," (3) "the author's estimation of the intended audience," and (4) "the currently preferred literary form" (p. 5). The first and second constraints are close to what I mean by focus on the ethnographic other and self, respectively. We differ in that I make explicit what he leaves implicit, namely, the kinds of data (empirical, experiential, or both) that ethnographers choose to use in their specific ethnography. By contrast, what I leave implicit, he makes explicit, namely concern for audience and anthropological fashions.

In sum, probing what happens (inside and outside of the self) while doing something is very much a matter of reading signs and signals, of engaging the symbolic faculties of metonymy in the context of the cultural schema of the other. As I point out elsewhere, it is what happens when we formulate hypotheses or hunches (1994). Thus an ethnographer who participates in an event heeds what is happening (to self and other) while s/he is participating (Hastrup 1987:292–294). Given the foreign cultural schema, what is happening during an event is the result of the effect of that culture on the researcher and the researched. To my mind, this effect has to do simultaneously with metonym and empathy. Ethnographers who surrender themselves to the happenings, therefore, really experience the workings of that culture in their lives (Cesara 1982). It opens in them an area of sensory perception that was hitherto unused. Should one be surprised that they might want to step away from a school of thought and explore this new area of perception in another style of writing?

Empathy and Memory

The story of ethnography is like the story of Adam and Eve. We bit into the textual apple of the tree of the knowledge of experience and rhetoric, and now there is no going back. Nevertheless, the causal and experiential aspects of metonym are often missed (Durham and Fernandez 1991:192), while empathy, in some ways associated with metonym, is almost completely misunderstood. Thus in North America, experimental ethnographers tend to focus almost entirely on metaphor and reflexivity.

If metonym has to do with the actualization of a schema through happenings so that the happenings are signs of, and/or are triggered by the schema, then empathy is the faculty that allows us to experience the happening. Broadly speaking, empathy is the ability to share in another's emotions and feelings. It is not, however, as it tends to be defined in Webster's dictionary, a matter of projecting one's own personality into the personality of another in order to understand him or her better.[15] More frequently, the reverse is the case. Empathy has to do with the projection, in the sense of impact, of the other's personality and culture on one's own. The other's personality and culture create a happening in the open-minded or receptive researcher that requires thoughtful exploration (Hastrup 1987:293). The result may be an increased illumination of both the other's and one's own personality and culture. Clearly, if an ethnographer wants to give expression to this increased illumination, the ethnographer is compelled to write a different kind of work from the kind that Evans-Pritchard made famous without, however, denying the important and essential, if separate role played by the latter.

The meaning of empathy is in fact more complex than that given above. It is also more than the expectation that the anthropologist be "an unmitigated nice guy" with "extraordinary sensibility, an almost preternatural capacity to think, feel and perceive like a native," as Geertz would have it (1983:56). And while I would contend that field work is a journey of discovery, it is not quite the quest story as satirized and dismissed by Geertz (1988:44–45). Let us look at empathy more closely.

According to T. Lipps (1851–1914), empathy is based on the assumption of a common humanity. This assumption is quite the opposite of that of reflexivity which depends on cultural differences and distance (even when none exist or are of minor importance) and is concerned with intersubjective meaning.

Empathetic researchers can experience themselves, in some manner, in the other's experiences and vice versa. As I converse or interact with the other, the other and/or I will recognize things in accord with our respective inclinations and needs.

It is not the case, as is often assumed, that experiencing oneself in the other's experiences and vice versa makes for identity. Nor is it the case that the experience is necessarily positive to be empathetic. Lipps distinguished between positive empathy or pleasure and negative empathy or pain.

Positive empathy refers to **agreement** between the stimulus derived from interaction with the other and one's inner activity. Negative empathy occurs when the suggestions implied in the interaction **conflict** with one's inner self. "Inner activity" or "inner self" refer to the complex activity which involves thought, feeling, intuition, sensation, imagination, and suspected or unsuspected attitudes. In other words, we use all human faculties to make sense of other (and self) and then translate these into written, oral, or visual media—if that is what we want to do.

Lipps (1902, in Zweig 1967:485–486) distinguishes at least three kinds of empathy each of which can be experienced negatively or positively.[16]

(1) **Empirical empathy** occurs when sounds of natural objects remind us of, for example, "howling" or "groaning." They can result in such metaphorical descriptions as "howling storm," "groaning trees," which call forth similar feelings in the experiencing self and other. Note the involvement of memory in matters of empathy.[17] One person, however, may experience "groaning trees" positively, the other negatively. The reminder becomes more powerful, that is metonymic, when it is experienced as, for example, the "groaning of all creation" or "the groaning" of the spirit, as charismatic Christians in Africa and elsewhere might say.

(2) **Mood empathy** occurs, for example, when color, music, art, conversation, and so on, call forth similar feelings or moods in the researcher and researched. Thus, I experienced Herero tunes as haunting, melancholy, and overall sad, which is what the Herero showed and said they felt (Poewe 1985). It increased my understanding of their culture, centered as it was on defeat and death, although it also distanced me personally from them.

(3) **Empathy for the sensible** (in the sense of perceptible) **appearance** of living beings occurs when we take other people's gestures, tones of voice, and other characteristics as symptomatic of their inner life (Malinowski 1967). We can talk about "appearance empathy" when we recognize, as in

a flash, by a gesture, or something external, the other's inner life; when we know that it could be, but need not be, part of our inner life. For example, this kind of empathy led to a real breakthrough in my understanding of the Herero. It struck me that their dress made a statement simultaneously about their superiority, sense of failure, and self-protection. This was confirmed by subsequent research and discussions with Herero women.[18]

Before concluding this section, let us look at some examples of negative empathy from the anthropological literature. Let us start with Malinowski's *Diary*. Malinowski was attracted to native women. The diary contains several sensually evocative descriptions of their bodies in walk and gesture. "I liked naked human bodies in motion, and at moments, they also excited me. But I effectively resisted ..." (Malinowski 1967:281; Kohl 1986:50–1; 1987). Yet, as Stocking (1986:26) and Kohl (1986:46) point out, it is precisely this sensual arousal that separated Malinowski from the Trobrianders. At the most empathetic point, Malinowski was aware of the gulf between him and the human beings around him. Furthermore, he saw this precisely because he knew himself to share in a common humanity.

The awareness of the gulf between self and other, at moments of intimacy, is what negative empathy is all about. It has much to do with surrender to the human condition and with making oneself vulnerable even at the risk of pain (Wolff 1964; Richardson personal communication). An example of negative empathy that was, however, transformed into positive empathy and led to a theoretical breakthrough will illustrate the point. The case is that of the South African Nico Smith, an Afrikaner dominee, who like an anthropologist moved into the black township of Mamelodi "to experience the other side of South African life" (personal interview, Mamelodi, summer 1989). He had an extraordinary empathy with blacks. Yet he suffered severe depression, a form of negative empathy, not only because the needs of blacks in townships were overwhelming, but because he learned that: "young blacks are becoming more brutal," that the "majority of black children are embittered," that they "do not value their own lives and therefore do not hesitate to take the life of another" (de Saintonge

1989:178; personal interview, summer 1989). "They did not mind committing suicide, nor did they mind killing each other," said Nico Smith during the interview.

What is curious about the Nico Smith story is that his negative empathy which resulted in severe depression came in time to be transformed into positive empathy. He achieved this by coming to terms with what he formerly regarded to be a painful and unacceptable reality, namely, that South Africa would not escape some sort of drastic violence.

Following his surrender to this threatening reality, he turned to action. It involved both doing something new and rethinking his theology. He remembered Christians in Germany who in early 1930 foresaw that Germany was headed for a catastrophe. They began then to build up a new system of values and relationships. When, in 1945, Germany was in ruins, its people demoralized, its industries and cities destroyed, these Christians played a vital role in the rebuilding of their country. They had already discovered an alternative way as, by the way, has Nico Smith (personal interview, summer 1989; de Saintonge 1989:218).

The unexpected feeling of separation from those to whom we are physically attracted, the deep sense of depression called forth in us by those we love and to whom we are committed, the highlighting of difference despite "mutual erotic attraction" between "an anthropologist and a person in the field" (Kulick 1995:19), epitomize negative empathy. Far from forcing ethnographers to pretend to something we are not, negative empathy may make us more human. Reflecting on her experience of "falling in love with an-Other lesbian" in the field, Blackwood writes:

> The ethnographic experience is about experiencing oneself with others, of knowing we are all different, yet recognizing the bonds among us rather than reifying the difference to make Others exotic or inferior (1995:72).

Lipps talks about other forms of empathy. Suffice it to say here that empathy has to do with those moments of clear perception of the other which powerfully stimulate our imagination. Consequently, we experience the other as part of something greater or of something in us, our past, our theoretical assumptions, our approach to research, or in the other's past, the other's way of life, that we could not see or face before. And this challenge is, as Kulick (1995:20) emphasizes, epistemologically productive. It encourages us as social scientists to formulate hypotheses, or hunches, that are thereafter subjected to falsification.

Writing Field Work: Metonymic Structure Clarified

Ethnography has its source in systematically researched, as well as experienced life. Choices about style of writing come later. Postmodernism, political correctness, and research in politically sensitive parts of the world highlight the problem of remaking experience into text. For example, a rapidly changing and politically volatile South Africa, before 1991, presented us with a situation where thought—of whatever discipline—quickly turned into sterile and stereotypic rhetoric. Metaphors died quick deaths. Words became mere badges for where the speaker stood on the political spectrum. Human beings, especially blacks and whites, were frequently quite alienated from one another. In such a situation it is words that violate, and experiences, being with the other, that heal. In short, it shows just how important it is to experience another side of life and to convey this experience to others, especially when it contradicts the quotidian flow of events and rhetoric.

Participant-observation and field work make for an anthropology of experience (Turner and Bruner 1986). It does not do away with sound research methods and falsification nor does it deprecate diverse schools of thought. It does, however, insist upon thoughtful exploration of ordinary and extraordinary experiences that occur in or are related to the field. Experiential situations, especially when they disturb because they have to do with something to which we have been, or prefer to be blind, lead to conceptual or theoretical breakthroughs (Cesara 1982; Tedlock 1990;

Kulick and Willson 1995). They are also instrumental, as said, in reshaping or transforming our world view.

In some sense, therefore, field work may involve surrender to the ethnographic other for the sake of illumination, if not identification. It prompts us to use the metonymic faculty and the realistic receptive imagination. It is with the use of metonyms that we transform mundane experiences into insights and ethnographic narratives. Consequently, the ethnographic other becomes a language of signs and signals about that which "is essential" in them and "in ourselves" (Malinowski 1967:119; also quoted in Stocking 1986:26–27).

This kind of anthropology is experiential because it is based on a relationship between ethnographer and ethnographic other so that the former experiences the latter through signs made manifest, or events brought about, by that which animates the ethnographic other. It inspires anthropologists, like other scientists, to use both the analytical and receptive imagination. By analytical imagination is meant the critical questioning of images taken from experiences of the world, psyche, and people (Degenaar personal interview, summer 1989). By receptive imagination is meant the snap elucidation of images through visions, dreams, or discernment of hunches and hypotheses (Tedlock 1991). This kind of imagination is not only used by the ethnographic other, but also by us. As Susanne Langer (1948) pointed out, it is used at times of shifting and uncertain social and intellectual circumstances: the kind of circumstances encountered in the field.

Given the important emphasis on the use of imagination, though it is very much subject to analytical reason, it follows that experiential anthropology is both deconstructive and reconstructive. It is deconstructive in the sense that it is an attack on logocentrism and ethnography for opting only for reason when the human being is clearly constituted of sensation, emotion, intuition, intellect and imagination. It is reconstructive because it leads to conceptual breakthroughs that are then tested against empirical data collected by established methods or that inspire future research.

In the Cesara book, I used the letters to my mother to "plough up" logocentrism in order to show the soil of "nourishing" emotion and intuition beneath:

> ... (And) he told of his childhood. How his father would take him to the Industrial Belt and how he would roam the streets and rummage through refuse cans of Europeans ... He told me about his peculiar European friend who ... sat for the longest time watching the sunset. How peculiar, he said, to watch the sun for hours (1982:55).

And so I comment:

> To lay hold of a culture through one's love of one individual may be an illusion, but there can be no doubt that love became a fundamental relation of my thoughts and perceptions to both, the world of the Lenda and myself (p.60).

This sequence of event and insight is then followed by a phenomenological explanation of "moods or states of mind of ... the researcher and those being researched." It is the phenomenological explanation that highlights the revelatory and epistemological qualities of experienced events and emotions (p.66). But events do not only lead to insights about the epistemological importance of phenomena like love or dread. Events, sometimes small and seemingly insignificant, also activate memories that throw us back upon our history. For example:

> ... He had malaria and felt weak and sick. Beads of perspiration trickled down his face. And as I looked at him I felt some recognition. It stirred my memory and took me into my past for I saw in him the image of my father.

> ... He returned from the war ... He was simply there one day. His

head was shaved, his face looked wan, and he was weak and ailing. And as he greeted my mother, cold sweat ran down his face (Cesara 1982:80).

There is not enough time nor space to develop further this sequence of event to emotion, insight, memory, history, or dream. Suffice it to say this. Some may condemn the simple act of being human in the field.[19] But no one can take away that moment, nor that experience, nor that insight, nor finally the knowledge of the past that I and others have gained from it. The knowledge that made us fully alive and led to further research.

The experiential field worker is at home with change. It is not only that it might attract field workers with ambivalent identities to research peoples with ambivalent identities (Agar 1980). Making identities, cultures, and languages ambivalent is precisely what this form of anthropology is all about. It makes ambivalent because these field workers allow themselves to experience the breakdown of their assumptions and the questioning of their identities in the field (DeVita 1992; Blackwood 1995; Cesara 1982; Malinowski 1967). We do not need to be forced onto the psychiatric couch because of it (Wengle 1988). More importantly, as Malinowski (1967) reveals and as Jackson (1989:2) argues, immersion in the field creates ambivalence because experience and concept are not necessarily identical. Above all, concepts cannot be tied to ideological and political categories.

Past and Gone

The major premise of eighteenth and nineteenth century positive philosophy (and science) held that human kind progressed to ever greater intellectual and moral development. It was based, as most premises are, on common place perceptions and observations of the times. It will be remembered that Victorian England was a time of rapid technological and social change, so much so that change was experienced as transformation. As Stocking (1987:203) points out, the sense of radical transformation lent itself easily to reasoning from opposites. The world was perceived as divided into now and then, civilization and savagery, prosperity and slum, monogamy and promiscuity, rationality and instinct. And the two were thought to be fundamentally different, at opposite ends of an evolutionary scale (Stocking 1987:208–210).

Linked to the premise of progress and development from savagery to civilization was the "scientific" method of observation, comparison and generalization. But if one observed in terms of, and compared and generalized from the premise of progress to ever greater intellectual and moral development, the ethnographic other would always be more or less intelligent or morally developed than the ethnographic self. The implied judgment on our part (Fabian 1983), and increased consciousness of ethnic worth and ethnic distinctiveness on their part (Said 1978), led not so much to improvement of research methods and understanding, as to corrections through language use and rhetoric. Far from easing tensions among ethnic groups, one wonders whether our century will not become known as the "age of the intellectual organization of ethnic hatreds."

At any rate, the last decades of the twentieth century remind me of Julien Benda's (1928:27) characterization of the nineteenth century. He called it the "age of the intellectual organization of political hatreds." He wrote:

> Anti-Semitism, Pangermanism, French Monarchism, Socialism are not only political manifestations; they defend a particular form of morality, of intelligence, of sensibility, of literature, of philosophy and of artistic conceptions ... every one today claims that his movement is in line with "the development of evolution" and "the Profound unrolling of history" (1928:27–8).

Furthermore, argued Benda (1928:99), "the cult for the particular and the scorn for the universal is a reversal of values quite generally characteristic of the teaching of the modern (intellectual)." Modern intellectuals, he lamented, exhort "the peoples to feel conscious of themselves in what makes them the most distinct from others" (p.83). It would result, he predicted quite accurately, in race, ethnic, and national wars.

If systematic research is so easily held capture by ideologies and paradigms, how else but by experience, intense even painful experience, can we break through the straightjacket to contemplate anew the human condition? And what else but an intense experience will motivate us to write against the times?

Conclusion

Experiential and experimental ethnographies may overlap, but at the core they are fundamentally different. For the production of knowledge and for epistemological reflection, experiential ethnographers depend on how the "self" of the anthropologist interacts with experiences, people, and the flow of events in the field. This multi-level reciprocal dynamic between anthropologist and the field is the source of the proliferation of experiential ethnographies and genres. By contrast, for their text-making, experimental ethnographers depend on rhetoric and on using "the self" as a device for realism or as a "source for narrative strength" (Stoller and Olkes 1989:xi). Deliberate invention of textual strategies is the source of the proliferation of experimental ethnographies. Marcus and Fischer (1986) and Clifford and Marcus (1986) encouraged this experimentation with the creation of a new anthropological culture and program. But while some experimental ethnographies are successful, the experimental program is a "cultural trap."

Restriction of writing style is most effective when it is imposed by a school of thought based on a clear sense of goals, methods, and resources. But the anthropologist has invested too much of his or her intellectual power in the field, to give up on the full exploration of its potential for discovery of knowledge and styles of conveying it. Look at what we still do not have. Solid comparative works based on **as firm** a knowledge of one's own history and tradition, **as on** that of the other (de Rosny 1985). Consequently, critiques of things Western are hardly credible, except, that is, to those who share the same ideological persuasion as postmodernists. We have not yet learned the simple lesson, that criticism is more effective when it is implicit and mutual, as in the method of reciprocal illumination, than when it is explicit and directed to those who are, or that which is, safe to criticize. Serious memoirs, biographies (Clifford 1982), histories (Stocking 1987; Langham 1981), and historical novels by anthropologists are rare. Those that exist are focussed almost entirely on British and American anthropology. Furthermore, the time has come to stop treating societies and countries, South Africa for example, as special cases when they have been part of global processes all along (Furlong 1991; Featherstone 1991; Östberg 1995:17; Poewe 1996). Participant-observation, "actual physical presence in their world" (Hastrup and Hervik 1994:3), immersion in archival material written in other languages, these **methods of presence** will continue to be central to the "anthropological project of comprehending the world" (ibid:3). So long as we are a social science, our primary concern must be to maintain a clear link between the reality we research and what we write. To eliminate this link means eliminating anthropology.

Comment 2018

After research in Zambia, I did two further field trips to Africa. I chose countries that led, as if perfectly planned, to archival research in Germany. For two decades Sub-Saharan Africa and German history, which was a constant undercurrent during my apprentice stay in Zambia, remained parallel, if also linked interests.

Then in the mid-nineties the focus became the development of National Socialism based on unpublished documents stored in various archives in Germany (Poewe 2006). Seeing the deceit of that worldview—and its horrendous consequences—was the light that I hoped for when I stood there in the Lenda valley baffled, because it was as if I looked at my own past.

When I read the recent work of ethnographers that were mentioned in this Chapter, for example Douglas Holmes and George Marcus (2008), I think that field work as I and uncountable others experienced it is finished. Its price was perhaps always too high not only in financial terms but also social and psychological ones.

It is very important, therefore, that this little book is read as part of the history of knowledge and, importantly, as one example of an episodic story in the life of millions of potential new immigrants to functioning democratic countries that will expect adaptation or integration. I anticipate—indeed it is already happening—many new apprentices of simply life if not ethnography.

APPENDIX

About the Title: The main title is inspired by Beatrice Webb "My Apprenticeship." 1926 Longmans, Green and Company. London: Great Britain. The sub-title comes from Jessica Riddell "Building resilience into the classroom." In *University Affairs* 5/17:43.

About Heidegger: In this revision, I excluded Heidegger's *Sein und Zeit* (*Being and Time*). My subsequent archival research in Marbach, Germany, convinced me that Heidegger's philosophy and politics were *völkisch*, a form of post-WWI German fascism, and thus Nazi (Poewe 2006; Faye 2009). His thought operated as "anthropology" within German fascism in the 1920s. For interesting recent research of European fascism see Douglas Holmes (2016).

About C. S. Lewis: C.S. Lewis, 2001 (1961), *A Grief Observed*. New York, NY: HarperCollins, p.72. An adaptation of Lewis' words expressing grief on the death of his wife. Although unintended, his is the best characterization of the anthropological enterprise. In my view, the latter is a tragi-comedy.

About author's loss of country: Gumbinnen is now Gusev. Under the Potsdam Conference 1945, northern East Prussia became part of the Soviet Union as did Gumbinnen, which was renamed Gusev after the Russian Army Captain and Hero of the Soviet Union. The suffering and sacrifices of Russia's people cut deeply into their lives.

About Johann Wolfgang Goethe: Johann Wolfgang Goethe (1749–1832) is a famous German poet and literary figure with whose work I grew up. His poem "Nur wer die Sehnsucht kennt …" (a poem about knowing the meaning of longing) has accompanied me throughout life. It is hard to tell whether this sense of yearning is also an aspect of Lenda psychology? We know from Laura Bohannon that Shakespeare could be told in tribal contexts of Africa, but the rightness of the relationship for the motivation of say, revenge, differed.

ENDNOTES: Chapter 22

1. This paper appeared in *Ethnos*, Vol. 61, No. 3–4, December 1996, pp.177–206.

2. I base my comparative remarks and analogies on research conducted in southern Africa, the southeastern US, western Canada, parts of Germany and Britain. In South Africa itself, I did field work and life history interviews among charismatic Christians of all shades of skin colour and among selected popular writers who were Afrikaans and English speaking. As well, I conducted archival research in the Berliner Missionswerk from January 2 to April 29, 1995. Based on usually ignored German documents, this has led to an intense examination of the affinities and links between Afrikaner and German nationalisms between 1870 and 1948 (Poewe 1996, 2000). Field work was conducted off and on from 1972 to 1991. In South Africa, specifically in 1986, 1987, 1989, field work was done for four months each year. My approach to research became historical and global as a result of my reflection on my first long field work in Zambia (see Cesara 1982).

3. I put Marcus and Fischer (1986), Tyler (1986), and Scheper-Hughes in the same camp vis-a-vis political commitment and ethics even though Scheper-Hughes abhors "cultural relativism" (1995:414). Consequently, she questions "two sacred cows": the proud, even haughty distance from political engagement and its accompanying, indeed, its justifying ethic of moral and cultural relativism. The latter has returned with a vengeance in the still fashionable rhetoric of postmodernism (p.414).

    To me the dogma of the inseparability of poetics and politics, that is political commitment to the experimental program, and political engagement, that is political commitment to one political faction in a political situation replete with other political factions, are in principle one and the same. See for example Nomavenda Mathiane's (1989) very different view to that of Scheper-Hughes.

Mathiane is a black woman who lived permanently in a black township and witnessed all kinds of political horrors, including the necklace. Scheper-Hughes does belong, however, in the experiential camp vis-a-vis her emphasis on an "anthropology of the *really real*" (1995:417).

4.   Numerous alternative terms are used for experimental ethnographers. They include: experimentalists, new ethnographers, textualists, postmodernists, and deconstructionists (Probyn 1993:72; Olivier de Sardan 1992:7). Tyler (1986) also uses the term anarchists.

5.   According to Bohannan (1995:181, 185), "An ideology is a set of doctrines, assertions, and intentions that undergird a social, religious, or political position." To quote further: "Ideologies differ from science (including social science) in that their propositions are not presented as theory to be criticized, tested, and improved, but rather as premises to be accepted on faith" (p.185). It is a superb criticism of Clifford (1986:2) without referring to him.

6.   I use metonym the way Leach (1976) defined it, but modify it in accordance with my field observations. According to Leach, metonymy includes sign, natural index, and signal. In the first, A stands for B as part for a whole; in the second, A indicates B; in the third, A triggers B so that the relationship between A and B is mechanical and automatic. What makes the metonymic operation powerful is the fact that, in practice, we do not carefully distinguish among sign, index, and signal, so that A stands for and indicates B, while B is seen to trigger A. In a happening, the happening (A) usually stands for and indicates the schema being actualized (B), while the schema (B) is seen to trigger the happening (A). For charismatic and African Christians, this schema is centered on the activities of the Holy Spirit so that events (A) are interpreted as evidence of the Holy Spirit (B) working in the life of a person. For experiential anthropologists, the schema (B) being actualized in happenings (A) is that of the culture or world of the people under study.

7.   The aim is to move beyond the view that metonym, a trope, is but "an assertion of an association based on contiguity of relation" (Fernandez 1986:173). The contiguity is **causal**. James Fernandez also recognizes the presence of metonymy in revitalization (p.172). Metonym is a turn of thought that is used to express a relationship between an aspect of **experienced reality** and the **larger reality**, visible or invisible, of which the experience is a manifestation. This position which was brought home to me by scientists who were charismatic Christians (1994), is very different from the postmodernity posture that celebrates copies and images predominating over, and usually cut from, originals and substance.

8.   The book is co-authored by Paul Stoller and Cheryl Olkes. I am assuming that the "I" of the Prologue refers to Stoller. It is just an additional ambiguity of their method.

9.   In *Barawa* (1986) Jackson uses hypotyposis, vivid description appealing to the sense of sight, to great effect (p.11–12, 29). While I am not going to define each term here Jackson uses epizeuxis, anaphora, gradatio (see p.19); ploche, epistrophe and epanalepsis (see p.22), among many others. Indeed, in my classes I found that students tend not to understand Jackson's books, especially, *Barawa* until the world of rhetoric is opened to them. In *Barawa* Jackson is the main character.

10.   My research of charismatic Christians was based on a global cultural perspective. See also Hexham and Poewe (1997). Consequently, I interviewed charismatic Christians from various sub-communities in South Africa, as well as in the southeastern US, in western Canada, and in Britain and Germany. In this paper, and for purposes of simplicity, I refer primarily to black, white, "coloured," and Indian South Africans who belonged to two kinds of churches: African Independent Churches, founded by black South Africans, and New Independent Churches, founded by people of all skin colours, but especially by white South Africans. The founding of African Independent Churches goes back to the nineteenth century. New Independent Churches began to be

founded from the nineteen seventies onward. Again, because I took a global perspective I interviewed charismatic Christians who lived in mud huts as well as scientists who were charismatic Christians. My generalizations come from this spectrum of interviews (see Poewe 1994).

11.   The inclusion of sexual intimacy and gender in the book seems to have eclipsed what I considered to be most important, namely, how my past history played into every significant experience and insight. Unfortunately, in my exuberance about new insights gained from immersion in field work, I showed my provincialism in matters that were not a direct part of my field work experiences and about which I should have remained silent. As Newton (1993) reminds her readers, she took me to task for that.

12.   It is important to understand that not all anthropologists give themselves over to experiencing the cultural schema of the other. Clearly, some anthropologists go to the field to test hypotheses, and so forth, that derive from the scientific schema of their discipline. Most of us do both.

13.   The kinds of ethnographies named in each box are **mere** suggestions. The reader might come up with better ones. This indeterminacy should be seen as part of the positive asset of participant-observation. It is a method that leaves us entirely open to discovery. If we heed doings and happenings in the culture outside, there is always the possibility that "the beautiful premises that are part of the culture within (our) heads" will be questioned and/or give way to new insights (Bohannan 1995:185).

14.   Reciprocal illumination is associated with the work of Joseph François Lafitau (1670–1740) who illuminated the customs and institutions of native Americans in terms of those of ancient Greece, at the same time that he illuminated the customs and institutions of ancient Greece in terms of those of native Americans (Mühlmann 1984:4). Looking at contemporary material, Tedlock's "Self/Other dialogue" may be an example of reciprocal illumination (1991:82).

15. Some anthropological texts have already eliminated the concept empathy from their glossary and replaced it by intersubjective meaning and reflexivity. See Schultz and Lavenda (1987:46) where they say, "Recognizing the humanity of one's informants has nothing to do with trying to empathize (sic) with and reproduce their inner psychological states. It is concerned with intersubjective meanings..." Yet, empathy has nothing to do with reproducing someone's psychological state. As well notice their limitation of understanding to "informants" and of "reflexivity" to "thinking about thinking." As if that is all there was to field work and the human being. My field work was certainly never limited to "informants." Why else should I have made such efforts to learn their language and to use quantitative as well as qualitative methods of researching society. Furthermore, we shall see that empathy implies reflection upon the experiences and thoughts of self and other. As for reflexivity, the conjoining of self and other through intersubjective meaning, its limitations are obvious in, for example, South Africa where black and white Christians believe themselves to have arrived at common intersubjective meaning only to discover that there is no agreement between them in action or experience to which the common meaning seemingly referred. (Poewe 1993).

16. While I give examples of different kinds of empathy following Lipps, I differ from him in that I move away from the idea that empathy means projection of our feelings into the other. Zweig (1967) continues the use of "projection."

17. See Cesara (1982). Field experiences and empathy called forth significant memories. Working through these had a great impact on my anthropological world view and theoretics. The potential importance of erotic subjectivity and reflexivity for our epistemology, methods, and theories is most competently discussed in a book edited by Kulick and Willson (1995).

18. "This dress identifies us immediately. We, the long-dresses, don't get paid well. We don't get good jobs. Men treat us worse."

Astonished I said, "then you are identifying yourselves as a certain type."

"Yes. The dress identifies us as washers and ironers for whites ... There are other jobs. But we don't know them. Therefore we wear this dress. In this way ... Others won't approach us ..."

"Look," said one Herero woman. "Our tradition too goes with wearing this dress. Tradition folds us in, makes us cower, cringe, grovel." They used the word *okuriyanga* which is reflexive and points simultaneously to an exterior condition and a psychological state.

"Likewise," she continued, "the dress folds us in and narrows our behaviour ... It goes with our life." And then they talked about how they use the dress to hold one another back.

The important point is that this conversation would not have occurred had their dress not called forth in me a feeling of empathy. It came as a hunch that the dress underlined the above inner life. The Herero-Victorian dress signalled to me, as said, their sense of tortured superiority, incapacity, self-imprisonment, and distinctiveness. It made a powerful statement about a major conflict in Herero character.

19.   Some in our profession pretend that a private life in the field is professionally unethical. The fact is, all of us, at home or abroad, have a private life in addition to our work related life. Indeed, many make no distinction. Furthermore, insights gained from people with whom we live our private lives often spill over into work related things and not infrequently this is explicitly acknowledged. No one would be narrow minded enough to call this unethical. Where is the mutually inspiring public-private life in the field different from the public-private dynamic at home? It troubles those who categorically, not experientially, assert that those we study are objects and inferior. Probyn (1993), Hastrup (1992), among many others, including Cesara (1982), have shown otherwise. Like Romantics, postmodernists have quite literally "enthroned the national (or ethnic) community and its utterly

individual, national (or ethnic) spirit" (Dooyeweerd 1979:179). This despite the fact that "under nazism we have experienced what it means when civil-legal freedom and equality are abolished and when a man's legal status depends upon the community of "blood and soil" (ibid:186). A full life lived under the dictum of universal human rights does not interfere with respecting the professional ethics of the discipline. In the business of respecting the human rights of people anywhere, we might even include those of the anthropologist. We are not a priesthood! I say this despite the fact that Newton (1993) reprimanded me for my ethical provincialism in the matter of homosexuality.

REFERENCES

Abrahams, Roger D.
Ordinary and Extraordinary Experience. *In the Anthropology of Experience*, edited by Victor Turner and Edward Bruner. Pp.45–72. Urbana: University of Illinois Press.

Agar, Michael H.
1980 *The Professional Stranger*. New York: Academic Press.

Andersen, Barbara G.
1971 Adaptive Aspects of Culture Shock. *American Anthropologist* 73, 1121–1125.

Ardener, Edwin
1982 Social Anthropology and the Decline of Modernism. In *Reason and Morality*, edited by J. Overing. ASA Monographs no. 24. London: Tavistock.

Arendt, Hannah
1969 *Hannah Arendt im Gespräch mit Günter Gaus*. https://www.youtube.com/watch?v=J9SyTEUi6Kw. Also in *Philososphie Magazin*: Hannah Arendt, Die Freiheit des Denkens. Sonderausgabe, 6 June 2016:16–26.

Barnes, Sandra T.
1989 *Africa's Ogun*. Bloomington: Indiana University Press.

Beauvoir, Simone de
1956 (1961) *The Mandarins*. Cleveland and New York: World Pub. Co.

1965 *The Prime of Life*. Harmondsworth: Penguin.

Bekker, Simon
1995 The silence of our scholars. In *Frontiers of Freedom*. 5:7–8.

Benda, Julien
1928 *The Treason of the Intellectuals*. New York: Norton & Co.

Blackwood, Evelyn
1995 Falling in love with an-Other lesbian: reflections on identity in field

work. In *Taboo: Sex, identity, and erotic subjectivity in anthropological field work*, edited by Don Kulick and Margaret Willson. Pp.51–75. London: Routledge.

Bohannan, Laura
1966 *Shakespeare in the Bush*. Available at www.sociology.morrisville.edu.

Bohannan, Paul
1995 *How Culture Works*. New York: Free Press.

Bowen, Elenore Smith (Laura Bohannan)
1964 *Return to Laughter*. New York: Doubleday.

Bruckner, Pascal
1986 *The Tears of the White Man*. Tr. William R. Beer. New York: The Free Press.

Bruner, Edward M.
1986 Experience and Its Expressions. In *The Anthropology of Experience*, edited by Victor W. Turner & Edward M. Bruner, pp.3–30. Urbana: University of Illinois Press.

1995 Introduction: The Ethnographic Self and the Personal Self. In *Anthropology and Literature*. Paul Benson, ed. Urbana: University of Illinois Press.

Camus, Albert
1948 *The Plague*. Translated by Stuart Gilbert, Harmondsworth, Middlesex, England: Penguin Press.

Castaneda, Carlos
1968 *The Teachings of Don Juan: A Yaqui Way of Knowledge*. New York: Ballantine Books.

1971 *A Separate Reality: Further Conversations with Don Juan*. New York: Simon and Schuster.

Cesara, Manda (Karla Poewe)
1982 *Reflections of a Woman Anthropologist: No Hiding Place*. London: Academic Press.

Chayanov, A.V.
1966 *On the Theory of Peasant Economy*. (D. Thorner, B. Kerblay, R.E.F. Smith, eds.) Richard D. Irwin, Inc. for the American Economic Association, Homewood.

Classen, Constance
1993 *The Worlds of Sense*. London: Routledge.

Classen, Constance, David Howes, and Anthony Synnott
1994 *Aroma: The Cultural History of Smell*. London: Routledge.

Clifford, James
1982 *Person and Myth: Maurice Leenhardt in the Melanesian World*. Berkeley: University of California Press.

Clifford, James & George E. Marcus.
1986 *Writing Culture: The Poetics and Politics of Ethnography*. Berkcley: University of California Press.

Cliggett, Lisa
2005 *Grains from Grass: Aging, Gender, and Famine in Rural Africa*. Ithaca and London: Cornell University Press.

Compton, John
2006 *The Giants of Philosophy Jean Paul Sartre Audiobook*. Narrated by Charlton Heston. Ashland, Oegon: Blackstone Audio Inc.

Crane, Stephen
1898 *The Open Boat and other Tales of Adventure*. New York: Doubleday & McClure.

D'Andrade, Roy
1995 Objectivity and Militancy: A Debate. *Current Anthropology* 36 (3):399–408.

Degenaar, Johan
1989 (conversation during research in South Africa).

de Rosny, Eric
1985 *Healers in the Night*. Maryknoll: Orbis Books.

de Saintonge, Rebecca
1989 *Outside the Gate: The Story of Nico Smith*. London: Hodder & Stoughton.

DeVita, Philip
1992 *The Naked Anthropologist*. Belmont: Wadsworth.

Dooyeweerd, Herman
1979 *Roots of Western Culture: Pagan, Secular, and Christian Options*. Toronto: Wedge Publishing Foundation.

Droogers, Andre
1980 *The Dangerous Journey: Symbolic Aspects of Boys' Initiation among the Wagenia of Kisangani, Zambia*. The Hague: Mouton Publishers.

Dube, Leela
1975 Woman's Worlds—Three Encounters. In *Encounter and Experience*. (A. Beteille and T.N. Madan, eds.) pp.157–177. Delhi: Vikas Publishing House PVT LTD.

Dubisch, Jill
1995 Lovers in the field: sex, dominance, and the female anthropologist. In *Taboo: Sex, identity, and erotic subjectivity in anthropological field work*. Don Kulick and Margaret Willson, eds. Pp.29–50. London and New York: Routledge.

Durham, Deborah and James W. Fernandez
1991 Tropical Dominions: The Figurative Struggle over Domains of Belonging and Apartness in Africa. *Beyond Metaphor: The Theory of Tropes in Anthropology*. James W. Fernandez, ed. Pp.190–210. Stanford: Stanford University Press.

Evans, Alice
2016 "'For the Elections, We Want Women!': Closing the Gender Gap in Zambian Politics." In *Development and Change* 47(2):388-411. DOI: 10.1111/dech.12224. International Institute of Social Studies.

Evans, Mary
1980. Views of Women and Men in the Work of Simone De Beauvoir. *Women's Studies* 3(4):395–404.

Evans-Pritchard, E.E.
1974 *Man and Woman Among the Azande*. London: Faber and Faber.

Fabian, Johannes
1983 *Time and the Other*. New York: Columbia University Press.

Faye, Emmanuel
2009 *Heidegger*. New Haven & London: Yale University Press.

Featherstone, Mike, ed.
1991 *Global Culture: Nationalism, Globalization and Modernity*.
London: Sage.

Feld, Steven
1982 *Sound and sentiment: Birds, weeping, poetics, and song in Kaluli
expression*. Philadelphia: University of Pennsylvania Press.

Fernandez, James W.
1986 *Persuasions and Performances: The Play of Tropes in Culture*. A
Midland Book: Indiana University Press.

Fikes, Jay Courtney
1993 *Carlos Castaneda, Academic Opportunism and the Psychedelic
Sixties*. Victoria, BC: Millenia Press.

Foucault, Michael
1972 *Archaeology of Knowledge*. Tr. By A.M. Sheridan Smith. New
York: Pantheon.

Freeman, Derek
1983 *Margaret Mead and Samoa: The Making and Unmaking of an
Anthropological Myth*. Cambridge, MA: Harvard University Press.

Friedrich, Paul
1989 Language, Ideology, and Political Economy. *American
Anthropologist*. 91(2):295–312.

Furlong, Patrick Jonathan
1991 *Between Crown and Swastika: the impact of the radical right on the
Afrikaner nationalist movement in the fascist era*. Middletown, CT:
Wesleyan University Press.

Gadamer, Hans-Georg
1976 *Philosophical Hermeneutics*. (David E. Linge, tr. and ed.) Berkeley: University of California Press.

Gatewood, John B.
1984 A Short Typology of Ethnographic Genres, or ways to Write About Other Peoples. *Anthropology and Humanism Quarterly.* 9(4):5–10.

Gauck, Joachim
2012 *Freiheit*. München: Kösel-Verlag.

Geertz, Clifford
1983 *Local Knowledge*. New York: Basic.

1984 Distinguished Lecture: Anti Anti-Relativism. *American Anthropologist.* 66:263–268.

1988 *Works and Lives*. Stanford: Stanford University Press.

Gill, Richard and Ernest Sherman
1973 *The Fabric of Existentialism*. Englewood Cliff, NJ: Prentice-Hall.

Goethe, Johann Wolfgang
1961 *Gedichte*. Zurich: Artemis Verlag.

Goldhagen, Daniel Jonah
1996 *Hitler's Willing Executioners*. New York: Alfred A. Knopf.

Goody, Jack
1976 *Production and Reproduction*. Cambridge: Cambridge University Press.

Gouldner, Alvin W.
1971 *The Coming Crisis of Western Sociology*. New York: Aron Books.

Green, Garrett
1989 *Imagining God*. New York: Harper & Row.

Griaule, M. and Germaine Dieterlen.
1954 The Dogon of the French Sudan. In *African Worlds*. Daryll Forde, ed. pp.83–110. London: Oxford University Press for IAI, International African Institute.

Griaule, Marcel
1965 *Conversations with Ogotemmeli*. London: Oxford University Press for IAI, International African Institute.

Hackett, Rosalind
1989 *Religion in Calabar*. Berlin: Mouton de Gruyter.

Hammarskjold, Dag
1964. *Markings*. (Tr. W.H. Auden and Leif Sjoberg). London: Faber and Faber Limited.

Handler, Richard
1984 Narrating multiple realities: some lessons from Jane Austen. *Anthropology and Humanism Quarterly*. 9 (4):15–21.

1986 Vigorous Male and Aspiring Female: Poetry, Personality, and Culture in Edward Sapir and Ruth Benedict. *Malinowski, Rivers, Benedict and Others*. George Stocking, ed. Madison: University of Wisconsin Press. Pp.127–155.

Hastrup, Kirsten
1987 The Reality of Anthropology. *Ethnos* 3–4:287–300.

1992a Out of Anthropology: The Anthropologist as an Object of Dramatic Representation. *Cultural Anthropology* 7(3):327–345.

1992b Writing ethnography: state of the art. In *Anthropology and Autobiography*. Pp.116–133. London: Routledge.

Hastrup, Kirsten and Peter Hervik, eds.
1994 *Social Experience and anthropological knowledge*. London: Routledge.

Hazleton, Lesley
1977 *Israeli Women*. New York: Simon and Schuster.

Heller, Scott
1992 Experience and Expertise Meet in New Brand of Scholarship. *The Chronicle of Higher Education*, 6 May:A7–A9.

Herskovits, Melville and Frances Herskovits
1934 *Rebel Destiny*. New York: Whittlesey House with McGraw-Hill.

Hexham, Irving, ed.
1994 *The Scriptures of the amaNazaretha of Ekuphakameni*. Calgary: The University of Calgary Press.

Hexham, Irving and Karla Poewe
1997 *New Religions as Global Cultures: the sacralization of the human*. Bolder: Westview Press. Pp.194.

Hobhouse, Emily
1901 *Die Zustände in den südafrikanischen Konzentrationslagern*. Berlin: Deutschen Burenhilfsbund.

1984 *Boer War Letters*. Rykie van Reenen, ed. Cape Town: Human & Rousseau.

Holmes, Douglas R.
2016 "Fascism 2." Guest Editorial. In *Anthropology Today*, April, Volume 32, Number 2.

Homans, George C. and David M. Schneider
1955 *Marriage, Authority, and Final Causes: A Study of Unilateral Cross-Cousin Marriage*. Glencoe: Free Press.

Honigmann, John J.
1976 *The Development of Anthropological Ideas*. Homewood: The Dorsey Press.

Horner, Winifred Bryan
1988 *Rhetoric in the Classical Tradition*. New York: St. Martin's Press.

Jackson, Michael
1986 *Barawa and the Ways Birds Fly in the Sky*. Washington: Smithsonian Institution.

1989 *Paths Towards a Clearing*. Bloomington: Indiana University Press.

Jules-Rosette, Bennetta
1980 *Rethinking Field Research: The Role of the Observing Participant*. Washington, DC: American Anthropological Association.

Jung, C.G.
1968 *Analytical Psychology: Its Theory and Practice*. New York: Vintage Books.

Kakar, Sudhir
1982 *Shamans, Mystics and Doctors*. Boston: Beacon Press.

Keesing, R.M.
1975 *Kin Groups and Social Structure*. New York: Holt, Rinehart and Winston.

Kelly, Raymond C.
1974 *Etoro Social Structure*. Ann Arbor: The University of Michigan Press.

Kleinschmidt, Kilian
2015 *Weil es um die Menschen geht*. Berlin: Econ.

Kleßmann, Eckart
1979 *Die deutsche Romantik*. Köln: DuMont Buchverlag.

Kohl, Karl-Heinz
1986 *Exotik als Beruf*. Frankfurt: Campus Verlag.

1987 *Abwehr und Verlangen*. Frankfurt: Qumran/Campus Verlag.

Kramer, Fritz
1986 Bronislaw Malinowski: Schriften zur Anthropologie. Frankfurt am Main: Syndikat.

Kulick, Don
1995 Introduction: The sexual life of anthropologists: erotic subjectivity and ethnographic work. In *Taboo*. Don Kulick and Margaret Willson, eds. Pp.1–28. London and New York: Routledge.

Kulick, Don and Margaret Willson
1995 *Taboo: Sex, Identity and Erotic Subjectivity in Anthropological Field Work*. London and New York: Routledge.

Landes, Ruth
1970 A Woman Anthropologist in Brazil. In *Women in the Field: Anthropological Experiences*. (Peggy Golde, ed.) Pp.118–139. Chicago: Aldine Publishing Company.

Langer, Susanne
1948 *Philosophy in a New Key*. New York: New American Library.

Langham, Ian
1981 *The Building of British Social Anthropology*. London: D. Reidel Publishing Company.

Leach, Edmund
1976. *Culture and Communication*. Cambridge: Cambridge University Press.

Lee, Richard B.
1978 Politics, Sexual and Non-Sexual in an Egalitarian Society. *Social Science Information* 17(6):871–895.

Lewis, C.S.
1940 *The Problem of Pain*. Glasgow: The Centenary Press.

2001 (1961) *A Grief Observed*. New York: HarperCollins.

2012 (1960) *The Four Loves*. New York: First Mariner Book Edition.

Lipps, Theodor
1902 *Vom Fühlen, Wollen, und Denken*. Leipzig.

Leach, Edmund
1976 *Culture and Communication*. Cambridge: Cambridge University Press.

Loubser, Jan J.
1968 Calvinism, Equality, and Inclusion: The Case of Afrikaner Calvinism. In *The Protestant Ethic and Modernization*. (S.N. Eisenstadt, ed.) Pp.367–383. New York: Basic Books.

Lounsbury, Floyd, G.
1964 A Formal Account of the Crow- and Omaha-Type Kinship Terminologies. In *Explorations in Cultural Anthropology*. (Ward H. Goodenough, ed.) Pp.351–393. New York: McGraw-Hill.

Malinowski, Bronislaw
1967 *A Diary in the Strict Sense of the Term*. Tr. N. Guterman. New York: Harcourt, Brace & World.

Mann, Thomas
1954 *Der Tod in Venedig*. (*Death in Venice*). Frankfurt: Fischer Bücherei.

1965 *Doctor Faustus*. (Tr. H.T. Lowe-Porter). New York: Alfred A. Knopf.

Marcel, Gabriel
1950 *The Mystery of Being*. Henry Chicago: Regnery Company.

Marcus, George and Dick Cushmann
1982 Ethnographies as Text. *Annual Review of Anthropology* 11:25–69.

Marcus, George and Fischer, Michael
1986 *Anthropology as Cultural Critique*. Chicago: The University of Chicago Press.

Mathiane, Nomavenda
1989 *South Africa: Diary of Troubled Times*. New York: Freedom House.

Mead, Margaret
1949 *Male and Female*. New York: William Morrow and Company.

1970 Field Work in the Pacific Islands, 1925–1967. In *Women in the Field: Anthropological Experiences*. (Peggy Golde, ed.) Pp.292–331. Chicago: Aldine Publishing Company.

1972 *Blackberry Winter: My Earlier Years*. New York: Simon and Schuster.

1977 *Letters from the Field*. New York: Harper & Row.

Michener, James A.
1971 *The Drifters*. New York: Fawcett Crest.

Muggeridge, Malcolm
1969 *Jesus Rediscovered*. London: Fontana Books.

Mühlmann, W.E.
1984 (1968) *Geschichte der Anthropologie*. Wiesbaden: AULA-Verlag.

Needham, Rodney
1962 *Structure and Sentiment*. Chicago: University of Chicago Press.

Neiman, Susan
2017 *Widerstand der Vernunft*. Salzbug: Ecowin Verlag.

Newton, Esther
1993 My Best Informant's Dress: The Erotic Equation in Field work. *Cultural Anthropology* 8 (1):3–23.

Nkrumah, Kwame
1970 *Consciencism: Philosophy and Ideology for De-colonization.* New York: Monthly Review Press.

Oberg, Kalervo
1938 Kinship Organization of the Banyankole. *Africa* 11(2):129–159.

Ohnuki-Tierney, Emiko
1991 Embedding and Transforming Polytrope: The Monkey as Self in Japanese Culture. In *Beyond Metaphor: The Theory of Tropes in Anthropology*, edited by James W. Fernandez. Stanford: Stanford University Press.

Okonjo, Kamene
1976 The Dual-Sex Political System in Operation: Igbo Women and Community Politics in Midwestern Nigeria, In *Women in Africa.* (edited by Nancy J. Hatkin and Edna G. Bay.) Pp.45–58. Stanford: Stanford University Press.

Olivier de Sardan, Jean-Pierre
1992 Occultism and the Ethnographic "I": The exoticizing of magic from Durkheim to "postmodern" anthropology. *Critique of Anthropology.* 12 (1):5–25.

Östberg, Wilhelm
1995 *Land is Coming Up: The Burunge of Central Tanzania and their Environments.* Stockholm: Department of Social Anthropology, Stockholm University.

Poewe, Karla, ed.
1994 *Charismatic Christianity as a Global Culture.* Columbia, SC: University of South Carolina Press.

Poewe, Karla
1978 "Religion, Matriliny and Change: Jehovah's Witnesses and Seventh Day Adventists in Luapula, Zambia," in *American Ethnologist* (Washington), Vol. 5, No. 2, Pp.301–321.

1985 *The Namibian Herero: A History of their Psychosocial Disintegration and Survival*. Lewiston, New York: The Edwin Mellen Press.

1988 *Childhood in Germany: the story of a little girl*. Lewiston, NY: The Edwin Mellen Press.

1989 On the Metonymic Structure of Religious Experiences: The Example of Charismatic Christianity. *Cultural Dynamics* 2(4):361–380.

1993 From Dissonance and Prophecy to Nihilism and Blame: A look at the work of Modisane in the context of Black South African writing. *Literature and Theology*. 7 (4):381–396.

1993 Theologies of Black South Africans and the Rhetoric of Peace versus Violence. *Canadian Journal of African Studies* 27 (1):43–65.

1994 "Rethinking the Relationship of Anthropology to Science and Religion," in *Charismatic Christianity as a Global Culture*, edited by Karla Poewe, University of South Carolina Press (Columbia, South Carolina). Pp.234–258.

1996 "From Volk to Apartheid: The Dialectic Between German and Afrikaner Nationalism," in *Missionsgeschichte-Kirchengeschichte-Weltgeschichte* [*Mission History-Church History-World History*], edited by Ulrich van der Heyden/Heike Liebau. Stuttgart: Franz Steiner Verlag. Pp.191–213.

2000 "The Spell of National Socialism." In Ulrich van der Heyden und Juergen Becher, Eds. *Mission und Gewalt: Der Umgang christlicher Missionen mit Gewalt und die Ausbreitung des Christentums in Afrika und Asien*. (Missionsgeschichtliches Archiv, Band 6) Stuttgart: Franz Steiner Verlag. Pp.268–290.

2006 *New Religions and the Nazis*. London/Oxford: Routledge Press. Pp. 218.

2008 A Curious Exercise in Archival Research: Missionary Martin Jäckel, the unravelling of his mixed genre novel, and the tragedies it revealed. In Ulrich van der Heyden and Andreas Feldtkeller, eds. *Border Crossings: Explorations of an Interdisciplinary Historian*. Stuttgart: Franz Steiner Verlag. Pp.221–252.

Polanyi, Michael
1964 *Personal Knowledge*. New York: Harper Torchbooks.

Probyn, Elspeth
1993 *Sexing the Self: Gendered Positions in Cultural Studies*. London: Routledge.

Rabinow, Paul
1977 *Reflections on Field Work in Morocco*. Berkeley: University of California Press.

Rao, Narahari
1988 Science: Search for Truths, or Way of Doing? *Cultural Dynamics* 1 (3):336–358.

Rappaport, R.
1967 *Pigs for the Ancestors: Ritual in the Ecology of a New Guinean People*. New Haven: Yale University Press.

Rattray, Capt. R.S.
1923 *Ashanti*. New York: Negro University Press (Reprinted, 1969).

Reck, Gregory
1984 Introduction to the special issue. *Anthropology and Humanism Quarterly* 9 (4):3–4.

Richardson, Miles
1996 Blurring the Line Between Fact and Fiction. *American Anthropologist*. 98 (3):623–624.

Riddell, Jessica
2017 Building Resilience Into the Classroom. *University Affairs* 5/17:43.

Said, Edward
1979 *Orientalism*. New York: Random House.

Sartre, Jean-Paul
1956 *Being and Nothingness* (Tr. Hazel E. Barnes). New York: Pocket Books.

Scheffler, Harold W.
1972 Systems of Kin Classification: A Structural Typology. In *Kinship Studies in the Morgan Centennial Year*. (Priscilla Reining, ed.) Pp.113–133. Washington DC: The Anthropological Society of Washington.

1973 Kinship, Descent, and Alliance. In *Handbook of Social and Cultural Anthropology*. (John J. Honigmann ed.) Chicago: Rand McNally and Company.

Scheper-Hughes, Nancy
1995 The Primacy of the Ethical: Propositions for a Militant Anthropology. *Current Anthropology* 36 (3):409–438.

Schmidt, Nancy
1984 Ethnographic Fiction: Anthropology's Hidden Literary Style. *Anthropology and Humanism Quarterly* 9 (4):11–14.

Schneider, David M.
1976 Notes Toward a Theory of Culture. In *Meaning in Anthropology*. (Keith H. Basso and Henry A. Selby, eds.) Pp.197–220. Albuquerque: University of New Mexico Press.

Schofield, Michael
1980 Patterns of Sexual Behavior in Contemporary Society. In *Human Sexuality*. (C.R. Austin and R.V. Short, FRS, eds.) Pp.98–123. Cambridge: Cambridge University Press.

Schultz, Emily and Lavenda Robert
1987 *Cultural Anthropology*. St. Paul: West Publ. Co.

Schumaker, Lynette
1996 "A Tent with a View: Colonial Officers, Anthropologists, and the Making of the Field in Northern Rhodesia, 1937–1960," *The History of Science Society*, OSIRIS; 2nd series, 11:237–258.

Schuster, Ilsa M. Glazer
1979 *New Women of Lusaka*. Palo Alto: Mayfield Publishing Company.

Smith, K.A.
2009 *Desiring the Kingdom: Worship, Worldview, and Cultural Formation*. Grand Rapids, Michigan: Baker Academic.

Stapel, Wilhelm
1933 *Die Kirche Christi und der Staat Hitlers*. Hamburg: Hanseatische
Verlagsanstalt.

Stocking, George
1986 Anthropology and the Science of the Irrational: Malinowski's
Encounter with Freudian Psychoanalysis. *Malinowski, Rivers, Benedict
and Others*. George Stocking, ed. Madison: University of Wisconsin
Press. Pp.13–49.

1987 *Victorian Anthropology*. New York: The Free Press.

1984 *Functionalism Historicized: Essays on British Social Anthropology*.
George Stocking, ed. Madison: University of Wisconsin Press.

1992 *The Ethnographer's Magic and Other Essays in the History of
Anthropology*. Madison, Wisconsin: The University of Wisconsin Press.

Stoller, Paul and Cheryl Olkes
1989 *In Sorcery's Shadow*. Chicago: Chicago University Press.

Stoller, Paul
1980 The Negotiation of Songhay Space: Phenomenology in the Heart of
Darkness. *American Ethnologist* 7(3):419–431.

Swiderski, Richard M.
1984 Malinowski's Tragic Ethnography. *Anthropology and Humanism
Quarterly* 9 (4):22–25.

Tedlock, Barbara
1991 From Participant Observation to the Observation of Participation:
the Emergency of Narrative Ethnography. *Journal of Anthropological
Research*. 47(1):69–94

1991 The New Anthropology of Dreaming. *Dreaming* 1(2):161–178.

Tedlock, Dennis
1990 *Days from a Dream Almanac*. Urbana: University of Illinois Press.

Thornton, R.J.
1985 "Imagine yourself set down …": Mach, Frazer, Conrad, Malinowski
and the role of imagination in ethnography. *Anthropology Today* 1(5):7–
14.

Troyat, Henri
1980 *Tolstoy.* New York: Harmony Books.

Turner, Victor W. and Edward M. Bruner
1986 *The Anthropology of Experience.* Urbana: University of Illinois Press.

Turner, Terence
1991 We are Parrots, Twins are Birds: Play of Tropes as Operational Structure. *Beyond Metaphor: The Theory of Tropes in Anthropology.* James W. Fernandez, ed. Pp.121–158. Stanford: Stanford University Press.

Tyler, Stephen
1986 Post-Modern Ethnography: From Document of the Occult to Occult Document. In *Writing Culture*, edited by James Clifford and George Marcus. Pp.122–140. Berkeley: University of California Press.

1996 The Essence of Aroma. *American Anthropologist* 98 (3):617–619.

Van Allen, Judith
1972 Sitting on a Man: Colonialism and the Lost Political Institutions of Igbo Women. *Canadian Journal of African Studies* 6(2):165–181.

1976 "Aba Riots" or Igbo "Women's War"? Ideology, Stratification, and the Invisibility of Women. In *Women in Africa.* Nancy J. Hatkin and Edna G. Bay, eds. Pp.59–85. Stanford: Stanford University Press.

Vickers, Brian
1989 *In Defense of Rhetoric.* Oxford: Clarendon Press.

von Gronicka, Andre
1970 *Thomas Mann: Profile and Perspectives.* New York: Random House.

Webb, Beatrice
1929 *My Apprenticeship.* London, New York, Toronto: Longmans, Green and Co.

Welch, James
1974 *Winter in the Blood.* New York: Harper & Row.

Wengle, John L.
1983 Fieldwork, Sunsets, and Death. *Anthropology and Humanism Quarterly* 8(2):2 12.

1988 *Ethnographers in the Field.* Tuscaloosa: University of Alabama Press.

White, Leslie A.
1959 *The Evolution of Culture.* New York: McGraw-Hill.

Wolcott, Harry F.
1995 *The Art of Field Work.* Walnut Creek: Altamira Press.

Wolff, K.H.
1964 Surrender and Community Study. *Reflections on Community Studies.* A.J. Vidich, J. Bensman, and M.R. Stein, eds. Pp.233–263. New York: John Wiley and Sons.

Woods, Donald
1978 *Biko.* New York and London: Paddington Press.

Zweig, Arnulf
1967 Lipps, Theodor. *The Encyclopedia of Philosophy.* Paul Edwards, ed. Pp.485–486. New York: Macmillan.

SUBJECT INDEX

ABOUT THE AUTHOR

Karla Poewe is professor emeritus at the University of Calgary. After her first fieldwork in Zambia, she received her Ph.D. in anthropology from the University of New Mexico. In this book she depicts that experience as an apprentice on an intellectual journey. It led to further work in Africa and archival research in Germany where she was born 1941 in what was then Königsberg, East Prussia. She lived in the Soviet Zone until 1948 and in the British zone from 1948 until immigration to Canada in 1955. She published numerous papers in professional journals and several books including *New Religions and the Nazis* (Routledge 2006). Karla met Irving Hexham in 1983 and they married in 1988. They live in Calgary.

93190865R00207

Made in the USA
Columbia, SC
06 April 2018